Church Court Records

An introduction for family and local historians

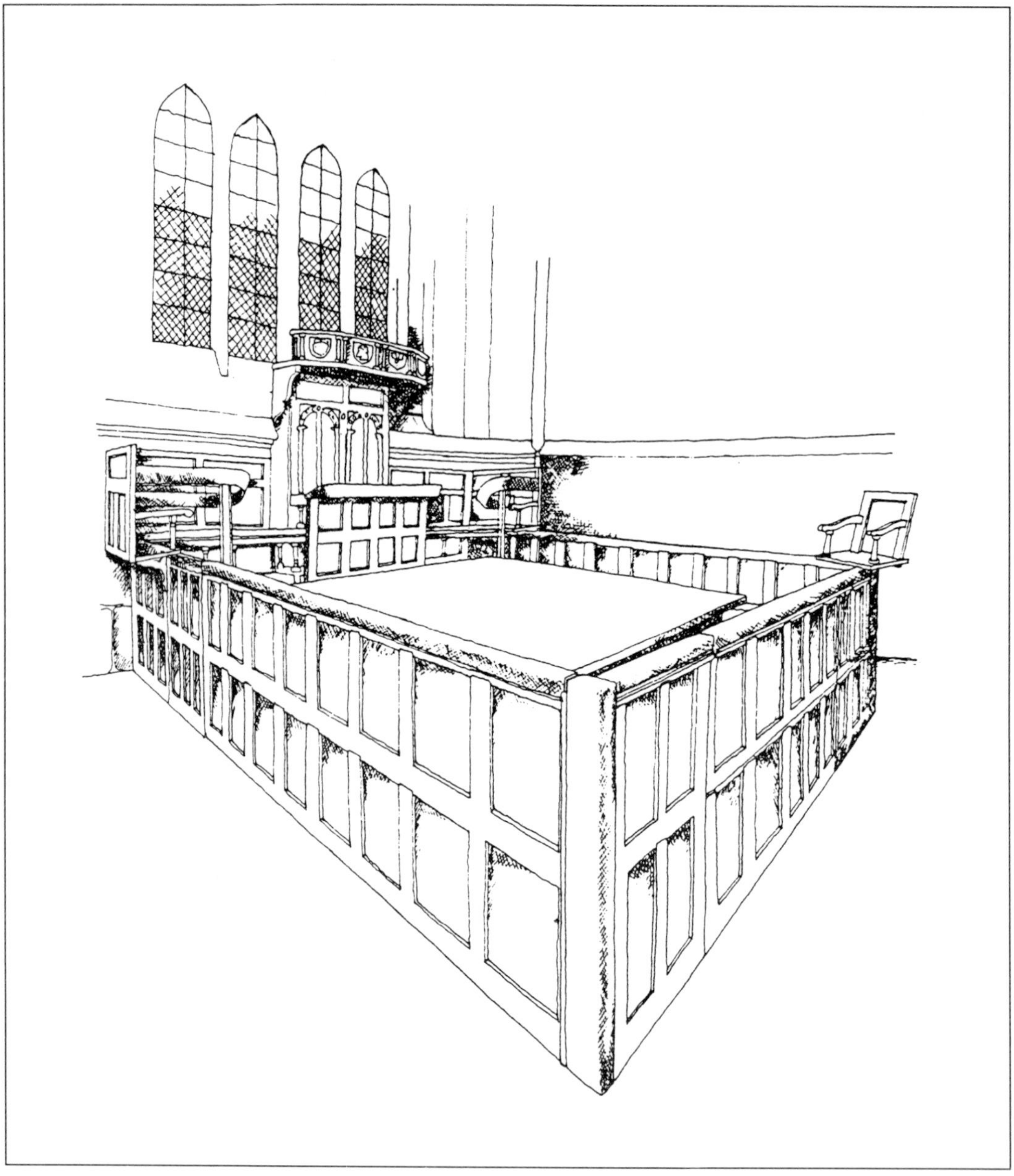

The Consistory Court in Chester Cathedral. This is housed in a room technically within the Cathedral building but with its own access to the street outside. The room still contains the original oak furniture, specially made for the purpose. The judge sat under the canopy, the dual nature of which probably suggests separate seats for the Official Principal and the Vicar General before the two offices were merged. The proctors and their clients would have been seated on opposite sides of the table. The chair precariously perched on one corner of the wainscot would have been used by the apparitor, one of whose duties was to summon individuals to the court.

Church Court Records

An introduction for family and local historians

Anne Tarver

Phillimore

1995

Published by
PHILLIMORE & CO. LTD.
Shopwyke Manor Barn, Chichester, Sussex

ISBN 0 85033 927 8

Printed and bound in Great Britain by
BOOKCRAFT
Midsomer Norton

To my husband
for his humour, patience and support

Contents

List of Documents and Diagrams in the Text

Frontispiece: The Consistory Court in Chester Cathedral

Size of original documents

For the purposes of publication the documents have been considerably, and variably, reduced in size. Most of the legal papers were written on a standard paper size of 12¼ in. x 7¾ in. (31 cm x 19.5 cm) used in both horizontal and vertical format. These include citations, articles of libels, personal answers, depositions, excommunications, absolutions, declarations, and guardianship papers. Larger sheets of 12½ in. x 15¼ in. were used in vertical format for citations with intimations, letters of request and larger citations *quorum nomina*. Odd pieces of paper of various sizes were used for miscellaneous items such as tenders for tithes, caveats, nuncupative wills and tickets for witnesses.

Transcriptions

In some cases it has been possible to produce a transcription with line lengths that match those on the original document. Hopefully, this will be of assistance in reading the documents concerned. Those with matching line lengths include Figs. 1.1, 1.2, 1.4, 1.5, 1.6, 1.8, 1.9, 1.12, 1.13, 1.14, 2.5, 2.7, 3.2, 3.3, 3.4, 3.5, 3.6, 3.8, 3.10, 3.12, 3.13, 4.2, 4.4, 4.5 and 4.6.

Acknowledgements

A great debt of gratitude is due to Dr. Nat Alcock and Dr. Joan Lane of Warwick University for establishing the Lichfield Consistory Court Project and the late Jane Hampartumian for her assistance in setting it up. Thanks are also due to Mark Dorrington, the present archivist of the Lichfield Joint Record Office for his continuing assistance, and his staff for their endless patience with the large numbers of documents involved.

My thanks also go to the staff of the Diocesan Record Offices of Lincoln, Leicester and Chichester, and the Nottingham University Manuscripts Department for their assistance in finding obscure documents so quickly and efficiently. Permission to use documents has been kindly given by Leicestershire County Record Office to use the records of the Archdeaconry of Leicester in their care, Nottingham University Manuscripts Department and the Lichfield Record Joint Record Office and the Lichfield Diocesan Registrar to use the Consistory Court Records of the Bishops of Lichfield and Coventry.

Narita Pike's comments on the chapter on matrimonial causes have been most welcome. Dr. Carl Trueman of the Department of Theology, Nottingham University has been most helpful with the Latin transcriptions.

Finally, without the funding of the Leverhulme Trust the research necessary to produce this book would not have been possible.

The views expressed and any errors are entirely my own.

ANNE TARVER

BELTON, LEICS

Introduction

The structure of the ancient ecclesiastical courts of England is likely to puzzle the enquirer ...
W.E. Tate.

Every local and family historian in the country is aware of the records generated by the Church if only from the use of parish registers, initiated in 1538 by Thomas Cromwell, and of the probate records relating to wills proved before 1858. Local historians also use the faculties granted for alterations to churches, the ordination papers of the clergy, churchwardens' accounts, and glebe terriers. Family historians find value in marriage licences, returns of dissenters and recusants, and the subscription books which record the names of schoolmasters, midwives and doctors, as well as those ordained into the church, all of whom had to testify to their allegiance to the church.

One large class of documents remains virtually unexplored—the records of the ecclesiastical courts. These courts were held by archdeacons and bishops, and by the archbishops of Canterbury and York. Areas outside the jurisdiction of the bishops were called peculiars and their landowners could also hold their own church courts. These areas were part of royal estates, or lands held by cathedral prebendaries as part of the temporal reward for their services. In cathedral towns, the dean and chapter were also permitted to hold courts for their areas of jurisdiction.

Church courts maintained spiritual discipline, dealing with the 'soul's health and the reformation of manners' of parishioners. Probate was granted to the executors or administrators of the affairs of the deceased, and the courts provided a means of negotiation in personal disputes of a moral nature, involving defamation, marriage and tithes. Within each diocese, the archdeacons were entitled to hold courts for their archdeaconries, but the main court of the diocese was that of the bishop, known as the consistory court. These courts were held regularly, usually fortnightly,[1] in the main church of the diocese and are, in fact, still in existence, being used to grant faculties for alterations to churches and for the discipline of the clergy, but their powers were severely curtailed in the 19th century by acts of Parliament.

The purpose of this book is to examine the documents produced by the church courts, to show examples of them, to illustrate their structure and to demonstrate the type of information they can give to the local and family historian. The first chapter will consider the process of canon law used in the courts and the documents that were generated by this process. The remaining chapters will examine the five major categories of court business, that of the Office which included the spiritual discipline of the clergy and their parishioners and administration of the church, testamentary business, matrimonial causes, tithes and defamation.

The problems

The problems which have resulted in the under-use of these documents are five-fold:

i) It can be difficult to decide where to begin a search for these papers. They are kept in diocesan record offices which cover areas that are not always coterminous with modern counties.

ii) The process of finding the relevant documents in the archives is not always easy. Some collections are still not adequately indexed and, in others, related papers are separated from one another.

iii) The process of law used in the courts was one of canon law and because the documents were legal evidence, their subtleties can make the extraction of information difficult.

iv) Many of the earlier documents were written in Latin, often in an abbreviated form, and this can be extremely frustrating to the beginner. The act books of some courts are also notoriously badly written, the details having been entered in great haste in a mixture of English and Latin.

Finding the record office

Since the Local Government (Records) Act of 1962, the records of the church courts have been housed in diocesan record offices, many of which are also county record offices, particularly where the diocese is a small one. Map 1 shows the post-Reformation dioceses of England which remained almost unchanged between the 16th and late 19th centuries, together with the contemporary county boundaries. In the case of larger dioceses, the appropriate record office is generally that of the county in which the cathedral is situated. One major exception to this is the diocesan record office for Lichfield and Coventry which is at Lichfield itself. The location of the relevant office can be checked using the directory of record offices produced by the Royal Commission on Historical Manuscripts.[2]

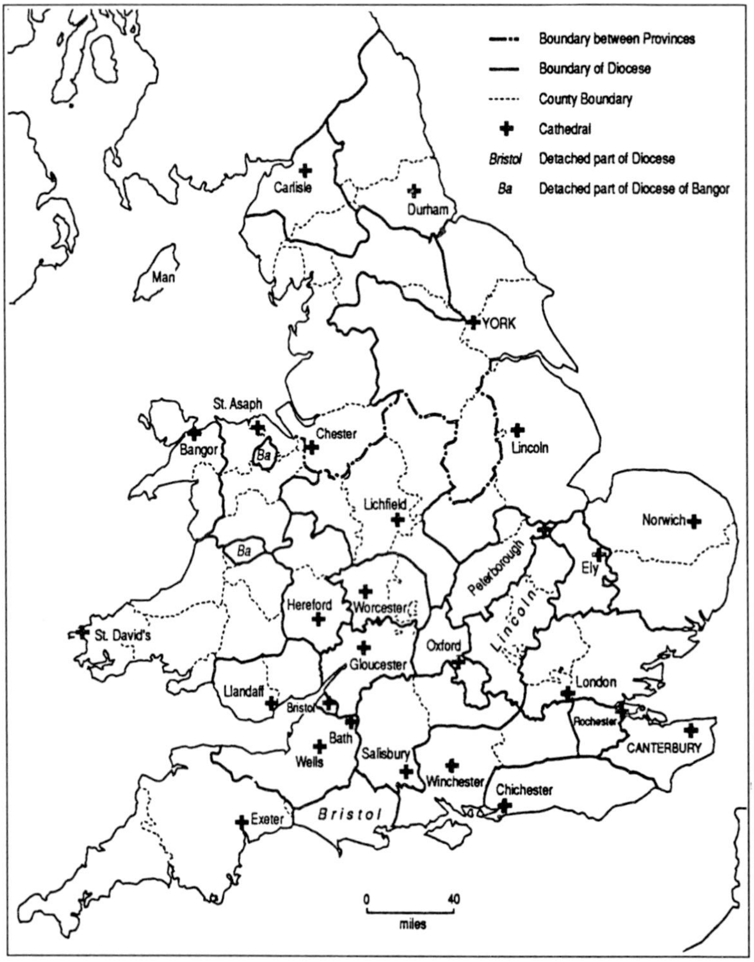

Map 1 The dioceses of England between the Reformation and the 19th century.

Finding the documents

Methods of locating documents vary widely between record offices. In some offices the papers have been listed by year and type of cause and, in some, card indexes which have been updated from time to time and contain varying amounts of information. In other offices finding aids are sparse and the collections poorly indexed. The situation is further complicated by the fact that, in some dioceses, prior to their deposition in diocesan record offices, the court records were stored in diocesan registries where some types of cause papers were bound together as separate books (particularly depositions and penances). Many record offices produce general handlists of their holdings and this can be the most useful starting point in a search for these documents.

The process of law

The concept of canon law is one which is difficult to understand in the 20th century, but this form of law is based on the legal validity of the canons, or rules of the church which were binding upon the clergy but could not override common law or custom. The canons are medieval in origin but were re-constituted after the Reformation to permit the king of England to act as head of the established Church. Legal treatises on canon law survive, particularly that of Richard Burn[3] whose alphabetically ordered work ran into many editions. Copies of these books can occasionally be found in university libraries, or on the shelves of antiquarian booksellers but they are neither easy to locate nor understand, and it is hoped that this book will explain the basic principles of law in the context of the documents generated by the courts.

One important point to emphasise is that these courts only dealt with moral offences. There was no criminal element in their business, as we would understand it today. Fornication, for instance, was described as a 'detestable crime' until 1733 at Lichfield and some court cases were referred to as 'criminal', but it should be remembered that these were seen as moral crimes. There were no cases of felony, debt, or assault tried in these courts.

The language of the documents

The documents pose three problems in terms of the language in which they are written. Firstly, the earlier papers are in Latin, secondly their writers used many abbreviations and finally the papers, being used in a court of law, have their own form of language.

There is no specialist Latin text book to assist with this material and, when turning to the earlier papers, a Latin dictionary from the 19th century will prove invaluable, as will Martin's book on the interpretation of records,[4] with its excellent list of Latin abbreviations, which were extensively used by the lawyers of these courts, simply to save time when writing out legal phrases.

As with all forms of law, its evolution was a slow process and this can be used to the advantage of the researcher. Instead of giving a great number of Latin transcriptions and their translations, it is proposed to give examples of the various documents generated during the 17th and 18th centuries, so that their legal sense and purpose may become evident, and their language may begin to become familiar. The general meaning of the earlier causes may then be understood in terms of their role in the proceedings of the courts. The use of these later documents also demonstrates more easily the type of information that is available to the 20th-century researcher, as well as the two main problems of extracting data from them. The first of these is the amount of detailed information that is given in some depositions, and the second, the conflicting nature of the evidence in those large causes where witnesses were produced by both parties. Reading the later court papers will give the reader some experience of the language of the court procedure, the layout of each type of document on the page, and the confidence to read the earlier causes.

Transcriptions of cause papers and act books as well as articles about them have been published in many widely scattered record society publications over the past century. Three of the most valuable articles are by Dorothy Owen, who has published transcriptions of a range of Latin cause papers from the late 16th and early 17th centuries,[5] Canon Purvis,[6] who has published transcriptions of depositions from tithe disputes in the York courts, dating from the 16th century, and Professor Helmholz who has produced a volume on defamation causes to 1600.[7]

Some help is often at hand on the documents themselves in that, after they were folded for storage, endorsements were made describing the contents: the type of document, type of cause, the surnames of plaintiff and defendant, and the year that the document was generated, often with the precise date.

The handwriting of the documents

The standard works on handwriting of the 16th and 17th centuries, especially that of Hilda Grieve,[8] are very useful when starting to read the 16th century documents which survive in some abundance between the reformation and the beginning of the civil war. The illustrations shown in this book are of necessity small, but the transcriptions of the documents enable the language and the expanded form of the abbreviations to be more readily understood. The reduced document size has the advantage of demonstrating clearly the layout of the text on the page which can help with the identification of the document. Recognising the type of document and the phrases used will also help to decipher the handwriting, although, as always, it is only with practice that the more difficult hands will become understandable.

The author is only too aware of the infinite variety of causes passing through these courts, and of the local and regional variations[9] in their business and procedures, but hopes to have distilled the basic practice into a form that applies to most courts. Each chapter of this book will deal with one of the major categories of business of the courts, looking at the information that can be gained and some of the pitfalls of interpretation, as well as the particular forms of document generated by that business. A glossary of the relevant Latin words and phrases is given at the end of the book, to assist in the identification of the various papers and the unravelling of the cause itself.

These documents may appear intimidating, but with a little patience, knowledge and practice they can reveal information available from no other sources for the family and local historian. The examples used in this book represent a mixture of the mundane and the extraordinary, and the reader may expect to find similar material in the records of every diocese. The records of the church courts and their implications have the potential to add considerably to the local historian's knowledge of his parish and to the history of individual families.

Chapter One

The Process of Law

The act books of the Church courts are among the more strikingly repulsive of all the relics of the past written in cramped and hurried hands, in very abbreviated and technical Latin, and often preserved (if that is the right word) in fairly noisome conditions, ill-sorted and mostly unlisted and sometimes broken in pieces. Cause papers, where they exist, are likely to be found in total confusion and with no guide to their contents.[1]

Canon law

The phrase canon law has tended to deter people from using the documents generated by the church courts, but the term simply means a form of law, based on the prevailing rules or canons of the Church, which ran parallel to the normal laws of the land. These rules evolved through the medieval period and relate to the life and spiritual discipline of the personnel of the Church and their parishioners, and were legally binding upon the clergy. Following the Reformation the canons were re-defined in 1603, to conform to the authority of the monarchy, whilst maintaining the disciplinary function of the bishop.

The law permitted these courts few powers of punishment. They were not entitled to harm the body of any individual or to fine them, although the bills for legal services may have been punishment enough for some. Excommunication and public humiliation, exemplified by the penance that had to be undergone after a defamation or immorality cause, were their main deterrents. Excommunication took two forms; the lesser excommunication in the form of exclusion from the church itself, which prevented an individual from taking part in divine service and communion, and the greater excommunication which involved the individual being excluded from the company of all christians; in effect, an early equivalent of being 'sent to Coventry'. Anyone who had dealings with someone who had been excommunicated by this form would have been liable to the lesser excommunication.

A penance was defined by Burn[2] as 'an ecclesiastical punishment, used in the discipline of the church, which doth affect the body of the penitent; by which he is obliged to give a public satisfaction to the church, for the scandal which he hath given by his evil example'. This usually involved standing in church apart from the congregation and reading a statement of apology either for their behaviour towards the community or to an individual that they had offended.

The process of a legal case (or cause as it was known) through the church courts was, to our eyes, lengthy, but it reflected the time required to prepare the cause and to write out the documents by hand. Contacting people prior to the invention of the telephone must have been extremely time consuming, as was the problem of informing those who could not read. It was also important that the legal procedures should be followed precisely, in order for decisions to be legally binding. Alongside ecclesiastical business, these courts formed an accessible method of litigation for the man in the street, within certain limitations. The main constraint on the business was that it had to have a moral interpretation. There were no cases of theft or bodily harm tried here but rather causes of moral defamation where sexual misconduct was inferred, failing to give the church its just dues (in the form of church rates, tithes and Easter offerings), and also nullity of marriage and separation from bed and board (the only form of divorce countenanced by the Church). These, together with arguments over wills, provided the courts with their business.

The courts

During the medieval period, the organisation of the church courts of most dioceses was very simple, those of the archdeacon formed the courts of the first instance, where cases were granted their initial hearing. The bishop's court was used as a court of appeal from the archdeacon's court, as well as an instance court in its own right. This arrangement seems to have continued until the disruption of the civil war in 1642. The relationship between these two courts after the Restoration in 1661 in many dioceses is not a clear one, due to the fact that the same personnel held posts in both courts. Some archdeaconry courts continued to function in the larger dioceses but business tended to gravitate towards the bishop's court. Those cases which explored difficult points of law would have been referred to the courts of the province—those of the archbishops of York or Canterbury, as would appeals to a higher ecclesiastical authority. Alongside the regular courts, those of the peculiars (arising in areas which were outside the bishop's jurisdiction) continued to function, but their records have rarely survived. We know of their existence through occasional references to them through letters of request from the main courts.

The work of the courts fell into two main categories, office and instance business. Office business related to disciplinary matters within the church, and causes were heard in three different categories described in Chapter Two (p.31). Some of these causes would probably have resulted from churchwardens' presentments, or from findings made at visitations. It is sometimes described as 'criminal business', but it must be re-emphasised that it related to moral crimes rather than those acts that we regard as criminal in the 20th century. Immorality, for instance, was described as the 'detestable crime of fornication' at Lichfield until 1733, a crime for which both clergy and laity could be subject to correction. Some office business could be promoted by a third party through the office of the judge and this included requests for the granting of faculties, which was the responsibility of the church court.

Instance business referred to the normal type of court procedure where one party was in dispute with another over such matters as defamation, unpaid tithes, matrimonial matters, and testamentary business involving unpaid legacies and disputed wills. In this form of cause the plaintiff was known as the *pars actrix* and the defendant the *pars rea*.

Forms of pleading

The courts worked by a system of pleadings, sub-divided into two major types, summary and plenary. Summary pleading was usually used for some forms of office business, which was mainly verbal and left comparatively few documents in the registry because proceedings were much shorter. Although the proceedings were less formal in nature, every event would be recorded in the act books. A cause heard by this form of pleading would usually arise from churchwardens' presentments and would commence with a citation issued from the Registry, requiring the presence of the defendant on a stated court day. If he failed to appear and was declared contumacious or was found guilty, then he would be excommunicated.

If an individual was brought to court to answer an office cause as a result of a 'common fame' or local rumour and there was insufficient evidence produced against him, he could undertake the process of compurgation. Five or six sober and honest neighbours, described as compurgators, had to be found to swear to the innocence of the defendant, a process which was often referred to as the 'wager of law'. On those occasions, where no compurgators could be found and the denial was sufficiently convincing, the case may have been dismissed. This type of defence was abolished in 1641.

The very formal method of written pleading was known as plenary pleading, which was used in instance causes and produced many more documents. Conset wrote of plenary pleading in 1708 that the 'order and solemnity of the law is exactly to be observed, so that if there be the least infringement or omission of that order, the whole proceedings are annulled'.[3] This was used in both instance business and more serious causes brought by the office of the judge and required that the process of law be observed very precisely to ensure its validity.

The people of the courts

The bishops and archdeacons with ultimate authority over the courts seldom appeared in person, being engaged in a variety of other business, and they both appointed officials to oversee the courts. The archdeacon chose a law officer known as the Archdeacon's Official to hear instance causes in his place. In larger dioceses, such as Lincoln, the bishop would elect his commissary 'one who supplies the office and jurisdiction of the bishop in the out places of the diocese' to hear the criminal causes in the archdeacon's court, one individual sometimes holding both posts.

The consistory court was led by the chancellor of the diocese, who was considered to act in the place of the bishop himself; his judgments in the consistory court were final, no appeal to the bishop being permitted. This single post was in fact a combination of the offices of official principal and vicar general. The official principal heard instance causes and the vicar general was responsible for those causes that dealt with the 'health of the soul'; in other words, office cases brought by the church.[4] At Lichfield the seals used on citations were those of the vicar general.

In spite of the requirements of canons 130 and 131 that advocates should work in the courts, very few actually did so and then only in the provincial courts of York and Canterbury. Their place was taken by proctors or procurators who worked almost universally in the consistory and archdeaconry courts. They were not necessarily graduates but were qualified in canon law; all of them would have been notaries public and would have served a seven-year apprenticeship to another public notary. These were defined by Burn as people who 'confirm and attest the truth of any deed or writings, in order to render the same authentick'. They were also responsible for writing down the acts of court.

The proctors themselves had to be admitted to the courts at the beginning of their careers and this would produce an act of court (Fig. 1.1).[5] Note the format on the page, sloping from right to left, in the same way as in the court act books, and also the use of abbreviations in the preamble. AM stood for '*Artis Magister*' or 'Master of Arts', WM for 'William Mott', NP for 'Notary Public' and DR for 'Deputy Registrar'.

The registrar (sometimes known as the register), or his deputy was responsible for the issue of citations, the maintenance of the act books and the storage of documents in the registry after causes had been completed. Their filing systems were not well developed, and the diary of Henry Prescott, deputy register of the Chester courts, refers to days spent 'in the dust' searching for lost items; in 1706 it took him four days to find a missing document, with the assistance of the bishop![6]

The courts also maintained officials known as apparitors whose main duties were two-fold, firstly to deliver the initial summons, known as a citation, to the defendant. Their second duty was to call witnesses on court days, and the mace of office of one such individual can still be seen in Lichfield Cathedral.

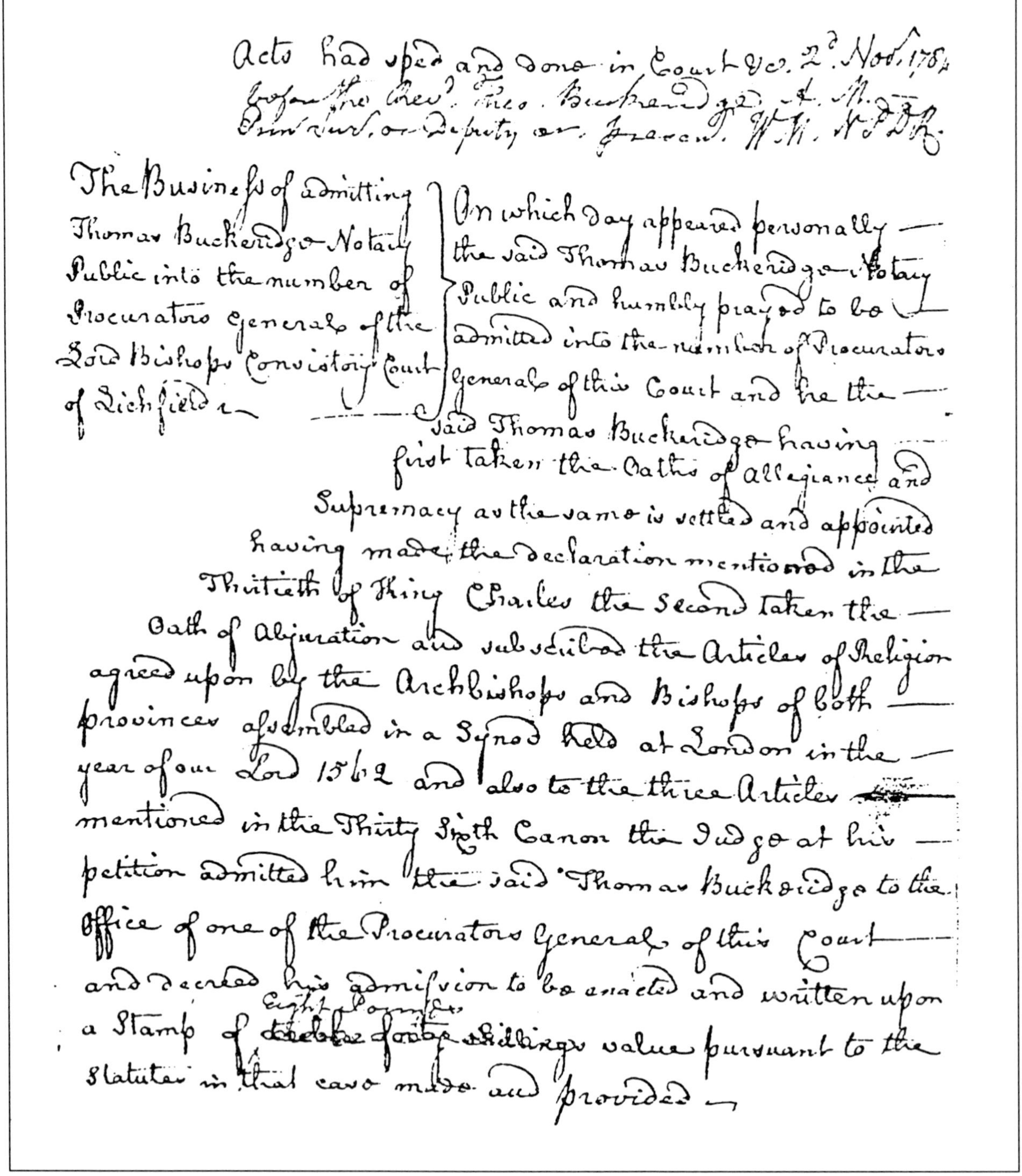

Acts had sped and done in Court &c. 2d. Nov. 1784
before the Revd. Theo. Buckeridge A.M.
Prin. Surr. or Deputy in presence W.H. N.P. D.R.

The Business of admitting Thomas Buckeridge Notary Public into the number of Procurators General of the Lord Bishops Consistory Court of Lichfield

On which day appeared personally the said Thomas Buckeridge Notary Public and humbly prayed to be admitted into the number of Procurators General of this Court and he the said Thomas Buckeridge having first taken the Oaths of Allegiance and Supremacy as the same is settled and appointed having made the declaration mentioned in the Thirtieth of King Charles the Second taken the Oath of Abjuration and subscribed the Articles of Religion agreed upon by the Archbishops and Bishops of both provinces assembled in a Synod held at London in the year of our Lord 1562 and also to the three Articles mentioned in the Thirty Sixth Canon the Judge at his petition admitted him the said Thomas Buckeridge to the Office of one of the Procurators General of this Court and decreed his admission to be enacted and written upon a Stamp of ~~twelve~~ ~~forty~~ Eight pounds shillings value pursuant to the Statutes in that case made and provided

Acts had sped and done in Court *&c.* 2nd. Nov. 1784
before the Reverend. Theophilus. Buckeridge A.M.
Principal Surrogate or Deputy *&c.* [etc], Present WM. NP DR.

The Business of admitting Thomas Buckeridge Notary Public into the number of Procurators General of the Lord Bishops Consistory Court of Lichfield

On which day appeared personally the said Thomas Buckeridge Notary Public and humbly prayed to be admitted into the number of Procurators General of this Court and he the said Thomas Buckeridge having first taken the Oaths of Allegiance and Supremacy as the same is settled and appointed having made the declaration mentioned in the Thirtieth of King Charles the Second taken the Oath of Abjuration and subscribed the Articles of Religion agreed upon by the Archbishops and Bishops of both provinces assembled in a Synod held at London in the year of our Lord 1562 and also to the three Articles mentioned in the Thirty Sixth Canon the Judge at his petition admitted him the said Thomas Buckeridge to the Office of one of the Procurators General of this Court and deceed his admission to be enacted and written upon a Stamp of Eight Pounds value pursuant to the statutes in that case made and provided.

Fig. 1.1 Act of Court: the admission of Thomas Buckeridge as proctor in the Lichfield court.

The course of a cause

Act Books

To understand the material produced by the courts, we must follow the development of an action and see how the documents were generated. All courts used act books, in which their daily business was recorded. These would often seem to have been written up in advance with lists of parties due to appear on each court day, and then a brief resumé of decisions taken would be added later; some of the books have obviously been copied out, with uniform handwriting throughout. Many of those at Lichfield have their pages folded vertically, implying that they were made up of individual sheets, copied in a fair hand and bound together at a later date, having been folded for storage until then. They were later indexed on completion of the volume, to help to find earlier events, which were sought either as precedents, or for reference if the cause continued after some lapse of time. The books at Lichfield were known as court books to differentiate them from the act books of the probate courts. The court clerks often wrote quickly in a mixture of English and Latin, using many abbreviations and initials for proctors and parties in the action, which renders them extremely difficult to understand, particularly when the type of cause is not stated from beginning to end! However, reading the cause papers will reveal the names of the proctors working at a particular period, as well as those of plaintiffs and defendants, who will all be recorded by their initials.

A typical court book entry from Lichfield would read as follows:[7]

Porter *con* Wood} Excom
Ha:

Here Porter and Wood would be Plaintiff and Defendant respectively. The use of '*con*' as a contraction for '*contra et adversus*' shows that this entry was probably made before 1733.[8] 'Excom' is an abbreviation for 'Excommunicate' and the defendant had probably failed to appear on more than one occasion, been declared contumacious,[9] or guilty of contempt of court, and was finally to be excommunicated. 'Ha:' beneath the protagonists refers to the proctor acting for the parties; in this cause George Hand of Lichfield would have been acting for Porter. Note also that the type of cause is not given, but it is probably an instance cause, no proctor being appointed by Wood who failed to respond to the citation.

A more complex entry[10] would read as follows:

Beighton against Beighton} The Decree being extracted under Seal by
Hand. Fletcher. Master Fletcher this day he returned the same duly executed with a Certificate of the execution thereof endorsed upon the back of the same, and the said Richard Beighton being called three times and not appearing the said Master Fletcher accused his Contumacy and prayed him to be reputed contumacious and in paid of his Contempt the Certificate of the said Decree to be continued to the next Court day, whereupon the Surrogate at his petition pronounced him contumacious and in Pain of his contempt continued the certificate of the said Decree to the next court day.

Once again, the type of cause is not stated, but it is obviously one between parties, and the legal action taken is described in minute detail. In this cause, both proctors are named, George Hand again acting for the plaintiff and John Fletcher for the defendant. In some act books, particularly the early ones, there is much more detail relating to the cause itself, but this varies from court to court and over time. This layout of the text on the page is typical of act books and of some of the related documents. The 18th-century books are much more readable than the earlier ones, both in writing style and language, and they form an excellent introduction to their predecessors.

Probate court act books are comparatively simple, as they deal only with grants of probate. They record the names of the deceased and the parish from which they came, as well as the names of those to whom probate or administration had been granted. The court books of the archdeaconry and consistory courts were generally kept separately from those dealing with probate, and it is important for the user to establish the nomenclature used in each diocese. In Lichfield, the probate court books are known as act books, and cease in 1638.[11] The court books here, all 118 of them from 1524 to 1800, refer to events in the consistory courts. The Oxford courts, consistory and archdeaconry, appear to have run concurrently by the later 17th century, and some act books relate to both courts. The information given at the beginning of each court day should give the name of the person presiding over the court, be they the official principal, vicar general or surrogate, as well as the name of the individual, usually the bishop or archdeacon, under whose authority the court was being held.

Cause Papers

The progress of an action through the courts was known as the *processus* and occasionally the papers generated were so prolific that they were bound together into book form, with the title '*Processus*, X *contra* Y' on the front. Many individual papers were endorsed with the names of plaintiff and defendant and the phrase '*contra et adversus*', abbreviated to '*cna*'.[12] Following a particular cause through the act books, the process of pleading a cause in plenary form under canon law gives the appearance of being a protracted one. However, many entries in the act books merely request a further period of time, or term probatory, in which to work on a cause.

Different court registries have stored their vast deposits of cause papers with a variety of filing systems over the centuries, prior to their being received by their present repositories. In some cases all examples of a single type of document have been grouped together i.e., citations, libels, allegations—often by individual years. In other offices, books of depositions survive, bound together, but without the original libels which help to give them structure. This can make the reconstruction of individual cases difficult if not well-nigh impossible, until all the records are stored electronically and can be searched quickly by this means. At Lichfield, the cause papers have all been stored more or less in their original groupings, although occasionally the papers are spread over the several years that a lengthy cause passed through the courts. These papers are grouped according to the type of business and stored in annual boxes, as are the archdeaconry court papers of Leicester.

The first stage of any case in the courts was to employ a proctor, which does not appear to have generated papers for storage in the registry at Lichfield, the agreement being between the lawyer and his client and not required for posterity. Proxies which gave a proctor or relative permission to act on the behalf of a minor do survive because of their legal importance.

The citation

The first duty of the proctor in a cause would be to call the defendant into court. A request would be made for their presence of the defendant, which produced an initial document called a citation, bearing a seal in the case of the Lichfield Consistory, that of the Vicar General. This summoned the defendant to appear in court on a specified day to hear the particular cause to be brought against him by the plaintiff before a named court official. The name of the parish in which the defendant lived would be given, firstly to confirm that he lived within the jurisdiction of the court, and secondly for the benefit of the apparitor who would deliver the paper. It would have been shown to the defendant and a note of its contents, known as a 'Note English' (from the time when citations were written in Latin), was left with him. The latter only rarely survive, as there was no reason to return them to the court, and they were probably consigned to the fire after the affair had been settled. The original citation was returned to the Registry of the court, having been signed and witnessed to confirm that it had been shown to the defendant.

To confirm that these documents had been shown to the individuals concerned, a sworn statement by the apparitor in the form of an endorsement was made on the earlier citations, confirmed by a surrogate. By the 18th century these endorsements were replaced by affidavits. The surrogate or lawyer before whom the affidavit was sworn signed and dated it, incidentally giving some indication of the time taken to deliver the documents. The slip of paper was then attached to the citation either by a pin or a small piece of wax. A surrogate was a beneficed minister, an MA with some knowledge of the law and of 'modest and honest conversation', deputed by the chancellor or archdeacon's official to exercise certain acts of jurisdiction, such as the granting of licences. Analysis of these signatures can show the rising influence through the 18th century of civil lawyers who signed these affidavits with increasing frequency.

A typical citation reads as follows (Fig. 1.2):[13]

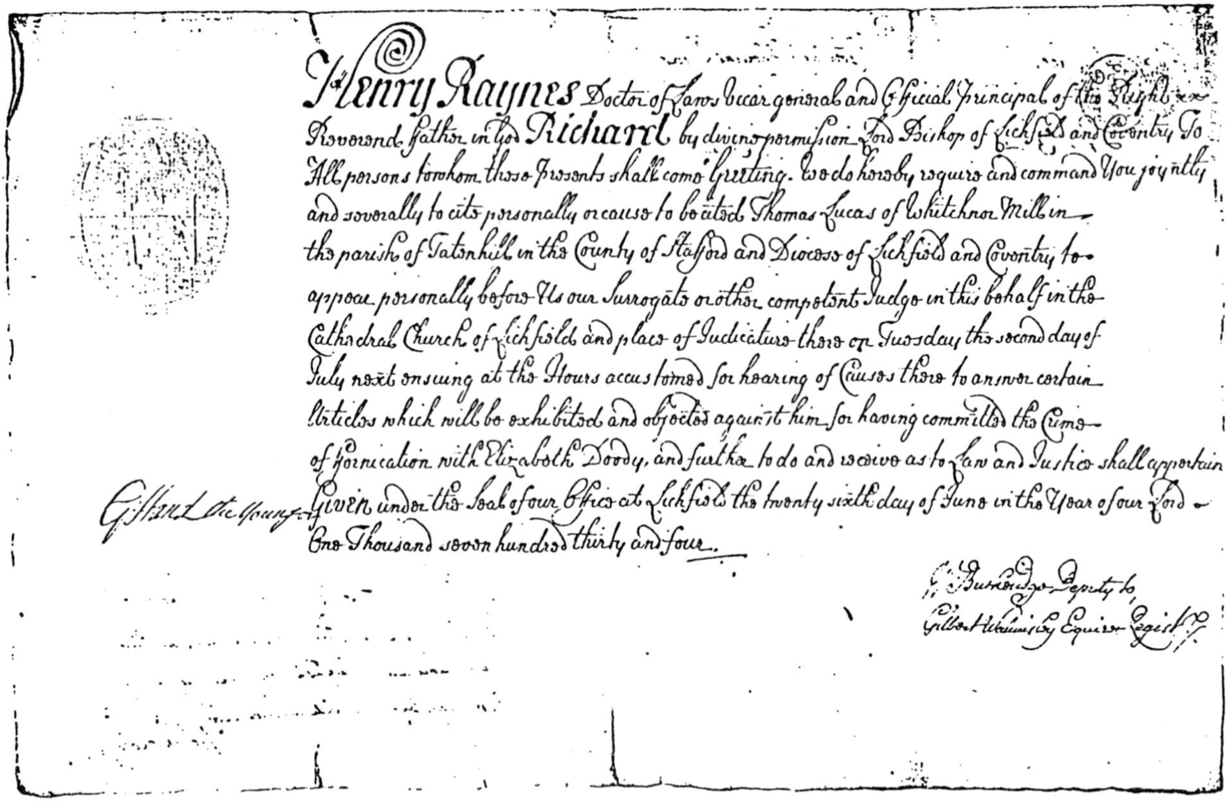

Henry Raynes Doctor of Laws Vicar general and Official principal of the Right
Reverend Father in God Richard by divine permission Lord Bishop of Lichfield and Coventry To
All persons to whom these presents shall come Greeting. We do hereby require and command You joyntly
and severally to cite or cause to be cited Thomas Lucas of Whitchnor Mill in
the parish of Tatenhill in the County of Stafford and Diocese of Lichfield and Coventry to
appear personally before Us our Surrogate or other competent Judge in this behalf in the
Cathedral Church of Lichfield and place of Judicature there on Tuesday the second day of
July next ensuing at the Hours accustomed for hearing of Causes there to answer certain
Articles which will be exhibited and objected against him for having committed the Crime of Fornication with
Elizabeth Doody, and further to do and receive as to Law and Justice shall appertain
Given under the Seal of our Office at Lichfield the twenty sixth day of June in the Year of our Lord
One Thousand seven hundred thirty and four.

W. Buckeridge Deputy to,
Gilbert Walmisley Esquire, Registrar

Fig. 1.2 Citation of Thomas Fox to answer the Judge in a cause of Immorality.

If, for some reason, the defendant could not be found or chose to ignore the summons, then a further citation was delivered by '*viis et modis*', by ways and means. This meant that the citation would be fixed for a short period of time to the door of the house of the individual sought, and then attached to the church door, again for a short period of time. In such cases, the document still retains the marks of the wax used to hold the document in place. In some dioceses it was customary for these documents to be read in church during divine service. If this still failed to produce any response, the individual would be declared contumacious, or in contempt of court, and be liable to excommunication. Occasionally this process would elicit some response; a note to the effect that the individual sought was away from home or with some other excuse. In 1784, one lady gave the following response:[14]

> Mary Bartlam's Comtaments to Mr. Coton [a lawyer in Coventry who was asked to deliver the original citation], and to let you no Hi be not fit to go out of doors, and my husband did not make any Will, and i hope you will excuse my not coming i being so very Hill.

Needless to say, this endearing response did not cut any ice with the courts and Mary was summoned to appear, not only to prove the will of her maltster husband, but also to answer George Hand on a charge of contumacy.

As well as the simple citation of an individual, a slightly different form, described as a *quorum nomina*, could be used in tithe or church levy disputes or as a result of presentments at visitations by archdeacons, bishops or the metropolitan himself. In this form a number of people from the same parish, all being cited by the same plaintiff, would be listed at the bottom of the document. A more elaborate form of this type of citation can be found amongst probate court papers, when the numbers of those who were cited to appear at the bi-annual probate courts were so numerous that they were listed alphabetically by parish.

On occasions, it was necessary to inform the parties in the cause that certain action would be taken, and this produced the 'citation with intimation'. The form of the normal citation was repeated, with the phrase, 'and further intimating', before a description of the procedure which was to follow. This form of citation was particularly common in faculty causes, where it was legally necessary for the document to be read out in church giving an opportunity for objections to the proposals to be raised. Physically the document is twice the size of the normal citation and the words 'further intimating' are slightly enlarged. Both of these types of citation would be suitably endorsed with their precise description, as well as with a statement from the officiating minister or clergyman confirming that the citation had been read out in church. The same procedure was also used in testamentary causes where there were no relatives of the deceased immediately apparent to undertake the administration of their estate. In this case the document was generally addressed to the population at large, giving notice of the action to be taken if no objections were forthcoming.

It was only possible for a bishop to cite the residents of his own diocese and, in those causes where it was necessary for plaintiffs, witnesses, or relatives to be brought from other dioceses, 'letters of request' would be extracted from the Registry, whereby the bishop requested the assistance of a fellow bishop in the issuing of the necessary citation for one of his flock to appear in the court of another diocese. These are generally of the same size as a 'citation with intimation', and the copy of the citation from the other diocese is often attached in the files, producing a document, bearing the name of the bishop or chancellor of another diocese and their seal. The following example relates to a witness in a testamentary cause (Fig. 1.3):[15]

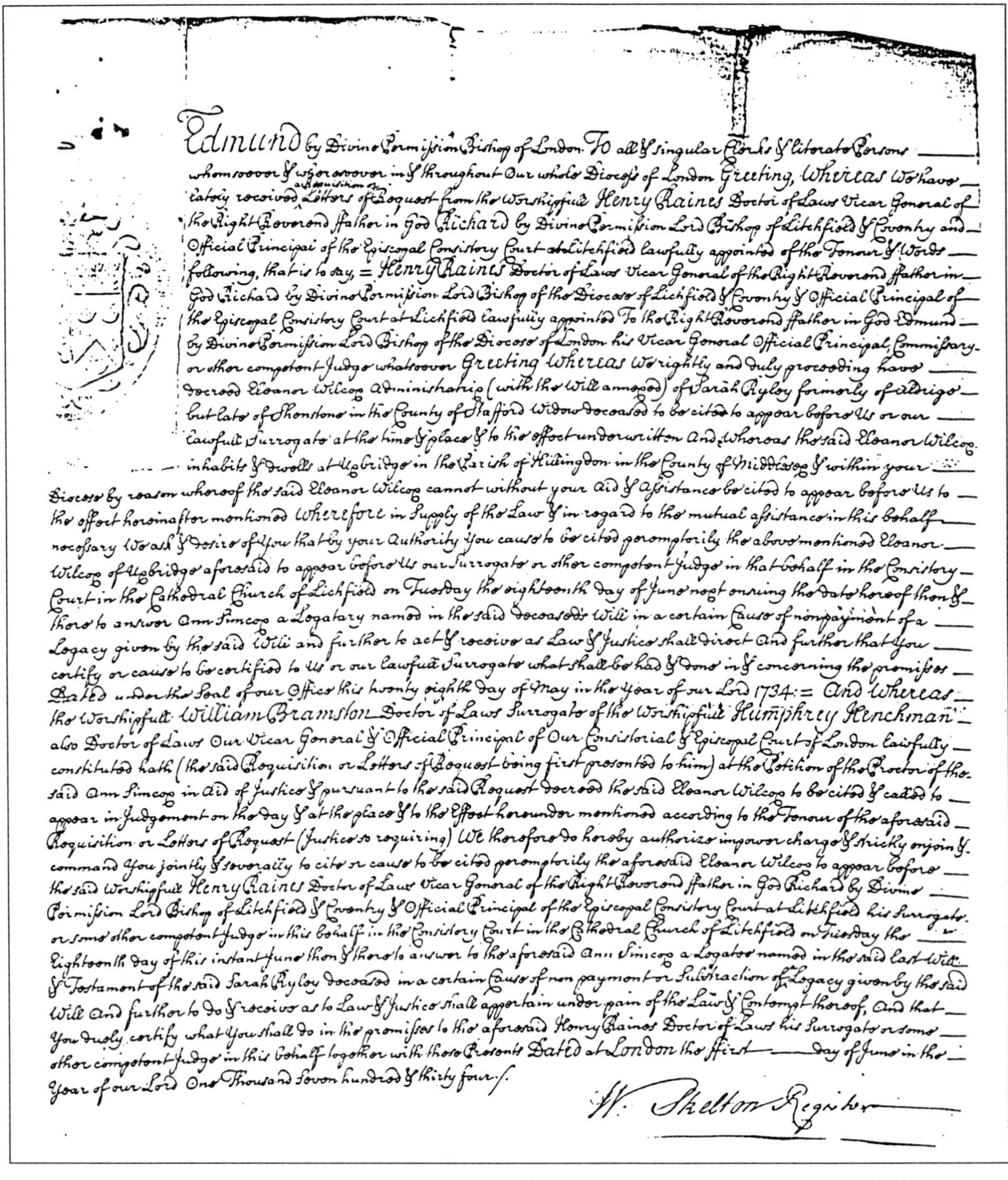

Edmund by Divine Permission Bishop of London To all & singular Clerks & literate Persons
whomsoever & wheresoever in & throughout Our whole Diocese of London Greeting, Whereas We have
lately received a Requisition or Letters of Request from the Worshipfull Henry Raines Doctor of Laws Vicar General of
the Right Reverend ffather in God Richard by Divine Permission Lord Bishop of Litchfield & Coventry and
Official Principal of the Episcopal Consistory Court at Litchfield lawfully appointed of the Tenour & Words
following, that is to say, = Henry Raines Doctor of Laws Vicar General of the Right Reverend ffather in
God Richard by Divine Permission Lord Bishop of the Diocese of Litchfield & Coventry & Official Principal of
the Episcopal Consistory Court at Litchfield lawfully appointed To the Right Reverend ffather in God Edmund
by Divine Permission Lord Bishop of the Diocese of London his Vicar General Official Principal Commissary
or other competent Judge whatsoever Greeting Whereas We rightly and duly proceeding have
decreed Eleanor Wilcox Administratrix (with the Will annexed) of Sarah Ryley formerly of Aldrige
but late of Shenstone in the County of Stafford Widow deceased to be cited to appear before Us or our
lawfull Surrogate at the time & place & to the effect underwritten And whereas the said Eleanor Wilcox
inhabits & dwells at Uxbridge in the Parish of Hillingdon in the County of Middlesex & within your
Diocese by reason whereof the said Eleanor Wilcox cannot without your Aid & Assistance be cited to appear before Us to
the effect hereinafter mentioned Wherefore in Supply of the Law & in regard to the mutual assistance in this behalf
necessary We ask & desire of You that by your Authority You cause to be cited peremptorily the above mentioned Eleanor
Wilcox of Uxbridge aforesaid to appear before Us our Surrogate or other competent Judge in that behalf in the Consistory
Court in the Cathedral Church of Litchfield on Tuesday the eighteenth day of June next ensuing the date hereof then &
there to answer Ann Simcox a Legatary named in the said deceased's Will in a certain Cause of nonpayment of a
Legacy given by the said Will and further to act & receive as Law & Justice shall direct And further that You
certify or cause to be certified to Us or our lawfull Surrogate what shall be had & done in & concerning the premisses
Dated under the Seal of our Office this twenty eighth day of May in the Year of our Lord 1734:= And Whereas
the Worshipfull William Bramston Doctor of Laws Surrogate of the Worshipfull Humphrey Henchman
also Doctor of Laws Our Vicar General & Official Principal of Our Consistorial & Episcopal Court of London lawfully
constituted hath (the said Requisition or Letters of Request being first presented to him) at the Petition of the Proctor of the
said Ann Simcox in Aid of Justice & pursuant to the said Request decreed the said Eleanor Wilcox to be cited & called to
appear in Judgment on the day & at the place & to the Effect hereunder mentioned according to the Tenour of the aforesaid
Requisition or Letters of Request (Justice so requiring) We therefore do hereby authorize impower charge & strictly enjoin &
command You jointly & severally to cite or cause to be cited peremptorily the aforesaid Eleanor Wilcox to appear before
the said Worshipfull Henry Raines Doctor of Laws Vicar General of the Right Reverend ffather in God Richard by Divine
Permission Lord Bishop of Litchfield & Coventry & Official Principal of the Episcopal Consistory Court at Litchfield his Surrogate
or some other competent Judge in this behalf in the Consistory Court in the Cathedral Church of Litchfield on Tuesday the
eighteenth day of this instant June then & there to answer to the aforesaid Ann Simcox a Legatee named in the said last Will
& Testament of the said Sarah Ryley deceased in a certain Cause of non payment or Subtraction of Legacy given by the said
Will And further to do & receive as to Law & Justice shall appertain under pain of the Law & Contempt thereof, And that
You duly certify what You shall do in the premisses to the aforesaid Henry Raines Doctor of Laws his Surrogate or some
other competent Judge in this behalf together with these Presents Dated at London the first day of June in the
Year of our Lord One Thousand Seven hundred & thirty four./

W. Skelton Register

Fig. 1.3 Letters of Request to the Diocese of London from the Bishop of Coventry and Lichfield requiring the presence of Eleanor Wilcox as administratrix of the estate of Sarah Ryley of Shenstone.

Edmund by Divine Permission Bishop of London To all & singular Clerks & literate Persons whomsoever & wheresoever in & throughout Our whole Diocess of London Greeting, Whereas We have lately received a Requisition or Letters of Request from the Worshipfull Henry Raines Doctor of Laws Vicar General of the Right Reverend Father in God Richard by Divine Permission Lord Bishop of Litchfield & Coventry and Official Principal of the Episcopal Consistory Court at Litchfield lawfully appointed of the Tenour & Words following, that is to say, Henry Raines Doctor of Laws Vicar General of the Right Reverend Father in God Richard by Divine Permission Lord Bishop of the Diocese of Lichfield & Coventry & Official Principal of the Episcopal Consistory Court at Lichfield lawfully appointed To the Right Reverend Father in God Edmund by Divine Permission Lord Bishop of the Diocese of London his Vicar General Official Principal, Commissary or other competent Judge whatsoever Greeting Whereas We rightly and duly proceeding have decreed Eleanor Wilcox Administratrix (with the Will annexed) of Sarah Ryley formerly of Aldridge but late of Shenstone in the County of Stafford Widow deceased to be cited to appear before Us or our lawfull Surrogate at the time & place & to the effect underwritten And Whereas the said Eleanor Wilcox inhabits & dwells at Uxbridge in the parish of Hillingdon in the County of Middlesex & within your Diocese by reason whereof the said Eleanor Wilcox cannot without your Aid & Assistance be cited to appear before Us to the effect hereinafter mentioned Wherefore in Supply of the Law & in regard to the mutual assistance in this behalf necessary We ask & desire of You that by your Authority You cause to be cited peremptorily the above mentioned Eleanor Wilcox of Uxbridge aforesaid to appear before Us our Surrogate or other competent Judge in that behalf in the Consistory Court in the Cathedral Church of Lichfield on Tuesday the eighteenth day of June next ensuing the date herefore then & there to answer Ann Simcox a Legatary named in the said deceased's Will in a certain Cause of non-payment of a Legacy given by the said Will and further to act & receive as Law & Justice shall direct And further that You certify or cause to be certified to Us or our lawfull Surrogate what shall be had & done in & concerning the premisses Dated under the Seal of our Office this twenty eighth day of May in the Year of our Lord 1734: And Whereas the Worshipfull William Bramston Doctor of Laws Surrogate of the Worshipfull Humphrey Henchman also Doctor of Laws Our Vicar General & Official Principal of our Consistorial & Episcopal Court of London lawfully constituted hath (the said Requisition or Letters of Request being first presented to him) at the Petition of the Proctor of the said Ann Simcox in Aid of Justice & pursuant to the said Request decreed the said Eleanor Wilcox to be cited & called to appear in Judgement on the day & at the place & to the Effect hereunder mentioned according to the Tenour of the aforesaid Requisition or Letters of Request (Justice so requiring) We therefore do hereby authorize impower charge & strictly enjoin & command You jointly & severally to cite or cause to be cited peremptorily the aforesaid Eleanor Wilcox to appear before the said Worshipfull Henry Raines Doctor of Laws Vicar General of the Right Reverend Father in God Richard by Divine Permission Lord Bishop of Litchfield & Coventry & Official Principal of the Episcopal Consistory Court at Litchfield his Surrogate or some other competent Judge in this behalf in the Consistory Court in the Cathedral Church of Litchfield on Tuesday the Eighteenth day of this instant June then & there to answer to the aforesaid Ann Simcox a Legatee named in the said last Will & Testament of the said Sarah Ryley deceased in a certain Cause of non payment or Substraction of a Legacy given by the said Will And further to do & receive as to Law & Justice shall appertain under pain of the Law & Contempt thereof, And that you duely certify what You shall do in the premisses to the aforesaid Henry Raines Doctor of Laws his Surrogate or some other competent Judge in this behalf together with these Presents Dated at London the First day of June in the Year of our Lord One Thousand Seven hundred & thirty four.

W. Skelton Register

Once the citation had been served, further action had to be taken. If no response was forthcoming, then the defendant would be declared contumacious, and if he still failed to respond he would then be declared excommunicate. At this point the defendant often resolved the matter, either by paying his tithes, making an apology for defamatory words spoken, attending to the administration of an estate or otherwise resolving the problem, and no more is heard of the cause. If an individual remained excommunicate for any length of time, his behaviour could be 'signified' to the local magistrate who would consign him to gaol.

The libel

If it was necessary to take matters further, a paper would then be produced, setting out the case to be preferred by the plaintiff, stating his name and occupation, the name of the defendant, the type of complaint and the name of the judge. This information was generally given in the preamble to the document, with the date of issue. The libel was only necessary in non-criminal causes pleaded in plenary form.[16] The facts of the cause would then be 'propounded', that is, listed in numbered paragraphs giving the legal justification for the cause and the details of the accusations that warranted the court's action. These paragraphs had to be clear, concise in their meaning and relevant to the matter in hand, and could run to over thirty in number. Transcriptions of libels for different types of causes are given in later chapters.

The libel begins an initial paragraph which gives the name of the person presiding over the court, their status and the parties concerned, and the parish in which they live (Fig. 1.4):[17]

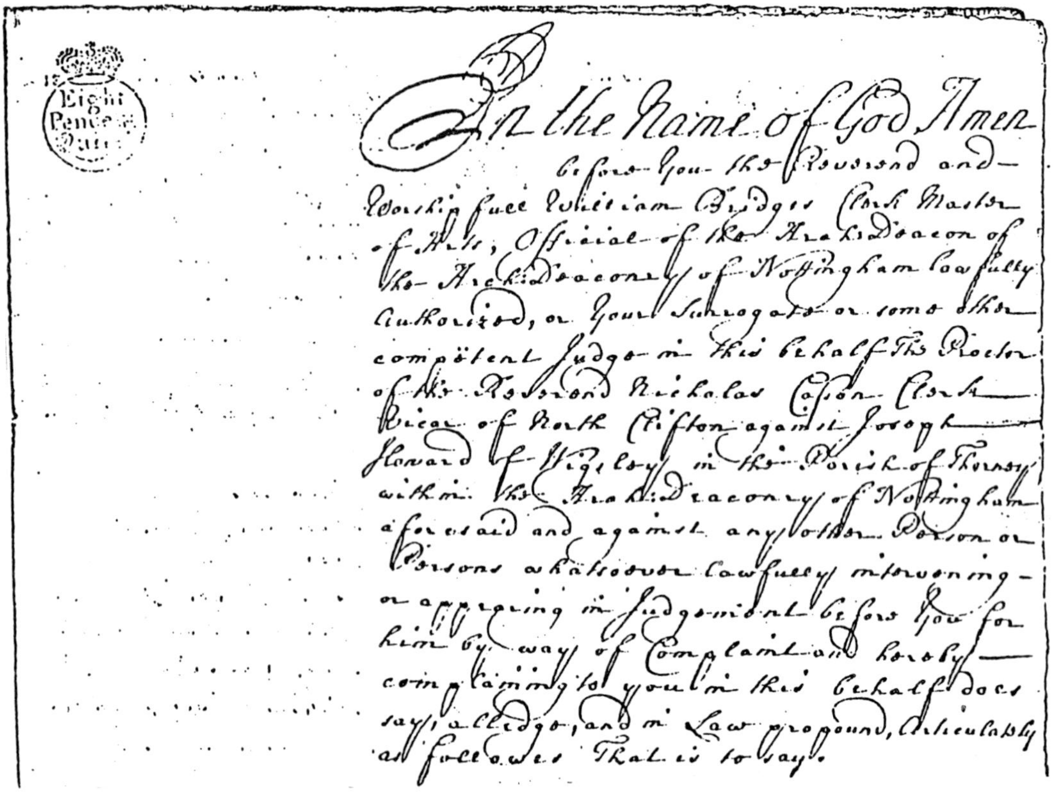
Eight Pence

In the Name of God Amen
Before You the Reverend and
Worshipfull William Bridges Clerk Master
of Arts, Official of the Archdeacon of
the Archdeaconry of Nottingham lawfully
authorized, or Your Surrogate or some other
competent Judge in this behalf The Proctor
of the Reverend Nicholas Cason Clerk
Vicar of North Clifton against Joseph
Howard of Wigsley in the Parish of Thorney
within the Archdeaconry of Nottingham
aforesaid and against any other Person or
Persons whatsoever lawfully intervening
or appearing in Judgment before You for
him by way of Complaint and hereby
complaining to you in this behalf does
say, allege, and in Law propound, Articulately
as followes That is to say.

Fig. 1.4 Introductory heading from a tithe cause in the Archdeaconry of Nottingham, giving the names of the Judge and the parties involved, the type of cause and the parish concerned.

> In the Name of God, Amen
> before You the Reverend and
> Worshipfull William Bridges Clerk Master
> of Arts, Official of the Arch Deacon of
> the Arch Deaconry of Nottingham lawfully
> Authorized, or Your Surrogate or some other
> competent Judge in this behalf The Proctor
> of the Reverend Nicholas Casson Clerk
> Vicar of North Clifton against Joseph
> Howard of Wigsley in the Parish of Thorney
> within the Arch Deaconry of Nottingham
> aforesaid and against any other Person or
> Persons whatsoever lawfully intervening
> or appearing in Judgement before You for
> him by way of Complaint and hereby
> complaining to you in this behalf does
> say, alledge, and in Law propound, Articulately
> as followes That is to say

This example was the preamble to a tithe cause, the vicar probably seeking payment for small tithes. This would be followed by the facts themselves, numbered and with formal wording for each type of cause.

After the numbered paragraphs on some libels, a tail piece follows, in similar form to that of an act book entry. This usually takes the form of a plea to the judge for the action the plaintiff's proctor would like to see followed (Fig. 1.5).[18]

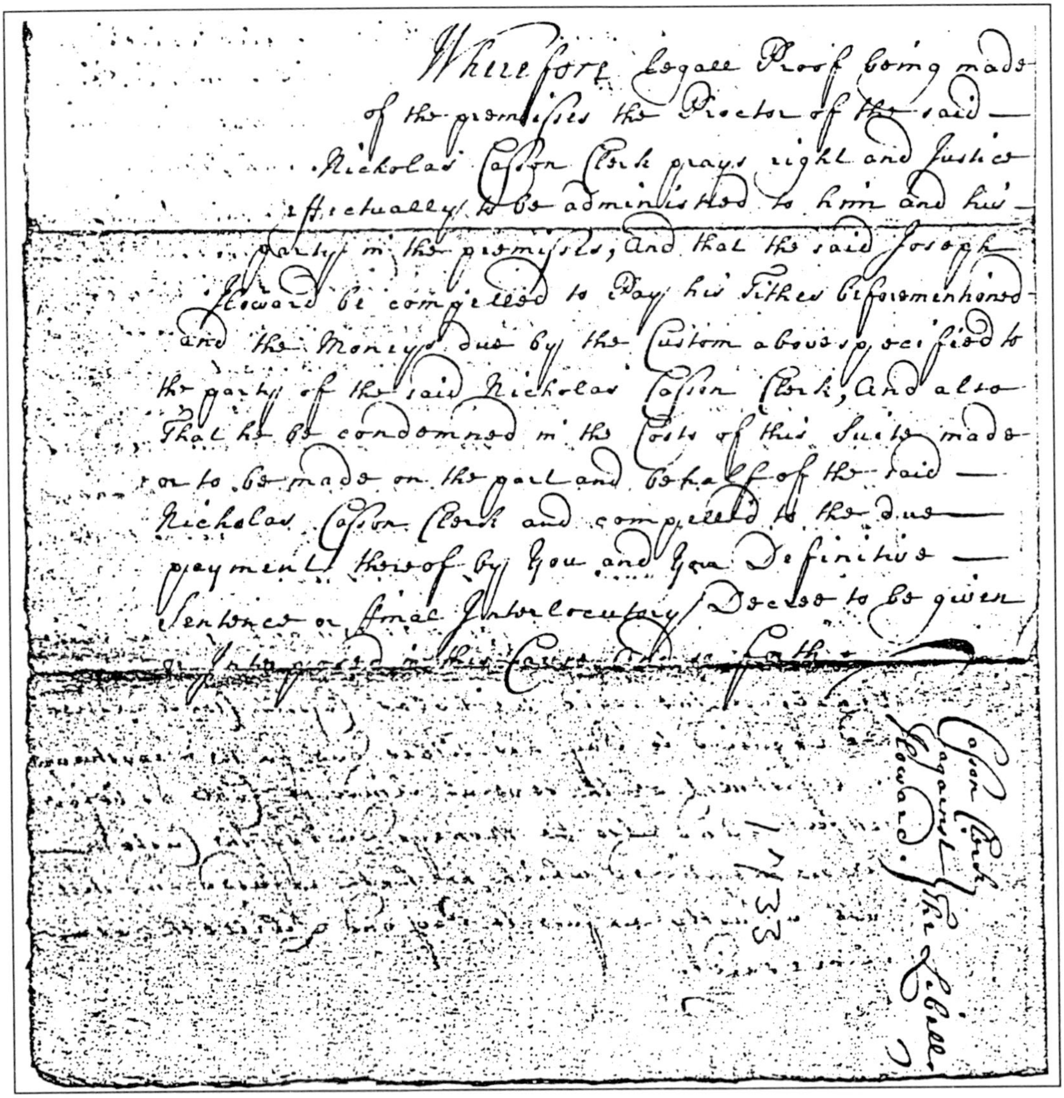

Wherefore Legall Proof being made of the premisses the Proctor of the said Nicholas Cosson Clerk prays right and Justice effectually to be administred to him and his party in the premisses, And that the said Joseph Steward be compelled to pay his Tithes beforementioned and the Moneys due by the Custom above specified to the party of the said Nicholas Cosson Clerk, And also That he be condemned in the Costs of this Suite made or to be made on the part and behalf of the said Nicholas Cosson Clerk and compelled to the due payment thereof by You and Your Definitive Sentence or final Interlocutory Decree to be given in and upon this Cause [illegible]

Cosson Clerk against Steward. The Libell 1733

Fig. 1.5 Tailpiece to the articles of libel from a tithe cause in the Archdeaconry of Nottingham. Note the endorsement on the outside of the folded document giving the names of plaintiff and defendant and the type of document.

Wherefore legall Proof being made
of the premisses the Proctor of the said
Nicholas Casson Clerk prays right and Justice
effectually to be administered to him and his
party in the premisses, And that the said Joseph
Howard be compelled to Pay his Tithes before mentioned
and the Moneys due by the Custom above specified to
the party of the said Nicholas Casson Clerk, And also
That he be condemned in the Costs of this Suite made
or to be made on the part and behalf of the said
Nicholas Casson Clerk and compelled to the due
payment thereof by You and Your Definitive
Sentence or Final Interlocutary Decree to be given
& Interposed in this Cause And so forth.

The personal answers

The responses of the defendant would be requested by means of a decree for 'personal answers' which were to be produced by the defendant's proctor. In these answers the facts of the libel would usually be denied, in order corresponding to the sequence of the paragraphs of the libel. Once a denial had been made, the suit would have to be contested '*contestio litis*'.

The allegation

Those facts which had been denied were then termed the allegation and the proctor requested a term probatory, or period of time in which to assemble the evidence.

The compulsory

It was often necessary for each party to produce witnesses who would be called by citations or by the use of a compulsory, which summoned them to give evidence in the cause. The form of a compulsory is as follows (Fig. 1.6):[19]

James Thomas Law Clerk Master of Arts Vicar General
and Official Principal of The Right Reverend Father in God
John by Divine Permission Lord Bishop of Lichfield and of his
Episcopal Consistory Court of Lichfield lawfully constituted To all
and singular Clerks and literate persons whomsoever Sendeth
Greeting Whereas we rightly and duly proceeding in a certain
Cause or business of defamation or Slander promoted by Frances
England Wife of Joseph England of Alfreton in the County of Derby
and Diocese of Lichfield the party agent and complainant of the
one part against William Simpson of Alfreton aforesaid Innkeeper
the party against whom the said Cause or business is promoted of the
other part have at the petition of the Proctor of the said Frances
England alledging that John Holley John Webster Samuel
Barrett and George Allen were and are necessary Witnesses to prove
the contents of a certain Libel given in and admitted in the said Cause
on the part and behalf of the said Frances England decreed the said
John Holley John Webster Samuel Barrett and George Allen to
be cited to appear in the manner and to the effect hereunder —
written justice so requiring We do therefore hereby authorize and empower
and strictly enjoin and command you jointly and severally peremptorily
to cite or cause to be cited the aforesaid John Holley John Webster Samuel
Barrett and George Allen that they and each of them appear personally
before Us our Surrogate or other competent Judge in this behalf in the
Lord Bishop's Consistory Court in the Cathedral Church of Lichfield and
place of Judicature there upon Wednesday the Seventeenth day of March
instant between the hours of nine in the forenoon and three in the
afternoon of the said day then and there to take the Oath of a
Witness usually taken and to testify the truth of what they know
in the said Cause or business And further to do and receive as Law and
Justice shall require under pain of the law and contempt thereof
And whatsoever you shall do or cause to be done in the
premises you shall duly certify to Us our Surrogate or other competent
Judge in this behalf together with these presents Given under
the Seal of our Office at Lichfield this Tenth day of
March in the year of our Lord One thousand eight hundred
and fifty two &c

J. Mott Regr.

James Thomas Law Clerk Master of Arts Vicar General
and Official Principal of the Right Reverend Father in God
John by Divine Permission Lord Bishp of Lichfield and of his
Episcopal Consistory court of Lichfield lawfully constituted. To all
and singular Clerks and literate persons whomsoever sendeth
Greeting. Whereas We rightly and duly proceeding in a certain
cause or business of defamation or slander promoted by Frances
England Wife of Joseph England of Alfreton in the County of Derby
and Diocese of Lichfield the party agent and complainant of the
one part against William Sampson of Alfreton aforesaid Innkeeper
the party against whom the said Cause or business is promoted of the
other part have at the petition of the Proctor of the said Frances
England alledging that John Rolley John Webster Samuel
Barrett and George Allen were and are necessary Witnesses to prove
the contents of a certain Libel given in and admitted in the said Cause
on the part and behalf of the said Frances England decreed the said
John Rolley John Webster Samuel Barrett and George Allen to
be cited to appear in the manner and to the effect hereunder
written justice requiring We do therefore hereby authorize empower
and strictly enjoin and command you jointly and severally peremptorily
to cite or cause to be cited the aforesaid John Rolley John Webster Samuel
Barrett and George Allen that they and each of them appear personally
before Us our Surrogate or other competent Judge in this behalf in the
Lord Bishop's Consistory Court in the Cathedral Church of Lichfield and
place of Judicature there upon Wednesday the seventeenth day of March
Instant between the hours of nine in the forenoon and three in the
Afternoon of the said day then and there to take the oath by
Witnesses usually taken and to testify the truth of what they know
in the said Cause or business And further to do and receive as Law and
Justice shall require under pain of the Law and contempt thereof
And whatsoever you shall be or lawfully cause to be done in the
premises you shall duly certify to Us our Surrogate or other competent
Judge in this behalf together with these presents Given under
the seal of our Office at Lichfield this Ninth day of
March in the year of our lord One thousand eight hundred
and fifty two.

John Mott Deputy Registrar

Fig. 1.6 A very late compulsory summoning witnesses to give evidence in a defamation cause, 1852.

The depositions and interrogatories

The statements of witnesses, known as depositions, were taken down verbatim, and in private, by the deputy registrar, in what was described as a 'foul draft' (or draught), a very appropriate description in some cases. However, they would have been copied out before being read in court and then signed by the witness and the registrar. In some later 18th-century causes, small slips of papers with the names of witnesses written on them with a list of articles are included with the depositions these are known as 'tickets for witnesses' (Fig. 1.7)[20] and represent the questions to which each witness was to respond. It was most important that there was no collusion between witnesses or influence on them by either of the participants and they were often questioned about this.

Depositions always give information about the witnesses, usually their name and occupation. The marital status of women is given, and sometimes their ages and the town or village where they lived. Occasionally, details of the residential movements of witnesses over a number of years are given, including the length of time spent in any one town or village. In some courts they also have to state how long they have known the parties in the dispute.[21] The depositions also had to be signed with a signature or mark, and therefore give a good indication of literacy at a particular period.

Witnesses could also be questioned by the opposing party and these questions are known as interrogatories. When these were administered, the replies sometimes follow on from the depositions, on the same sheet of paper. Typical lines of questioning involved in a dispute can be seen from the examples given in later chapters. These may involve some pertinent questions about the wealth of the witness, and their relationship to the parties in the cause. To separate the depositions of each group of witnesses is not difficult, as a brief description of the cause and for which party they appeared is given along the top of the paper. In more protracted causes, additional articles of libel would be propounded and witnesses produced by both parties.

The allegation *apud acta*

Occasionally an act of court would contain an allegation, described as an 'Allegation *apud Acta*' (Fig. 1.8):[22]

The mere Office of the Judge against Edward Robinson of Beeston and Martha Robinson his pretended Wife }	The Second Day of April in the Year of our Lord One Thousand Seven Hundred Thirty and Three

On which Day Stockdale Proctor for the Office
in supply of Proof of the Contents of certain
Articles given in and admitted by him in this
Cause Exhibited a certain Paper writing hereto
annext purporting to be a Bill of Presentment
beginning thus Beeston 9. October 1732: Wee
the Church Wardens there whose Names are hereunto
subscribed And so forth, And Ending William Constable
Henry Cox, and alledged that all and singular the
Contents of the said Paper Writing were and are true,
And that the Names and Sirnames subscribed to the
same were respectively wrote by the said William
Constable and Henry Cox on the Day of the Date thereof,
And that the same was Exhibited by them upon Oath
before the Worshipfull the Judge of this Court, All
which he alledged and propounded jointly and
severally, And did request or petition as is before
by him requested or petitioned in this Cause, or
otherwise that right and Justice be administred
And this Allegation be admitted.

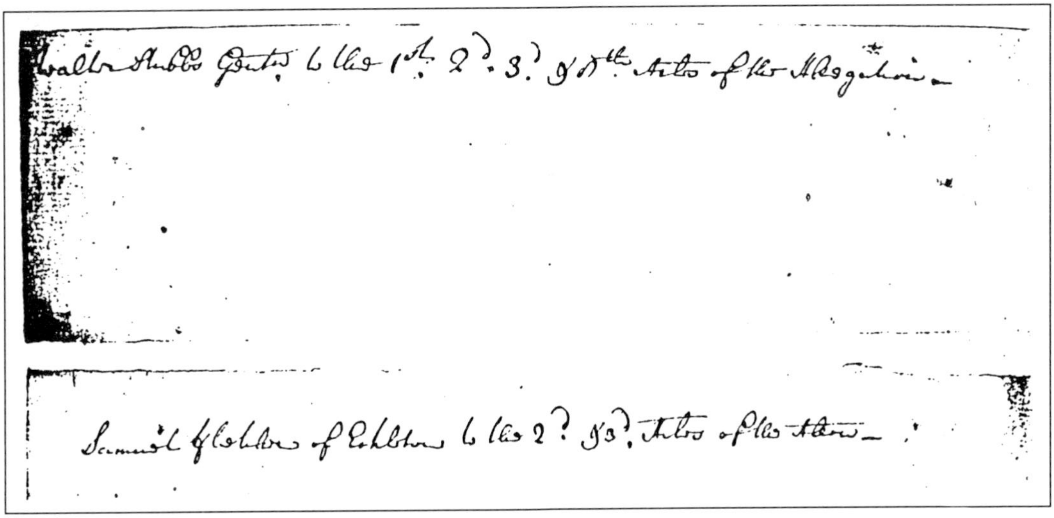

Fig. 1.7 Tickets for witnesses. These will only give the name of the witness and the number of the articles of allegation that they were to respond to.

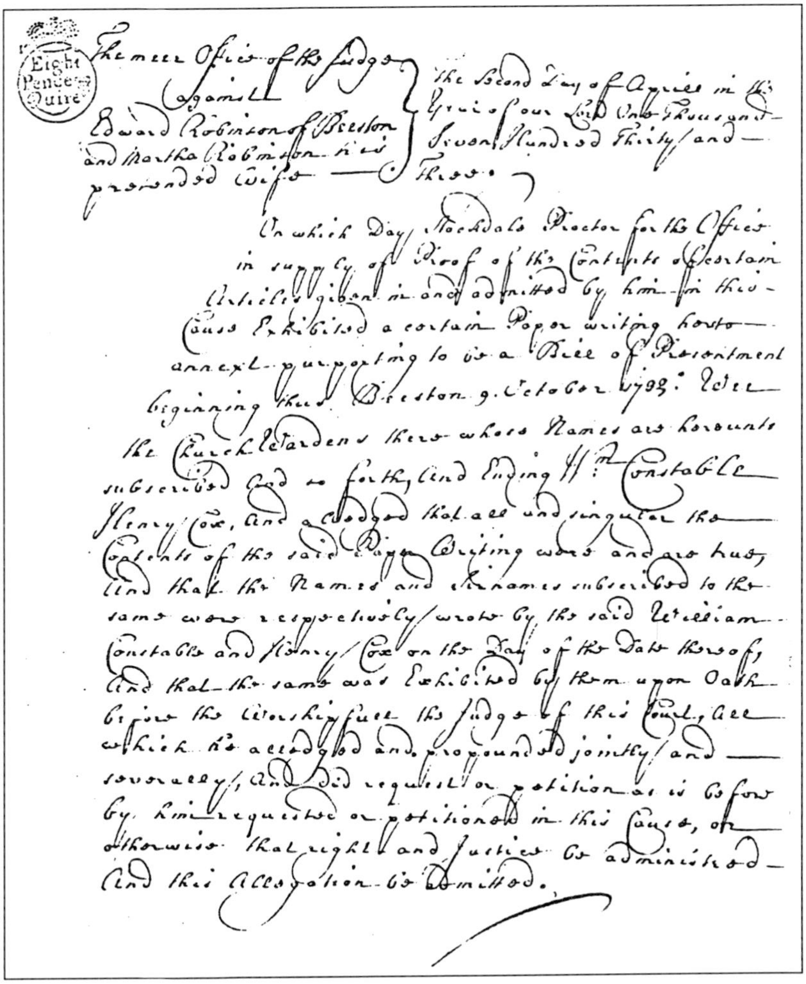

Fig. 1.8 Allegation *apud Acta*. This is an act of court containing an allegation. They are usually quite short.

Positions additionales sive Declaratories ad Articulares ex parte George Hand Notary Public contra Thomas Burbeck parochia Chesterfield in Comitatu Derbiae datus aet admissus sequuntur vidilicet

[Positions additional or remonstrations to the articles drawn up on the part of George Hand Notary Public against Thomas Burbeck of the parish of Chesterfield in the County of Derby given and admitted as follows, namely]

Imprimis That in ye Months of July August & September last past
some or one of them Anne Champernoon mentioned in ye articles
exhibited in this Cause being one Sunday Evening together
with one Hannah North walking in a meadow near to ye Town
of Chesterfield in ye County of Derby hard by an Indigo Mill
which he said Thomas Burbeck has in his possession &
meeting with the said Thomas there he came to them & desir'd
the said Hannah North to go to Charles Bantings an
ale house in ye said Town of Chesterfield & fetch a pint
of ale and bring it to him to his said Mill, and then gave
her money to pay for ye ale & an halfpenny for her
pains in fetching it, and the said Hannah at his Request
went accordingly, and so soon as ye said Hannah was gone
he ye said Thomas tooke ye aforesaid Anne Champernoon
who is blind of her Eyes, & lead her into the mill & locked
the doore upon her & then tooke her in his armes and threw
her down & put his hand upon her mouth to prevent her
crying out, & then & there had ye carnal knowledge of her body
& committed ye grievious Sin of Adultery
with her (he being then as he still is a marry'd man)
and then gave her money to conceal ye matter & not
discover him, telling her that if she prov'd with child
he wou'd take care of her or used words to this effect
Hoc qr etc pr tamen etc Et obmus et arlamur viy divy et de quolet[23]

2. Item that ye said Anne Champernoon sometime after ye
premisses in the foregoing article deduced finding her self
after an unusual manner did complain to one Mary Adsitt
who was then her bedfellow of great pains & uneasiness
in her belly & communicated to ye said Mary all ye particulars
which had been transacted between ye said Thomas & her
and quickly after the said Anne miscarry'd, which being
since discover'd. Hereupon a publique discourse arose in ye
said Town of Chesterfield, that the said Anne was begotten
with child by ye said Thomas Burbeck & had miscarry'd of ye same

Positions additional

In a long dispute, 'positions additional' could also be generated at this stage giving further information provided by one of the parties (Fig. 1.9)(opposite).[24]

When all the evidence had been produced, an entry in the act book would record a 'term to propound all acts' or the assignment of a period of time for the proctors to gather information together, after which date no further evidence was to be produced. After this a 'term to conclude' would be assigned, when the outcome of the cause would be decided.

The sentence

The sentence at the end of the cause 'puts an end to the suit in controversy'[25] and is known as a definitive sentence. This had to be produced in writing and to be read in the presence of both parties. The documents can often be confusing in that two versions were produced, one by each party. At Lichfield, a space would be left in the centre of the first page requiring the word 'Justice' to be inserted, which would have been completed on the version signed by the judge. This would be legally binding; those incomplete and always unsigned versions relate to the defeated parties, and were often left with the papers in the registry. However, some sentences do remain in the cause papers giving the decisions of the judge. All begin with the phrase '*In Dei Nomine, Amen*', and continue down the page, discussing in great and stylised detail the trouble that had been taken to reach the verdict. The wording of the actual decision may also be confusing and, even when in English, requires some thought to understand it.

Not all '*sententia*' were pronounced at the end of the cause; on some occasions it was necessary to give some firm decision on a point of law at an intermediate stage of the proceedings; such decisions are known as interlocutory decrees. The following example gives some indication of the complexity of wording of a definitive sentence (Fig. 1.10).[26] [The dots and lettering in a bold typeface indicate where insertions were made in the text.]

Fig. 1.9 (opposite) Positions additional, showing the amount of information that can sometimes be given when the cause is contested.

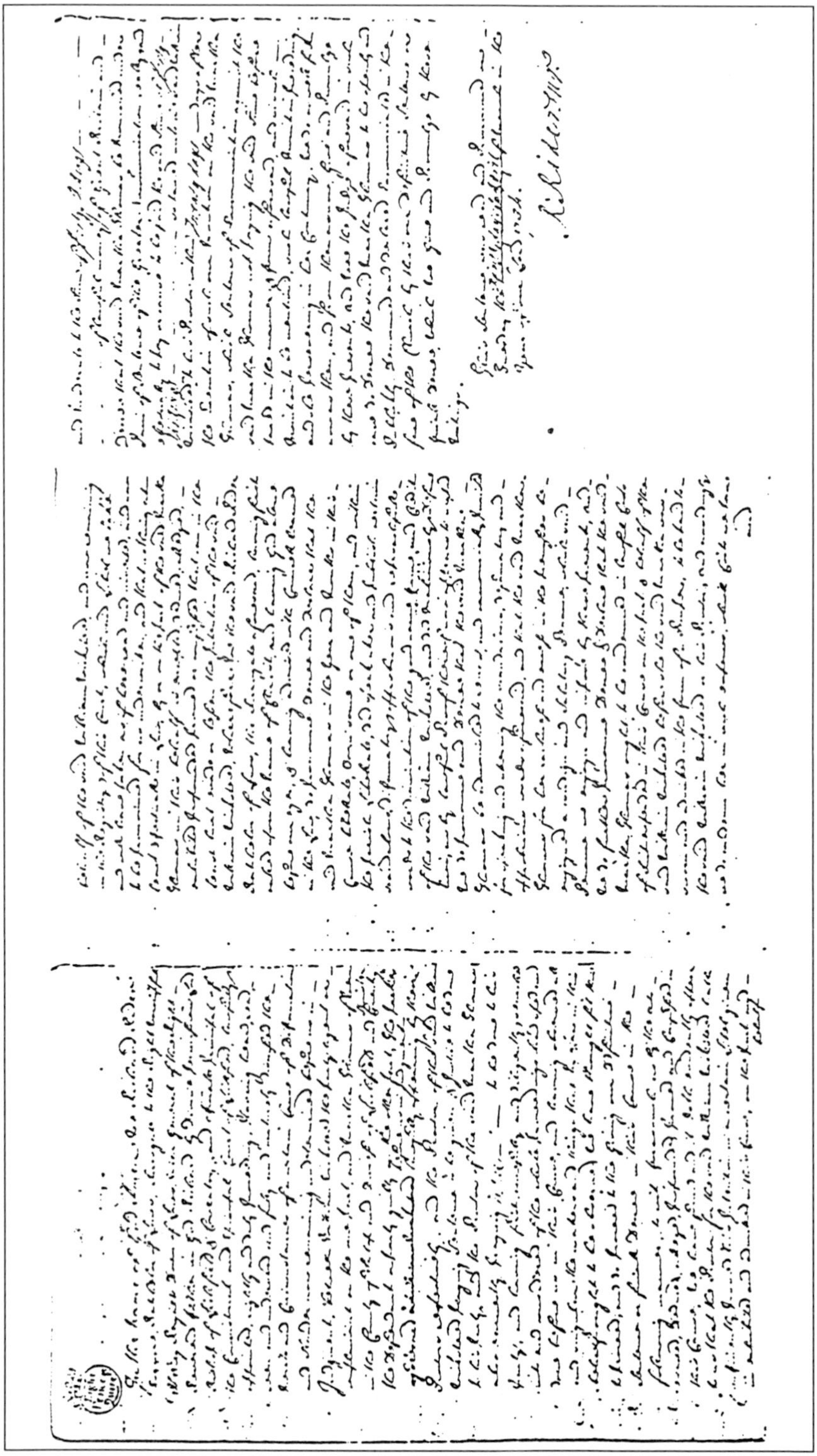

Fig. 1.10 Sentence in defamation cause, showing insertions made into the text. In this cause, Martha Thomas had decided, during the proceedings, to plead in *'forma pauperis'*.

In the Name of God Amen We Richard Rider Esquire, Batchelor of Laws, Surrogate to the Right Worshipfull Henry Raynes Doctor of Laws, Vicar General of the Right Reverend Father in God Richard by Diving Permission Lord Bishop of Lichfield & Coventry, and Official Principal of the Consistorial and Episcopal Court of Lichfield, lawfully appointed, rightly and duly proceeding, Having heard, read, seen and understood and fully and maturely discussed the Merits and Circumstances of a certain Cause of Diffamation and Slander now remaining undetermined before us in Judgement, between William Wicksteed the party agent or complainant on the one part, and Martha Thomas of Wem in the County of Salop and Diocess of Lichfield and Coventry, spinster, the Defendent or party guilty on the other part, The parties aforesaid lawfully appearing before us in Judgement by their Proctors respectively, and the Proctor of the said William Wicksteed praying Sentence to be given & Justice to be done to his party, and the Proctor of the said Martha Thomas also earnestly praying **...Justice...** to be done to his party, and having first carefully and diligently searched into and considered of the whole proceedings had sped and done before us in this Cause, and having observed all and singular the matters and things that by Law in this behalf ought to be observed, We have thought fit then to proceed, and do proceed to the Giving our Definitive Sentence or finall Decree in this Cause in the following manner, to wit, Forasmuch as by the Acts enacted, Deduced, alleged, propounded, proved and Confessed in this Cause, We have found and it doth evidently appear to us that the Proctor for the said William Wicksteed hath sufficiently proved his Intention in a certain Libel given in exhibited and admitted in this Cause, on the part and behalf of the said William Wicksteed, and now remaining in the Registry of this Court, which said Libel we take and will have taken as if here read and inserted, and now to be pronounced for as underwritten, and that nothing at least efectuall in Law, by or on the part of the said Martin Thomas in this behalf is excepted, deduced, alledged, exhibited propounded proved or confessed that can in the least hurt evade or lessen the Intention of the said William Wicksteed, Wherefore We the said Richard Rider Batchelor of Laws, the Surrogate aforesaid, having first called upon the Name of Christ, and having God alone before our eyes, & having advised with Counsell learned in the Law, do pronounce Decree and Declare that the said Martha Thomas in the Year and Months in this Cause libellate, Or in some or one of them, and within the parish Libellate, did speak utter and publish certain scandalous, diffamatory & opprobrious and reproachfull words to the diminution of the good name, Fame and Credit of the said William Wicksteed, and did Maliciously Defame him, as by lawful Proof thereof now appears to us, And We do pronounce and Decree that the said Martha Thomas be admonished to recant, and canonically punished for speaking and uttering the scandalous, defamatory and opprobrious words aforesaid, and that the said Martha Thomas for her rashness and excess in the premisses be enjoyned a condign and Salutary Penance, which said Penance we enjoyn and impose by these presents, and We do further pronounce Decree & Declare that the said Martha Thomas ought to be condemmed in lawful Costs of Suit expended in this Cause on the part & behalf of the said William Wicksteed before she the said Martha was sworn and admitted in the Form of a Pauper, to be paid to the said William Wicksteed or his Proctor, and accordingly we do condemn her in such expenses, which Costs we tax and moderate to the Sum of **..Forty Shillings..** of lawful money of Great Britain and Decree that the said Martha Thomas be Monished under Pain of Sentence of the Greater Excommunication really and effectually to pay or cause to be paid the said Summe of **..Forty Shillings..** so taxed unto the said William Wicksteed or to his Proctor within **..Twenty days..** days after the Execution of such our Monition on the said Martha Thomas, which Sentence of Excommunication against the said Martha Thomas not paying the said Summe before taxed in the manner & Form aforesaid, and in such Monition to be mentioned, such lawful Monition proceeding, and she perservering in her Contumacy, We do as well from now as then, and from then as now, Give and Promulge by these presents, and Wee the Judge aforesaid in such case do Decree the said Martha Thomas to be openly and Publickly Denounced and declared Excommunicated in the face of the Church by this our Definitive Sentence or Final Decree, which we give and Promulge by these writings.

This Sentence was read and Pronounced on Tuesday the ..Ninth day of April, in the Year of our Lord 1734

R. Rider Surrogate.

From the wording it can be seen that Martha was pleading in '*forma pauperis*'; in other words she was not worth more than £5, but if she did not pay the costs of the cause incurred before she was sworn to be a pauper, she would be declared excommunicate. She was also to perform a penance, the normal punishment in such causes. We can tell that this was the sentence actually passed, as it was signed and dated by the surrogate in this case, and the word 'Justice' on the front of the document has been filled in, together with the amount of costs and the period of time in which they were to be paid. This form of pleading in '*forma pauperis*' is unusual, and where there was any doubt on this subject witnesses would be brought to testify to the plaintiff's poverty, which occasionally involved listing and valuing their goods, almost in the form of an inventory taken for probate purposes.

In those cases where there is no sentence the alternatives are: that the dispute was settled out of court, that the documents have not survived, or that the victorious party took the document away. For the last two possibilities the relevant act book should record that the sentence was pronounced.

The bill of costs and monition

Bills of costs could be prepared at intervals throughout a long cause, but were generally produced after the 'sententia' had been read. The bills were always carefully itemised, listing the legal actions carried out and the types of document produced, with the cost of each. If sentence had been read, there is often a statement of the taxation of the bill at the bottom of the page, signed by a surrogate. The taxation was on a sliding scale in proportion to the costs incurred, and formed a source of revenue for the court. The tax payable was sometimes moderated, or reduced, and this is noted on some documents. The following bill is a comparatively small one, relating to the sentence above (Fig. 1.11):[27]

Fig. 1.11 Bill of costs relating to the defamation cause.

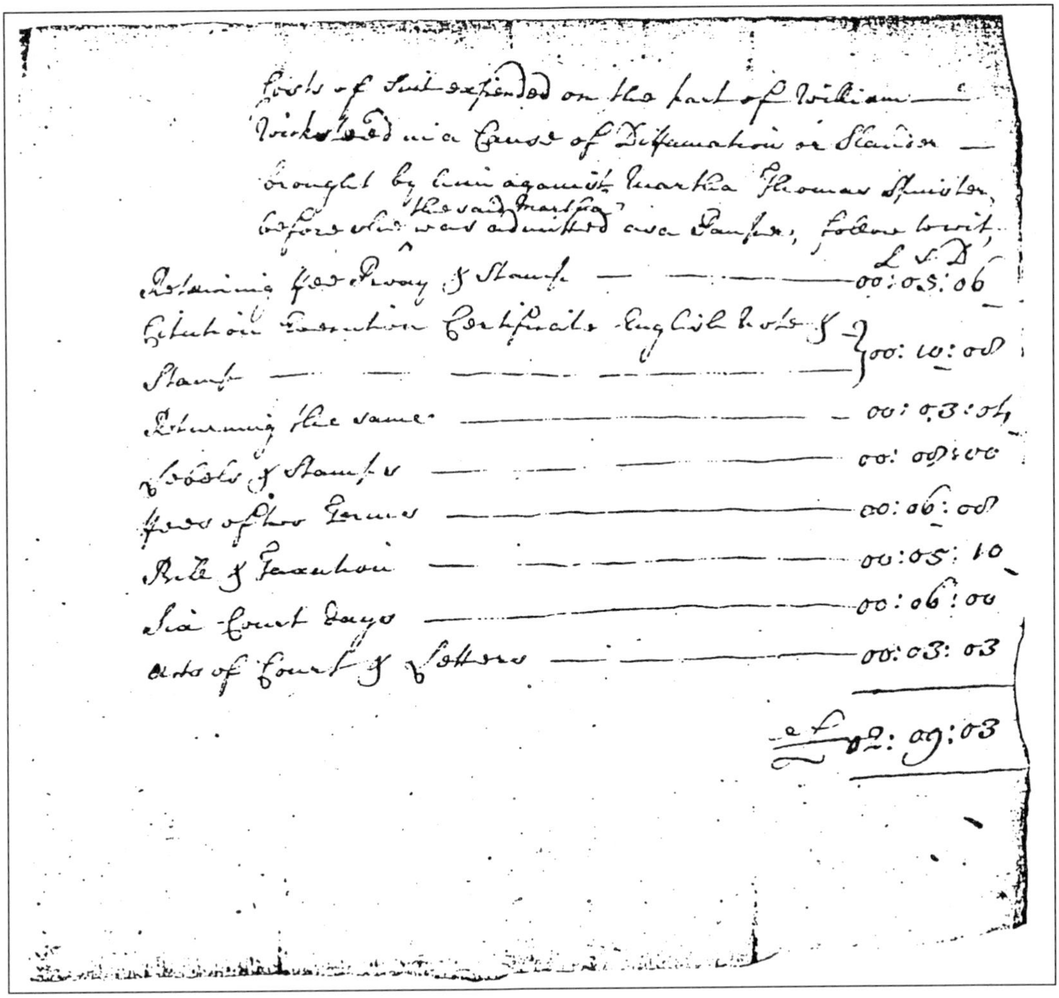

Costs of Suit expended on the part of William
Wicksteed in a Cause of Diffamation of Slander
brought by him against Martha Thomas Spinster,
before she the said Martha was admitted as a Pauper, follows to wit,

	£	s	d
Retaining Fee Proxy & Stamp	00	:05	:06
Citation Execution Certificate English Note & Stamp	00	:10	:08
Returning the same	00	:03	:04
Lebels* and Stamps	00	:08	:00
Fees of two Terms	00	:06	:08
Bill & Taxation	00	:05	:10
Six Court days	00	:06	:00
Acts of Court and Letters	00	:03	:03
	£02	:09	:03

* Possibly a spelling error, the word should read libels.

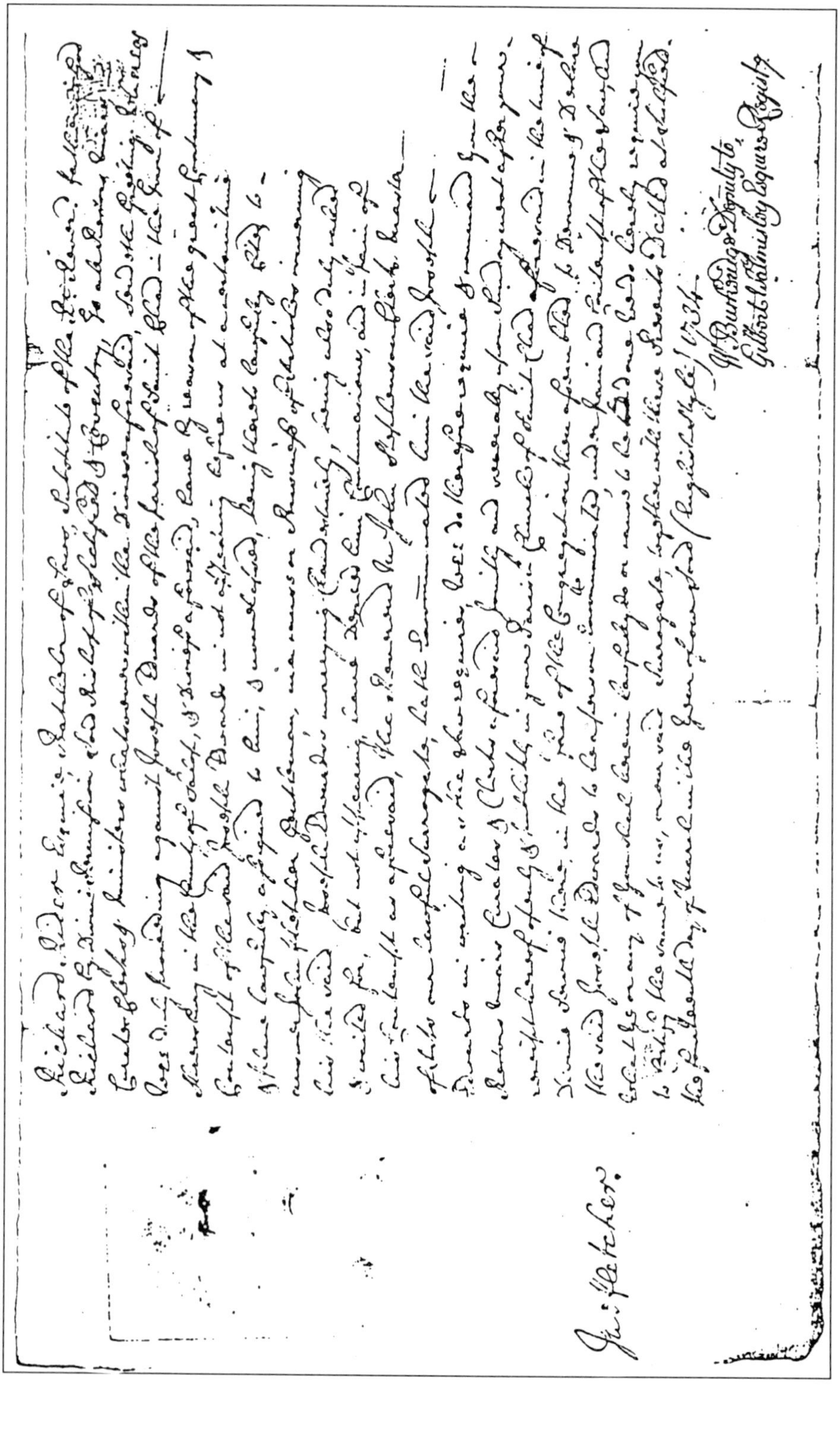

Fig. 1.12 Excommunication to be read in church, Joseph Edwards having failed to appear in court concerning his clandestine marriage.

A monition, or warning, to pay the costs was then taken out and delivered to the party paying the bill, who was then further charged for the privilege! Failure to pay up could lead to further action by the proctor in the church court, by means of an office cause seeking redress for non-payment of fees, stipend and salary.

The excommunication

Where payment was not forthcoming, or one of the parties was declared contumacious by non-attendance at court, the penalty of excommunication was incurred. This required a statement to be read out in church at the time of divine service as shown opposite and below (Fig. 1.12):[28]

Richard Rider Esquire Batchelor of Laws, Substitute of the Right Reverend Father in God
Richard by divine Permission Lord Bishop of Lichfield and Coventry, To all Rectors, Vicars,
Curates Clerks & Ministers whatsoever within the Diocese aforesaid, Sendeth Greeting Whereas
Wee duly proceeding against Joseph Edwards of the parish of Saint Chad in the Town of
Shrewsbury in the County of Salop, & Diocess aforesaid, have by reason of the great Contumacy &
Contempt of the said Joseph Edwards in not appearing before us at a certain time
& place lawfully assigned to him, & nowe lapsed, being thereto lawfully Cited to
answer John Fletcher Gentleman, in a cause or Business of Articles concerneing
his the said Joseph Edwards's marrying Clandestinely, being also duly called
& waited for, but not appearing have Decreed him Contumacious, and in pain of
his Contempt as aforesaid, the Reverend Mr. John Stephenson Clerk, Master
of Arts our lawful Surrogate, hath Excommunicated him the said Joseph
Edwards in writing as the Law requires, Wee do therefore require & command you the
Rectors, Vicars, Curates & Clerks aforesaid Jointly and severally upon Sunday next after your
receipt hereof openly & publickly in your Parish Church of Saint Chad aforesaid in the time of
Divine Service there, in the face of the Congregation then assembled, to Denounce & Declare
the said Joseph Edwards to be a person Excommunicated, under pain and Contempt of the Law, And
what ye or any of you shall herein lawfully do or cause to be done We do hereby require you
to Certify the same to us, or our said Surrogate, together with these Presents Dated at Lichfield
the fourteenth day of March in the Year of our Lord (English Style) 1734.

W. Buckeridge Deputy to
Gilbert Walmisley Esquire Registrar

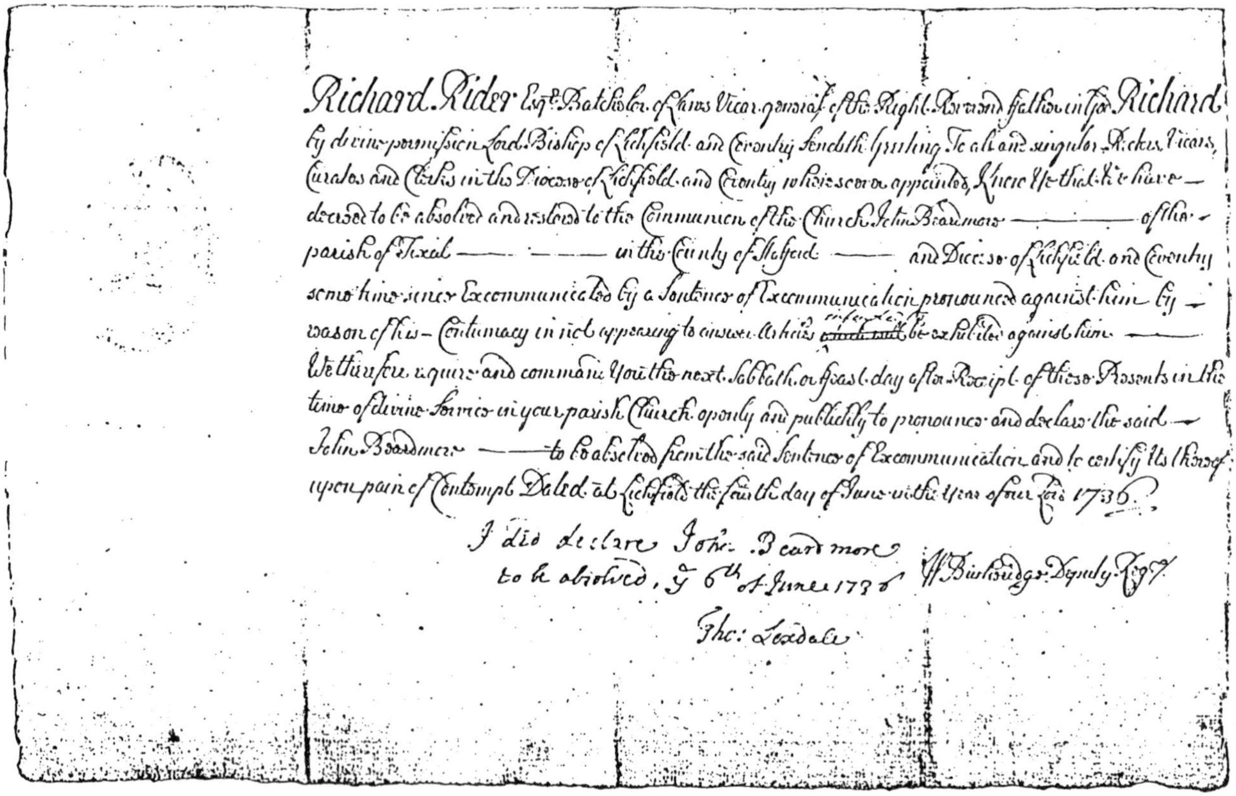

Richard Rider Esquire Batchelor of Laws Vicar General of the Right Reverend Father in God Richard
by divine permission Lord Bishop of Lichfield and Coventry Sendeth Greeting To all and singular Rectors, Vicars,
Curates and Clerks in the Diocese of Lichfield and Coventry wheresoever appointed, Know Ye that We have
decreed to be absolved and restored to the Communion of the church John Beardmore of the
parish of Tixal in the County of Stafford and Diocese of Lichfield and Coventry
some time since Excommunicated by a Sentence of Excommunication pronounced against him by
reason of his Contumacy in not appearing to answer Articles intended to be exhibited against him
We therefore require and command You the next Sabbath or Feast day after Receipt of these Presents in the
time of divine Service in your parish Church openly and publickly to pronounce and declare the said
John Beardmore to be absolved from the said Sentence of Excommunication and to certify Us thereof
upon pain of Contempt Dated at Lichfield the fourth day of June in the Year of our Lord 1736.

I did declare John Beardmore
to be absolved, ye 6th of June 1736 — W. Buckeridge Deputy Registrar
Thomas Loxdale

Fig. 1.13 Absolution from excommunictation, after a bonfire caused a disturbance in the churchyard of Tixal.

As with a citation, the name of the proctor, in this case John Fletcher, drawing the document from the registry would be signed on the left-hand side, near the end of the document, directly below the seal of the vicar general. Most of these excommunications simply relate to the lesser form, or exclusion from divine worship and the sacrament, sometimes described as *ab ingressu ecclesiae* [from entry into church]. This punishment did have legal implications in that any individual standing excommunicate could not be presented to a benefice, or act as a lawyer, a witness or executor of a will until they had been absolved. Christian burial could also be refused to any who died excommunicate. The sentence of greater excommunication also rendered the will made by an individual invalid.

The absolution

At some time, anything up to ten years later, the individual would be absolved from excommunication and the following statement would be read in church, signed and returned to the registry (Fig. 1.13):[29]

Note the use of the term vicar general in this document, wherein Richard Rider was acting in his role of correction only. John and his friend John Malpas had been brought to court for their involvement in making a bonfire in the churchyard. They both suffered excommunication and were later absolved.

The significavit

The final sanction against those who refused to co-operate with the courts was the 'significavit',[30] or writ of '*de excommunicato capiendo*', directed to the local magistrates to detain individuals in the local gaol after they had stood excommunicate for a period exceeding forty days, and pending their remorse and absolution. Examples are rare because the documents were sent to the justices of the peace, in whose records they would have been kept (Fig. 1.14).[31]

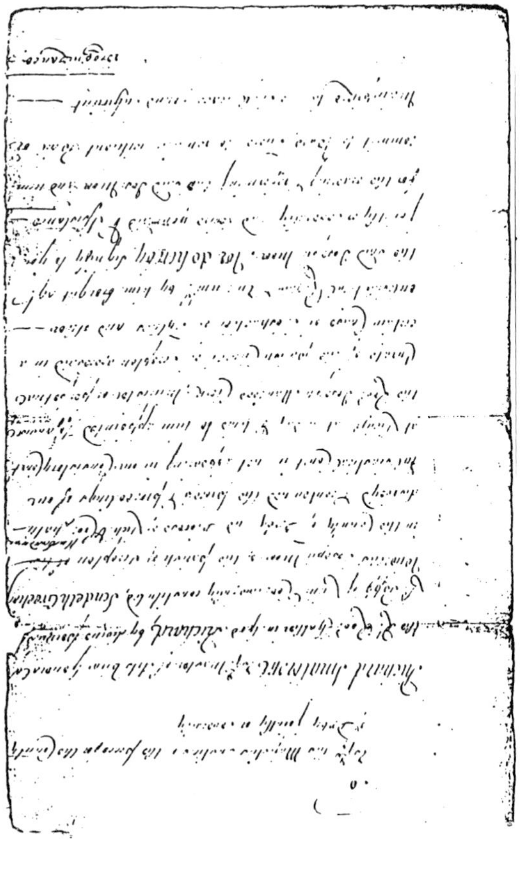

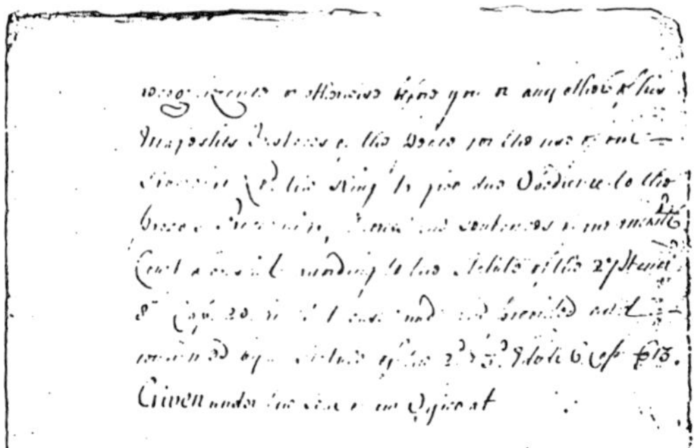

Fig. 1.14 Significavit from a tithe cause. Joseph Moor was to be imprisoned for failing to pay his tithes to Rev. Joseph Manlove, clerk of Scropton.

To
Esquires his Majesties Justices of the peace for the County
of Derby jointly or severally
Richard Smalbroke Esquire Master of Arts Vicar General of the
Right Reverend Father in God Richard, by divine permission
Lord Bishopp of Lichfield & Coventry lawfully constituted, Sendeth Greeting
Whereas Joseph Moor of the parish of Scropton
in the County of Derby and Diocese of Lichfield & Coventry husbandman hath
disobey'd & contemned the process and proceedings of our
Ecclesiastical Court in not appearing in our Consistory Court
at Lichfield at a day & time to him appointed to answer
the Reverend Joseph Manlove Clerk, Minister or perpetual
Curate of the parish church of Scropton aforesaid in a
certain Cause of Substraction of Tythes and other
ecclesiastical Rights & Emoluments by him brought against
the said Joseph Moor. We do hereby signify to you
jointly or severally and desire your aid & Assistance
for the ordering and reforming the said Joseph Moor and him
commit to Ward, There to remain without Bail or
Mainprize[32] till he shall have found sufficient
recognizance or otherwise before you or any other of his
Majesties Justices of the peace for the use of our
sovereign Lord the King to give due Obedience to the
process, Proceedings, Decrees and Sentences of our ecclesiastical
Court aforesaid according to the Statute of the 27 Henry
8th Cap. 20 in that case made and provided and
confirmed by a statute of the 2d and 3d Edward 6 Cap 13.
Given under the seal of our Office at

This item probably survived in the Lichfield records because it was incomplete, being unsigned.

The prohibition

Some causes were transferred to the secular courts, particularly tithe causes and other business involving financial damages which were outside the remit of the church courts. This generated one of the most fearsome documents in the repertoire, the prohibition. This was a procedure intended to prevent any further action in the church courts, prior to the transfer of the cause to the civil courts. During the late 16th and early 17th centuries the prohibition was written on parchment in a small, late medieval hand, in Latin in closely packed lines often on a large page. A late example is given in the chapter relating to tithe disputes (see Fig. 5.4, p.110).

This action required copies to be made of the existing documents that had been generated during the church court proceedings. The papers had to be copied out by hand in their correct sequence, and the spacing of the words and lines on the page was such that it was often said of these documents that 'the words were afraid of each other'! It may also have had something to do with the cost of the copies, which were charged by the page.

Evidence

Some of these causes produced items used in evidence. Extracts from baptismal and marriage registers were the most common, as well as testimonials for individuals, often members of the clergy. A 'gold' ring which figured large in one case was also kept with the documents at Lichfield, although this is a very rare find. (It was, incidentally, brass!)

Chapter Two

Office Business

There were two major themes in the Office business of the spiritual courts. The primary concern of the courts was the spiritual discipline both of the clergy and of their parishioners, and their second concern was the administration of the church. Causes relating to discipline were generally described as 'correction' business, one of the functions of the bishop being to correct the manners and morals of his flock *pro salute animae* for the 'health of their souls'. These causes were heard by the chancellor of the diocese in his role as vicar general being concerned with the souls of the faithful. The causes were also described as criminal but in a highly specialised sense, in that they offended against the canons of the church, but this should on no account be confused with the meaning of the word in relation to the secular courts. Causes were generally heard in summary form, thus leaving few documents (these mainly citations) but the proceedings were also noted in the act books. Some types of business were heard in plenary form and produced depositions by witnesses, and these will be noted later.

Types of cause

The causes in this group were heard in three different categories as defined by Grey.[1]

> In criminal Causes the Proceedings of the Ecclesiastical Courts are
> by Inquisition, or *ex Officio mero*;
> or by Accusation, or *ex Officio promoto*;
> or by Denunciation or Presentment of Church-wardens in Visitations, etc.

The first two types of cause are indentified as such in the citations and the act books. Causes proceeding *ex officio mero* and by denunciation came to the spiritual courts by way of churchwardens' presentments at visitations by archdeacons, bishops and metropolitans. The archdeacon visited his deaneries every year, and episcopal visitations took place in the bishop's first year in office and every third year thereafter. Until the civil war the churchwardens' presentments made on these occasions were listed in the '*libri comperta*' or books of detections. These presentments reported any residents involved in any 'common fame' in the parish, and included those who had failed to attend church or who had committed any of a wide range of offences against canon law. During bishops' visitations the business of the archdeacons' courts would have been suspended by an inhibition[2] for six months and the jurisdiction was exercised by the bishop. A similar process took place during the visitation of the metropolitan, or archbishop. With the decline of the archdeacons' courts after the civil war, fewer presentments were made. The churchwardens had to respond to a series of printed questions issued by the archdeacon, but many were returned simply signed *omnia bene* or 'all is well'.

By the nature of the court procedure, instance business in this category of causes did not arise. However it was possible for an individual to 'promote' a cause through the office, particularly where there was opposition to the granting of a faculty for the confirmation of a church seat.

Range of office business

Office business covered a wide range of causes, but most did not occur frequently, and they also tended to vary with time and from diocese to diocese. By the 18th century in Lichfield, office causes focused on the granting of faculties, the collection of church levies, clandestine marriage and immorality. The number of causes heard by the archdeaconry courts also diminished quickly after the Restoration, probably due to the type of administrative arrangements which have been noted in the Oxford diocese,[3] and at Lichfield, whereby officers of the archdeacons' courts also held positions in the consistory courts, and business gradually moved to the higher court.

Some idea of the wide variety of offences in office business can be seen from the list below, grouped by broad types of defendant:

Clergy:
- Preaching without a licence
- Intrusion into the cure[4]
- Discipline of the clergy for incontinence, gaming, drunkenness

Parishioners:
- Excommunication/Absolution
- Standing excommunicate for a long period of time
- Non-attendance at church
- Failure to receive the sacrament
- Failure to attend catechism
- Failure to be churched after childbirth
- Failure to have child baptised into the Anglican church
- Scolding
- Hindering preaching
- Recusancy
- Brawling in the church or churchyard
- Laying violent hands upon a clergyman
- Scandal to the Ministry and its Function (a form of defamation against the clergy)
- Church seat disputes: perturbation of sitting; intrusion into seat
- Clandestine marriage
- Immorality, including fornication and adultery
- Incest
- Rash administration of wills
- Perjury
- Untimely ringing of bells

Parish officers and professional individuals:
- Unlicensed curates, schoolmasters, midwives, and surgeons
- Parish clerks, election of and intrusion into office
- Churchwardens—not properly sworn

Fabric of church and associated buildings:
- Faculties for alterations to the fabric of the church and its seating re-building or alterations to parsonage houses and their farm buildings
- Failing to maintain the churchyard, its walls and gates
- Dilapidations of parsonages

Revenues of the church:
- Church levies
- Churchwardens' accounts
- Sequestration accounts
- Fees, stipend and salary, claimed by court officials, parish clerks, and clergy

The Clergy

The control of the clergy was an important facet of the work of the spiritual courts, particularly between the Reformation and the end of the 16th century, when political events tended to dominate the church. During this period unlicensed preaching was the subject of many causes and intrusions into a cure were also regarded as 'criminal' offences. By the 18th century clerics who had been a little lax in applying the rules with regard to the issue of marriage licences, or performed irregular ceremonies, would be summoned to appear and explain their activities. Other causes could result from discontent within the parish, or of the patron of the living either as a direct result of the behaviour of the cleric or of parochial politics. The vicar of Ellesmere, John Ottiwell, was the subject of a disciplinary hearing in 1706 when depositions were made describing various incidents which occurred in the parish (Fig. 2.1) (below and overleaf).[5]

Elizabeth Evans, uxor Thoma Evans de Elsmere in Comitatu Salop English Schole Master 60 annos ad circuiter nata noscens Arthuru Dickin 2 annos et Johem Ottiwel partes 30 annos super allegacionis predicta 12 die Septemb 1706 examinata

[Elizabeth Evans, wife of Thomas Evans of Ellesmere in the County of Shropshire English School Master born 60 years ago or thereabouts and has known Arthur Dicken for 2 years and John Ottiwel 30 years parties upon an allegation aforesaid examined on the 12th day of September]

Ad Secundum Articulum allegationis predict dicit et deponit [To the second article of the aforesaid allegation she says and deposes] That about a dozen yeares agoe the deponent being at the house of Dorothy Mare an Alehouse in Elsmere at two several Cockfights saw the articulate Mr. Ottiwel at those Cockmatches at which he fought several Cocks of his own, he then bred or kept fighting cocks and set them out to walks. The deponent had one of his Cocks in keeping which was Stolen and the said Mr. Ottiwel said he would not have taken 5 pounds[6] for it. The said Mr. Ottiwel is accounted a quarelsome man in the neighborhood where he lives but the deponent knows nothing of her own knowledge as to that particular Saving that as he was coming from one of the aforesaid Cockings he was invited into the deponents house where he fell in company with one Joseph Davies who being in drinck gave the said Mr. Ottiwel some small affront in Saying that for all the said Mr. Ottiwel was a Clergy man he had more money in his pocket than he, whereupon the said Mr. Ottiwel watching the said Joseph out of doors followed him and beat him as the Deponent beleives, for when the said Joseph came into the house again he was all bloody *aliter nescit deponere* [and further knows not how to depose]

Ad cætera non Examinater ex directione produdenti [Not examined on the rest at the direction of the producent]

Repetit coram nobis [Repeated before us]

Richard Lloyd — Signum [Signed]

John: Collier — Elizabeth (mark) Evans

In presentia Richard Rider [In the presence of Richard Rider]
Notary public:

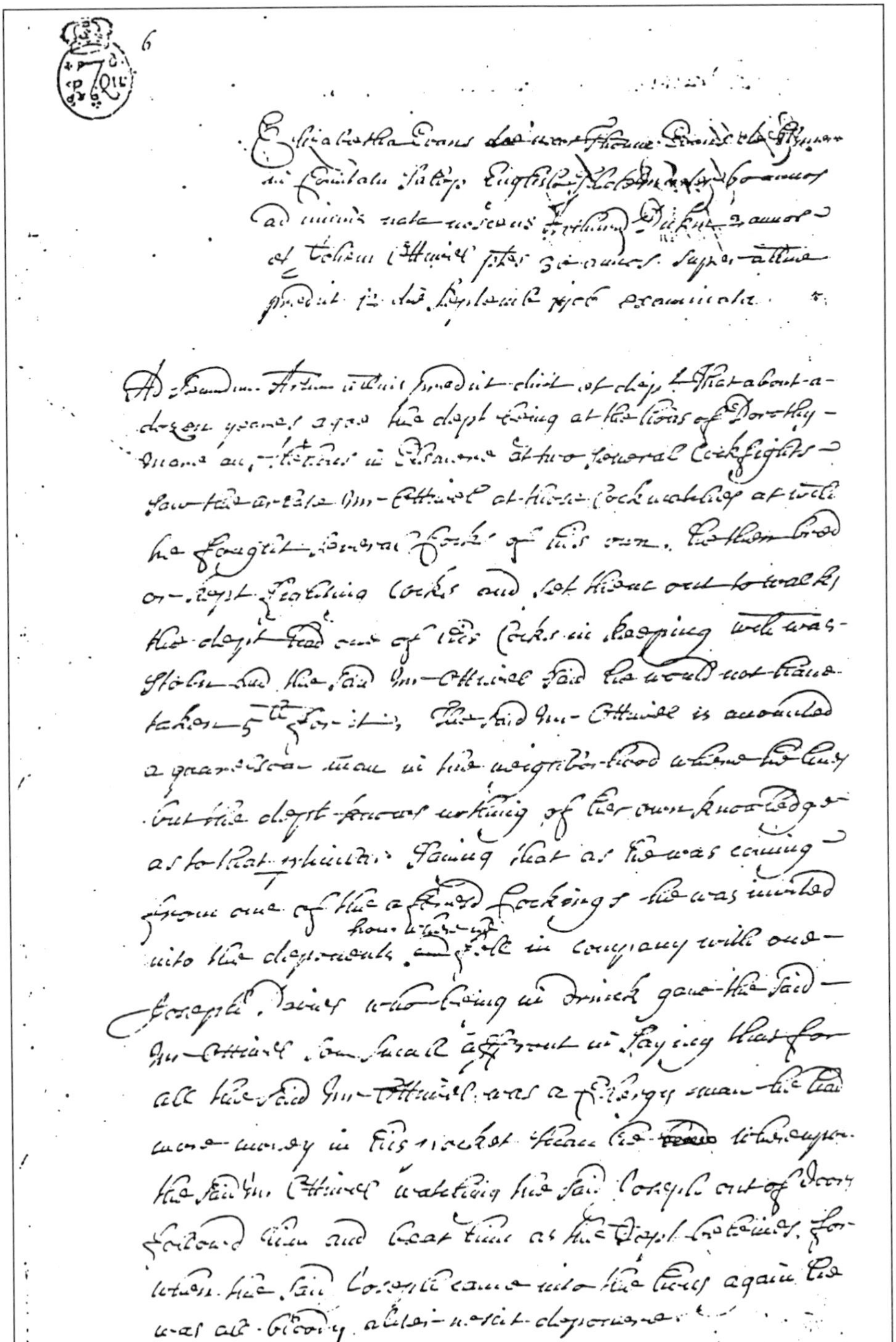

6

Elizabetha Evans de [illegible] in Comitatu Salop. [illegible] ad minus nata [illegible] Arthurum Dickin [illegible] et Johem Ottiwell [illegible] super articulo producta [illegible] examinata

Ad quintum Articulum libelli predict dicit et dep[onit] That about a dozen yeares agoe this dep[onen]t living at the house of Dorothy Evans [illegible] at two severall Cockfightes saw the article Mr Ottiwell at those Cockmatches at which he fought severall Cocks of his own, he then bred or kept fighting Cocks and sett them out to walk, this depon[en]t had one of his Cocks in keeping which was stolen and the said Mr Ottiwell said he would not have taken 5li for it. The said Mr Ottiwell is accounted a quarrellsome man in the neighbourhood where he lives but this depo[nen]t knowes nothing of her own knowledge as to that [illegible] saving that as he was coming from one of the aforesaid Cockings he was invited into this deponents house [illegible] in company with one Joseph Davies who being in drinck gave the said Mr Ottiwell some small affront in saying that for all the said Mr Ottiwell was a Clergyman he had more money in his pocket than he ~~[illegible]~~ whereupon the said Mr Ottiwell watching the said Joseph out of doors followed him and beat him as this depon[en]t beleives, for when the said Joseph came into the house again he was all bloody. aliter nescit deponere.

Fig. 2.1 Deposition of Elizabeth Evans in a cause of clergy discipline, reporting on his cockfighting activities, and his proclivity towards violence.

Feelings would often run high in this type of dispute and both sides would produce many witnesses and, in some causes, testimonials as to the character of the cleric involved, signed by his supporters in the congregation. Such documents, on occasion, would be produced by clergy from adjoining parishes in support of their colleague. One example of such a testimonial can be seen in Fig. 2.2.[7]

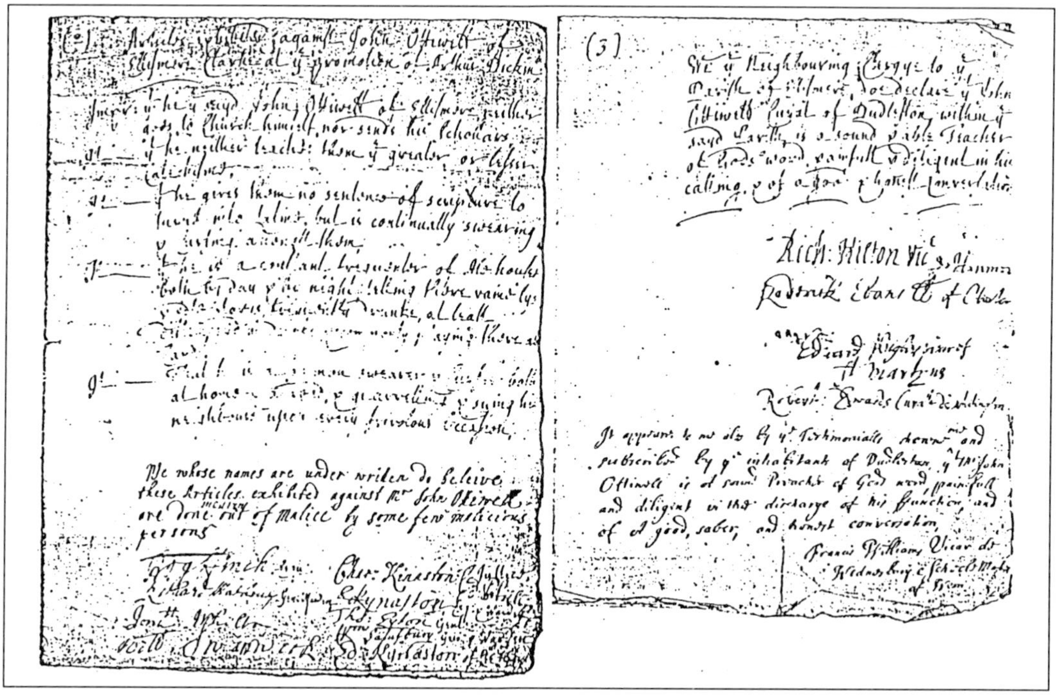

Fig. 2.2 Testimonials produced in support of John Otiwell, Curate of Dudlaston.

Parishioners

Political changes in this area of the work of the courts are well illustrated by the types of cause heard as office business during the 16th century and the immediate Restoration period. In the former period parishioners were cited for non-attendance at communion and attending conventicles. After the Restoration, large numbers of parishioners were cited to appear before the courts of the Oxford and Peterborough dioceses for non-attendance at church, failing both to baptise children and to receive the sacrament.[8] This can be seen as part of a concerted effort to re-establish the church after the comparative freedom of the civil war and interregnum, and Jones has shown that many of those cited were from parishes with a high recusant population.[9] A hint of problems can be seen at Lichfield where a visitation inhibition, dated 1686, has the following note written on the bottom, obviously addressed to the churchwardens, where they are encouraged:[10]

> to cyte all persons for fornication for Clandestine Marriage and for wills and Administrations and Endeavour to find out the same crimes and citye [sic] the persons that are gylty of the Crimes aforesaid and likewise once more I doe desire you to bring in your Excommunications and be careful of the Chancellors angre

This note was signed by Nathaniel Hinckes, one of the proctors of the consistory court. This document was drawn up in the year of the re-instatement of Bishop Wood after his suspension by the Archbishop of Canterbury, and there may have been a desire to re-establish the authority of the bishop on his return to the diocese.

Brawling

The comparative serenity of our rural churches today gives a very misleading impression of events in the past. Churches were far from quiet places, even during divine service. There are many citations for 'brawling in the church or churchyard' but often no more information survives. One exception relates to the parish church of Wirksworth in Derbyshire and produced the following articles of libel (Fig. 2.3):[11]

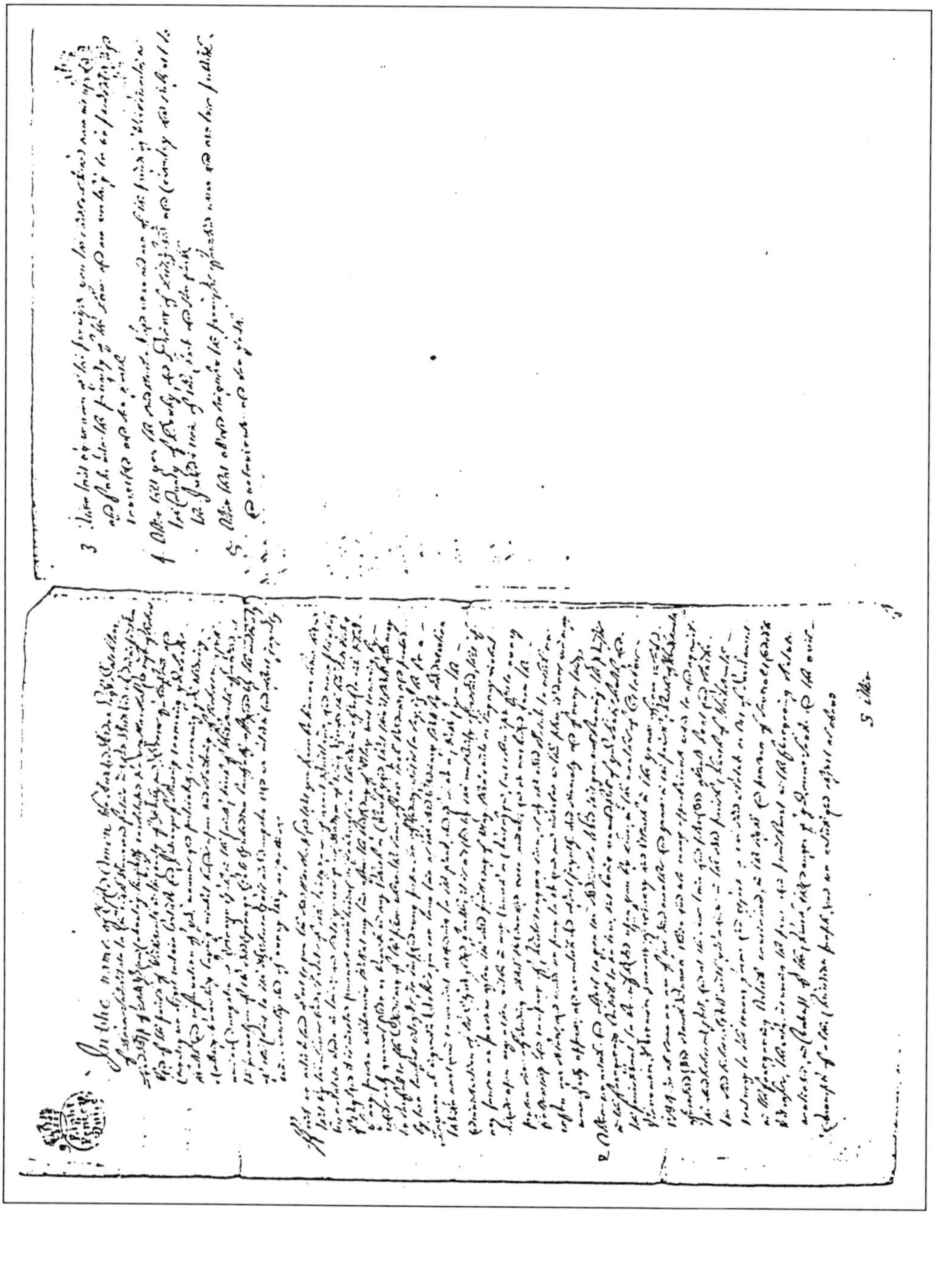

Fig 2.3 Brawling in church at Wirksworth, where an argument between Martha Wood and Rebecca Gell ended in violence.

In the name of God Amen We Richard Rider Esquire Batchlour of Lawes Substitute to the right Reverend father in God Richard by divine permission Lord Bishopp of Lichfield and Coventry lawfully constituted To you Martha Ward wife of Robert Ward of the parish of Wirksworth in the County of Derby and Dioces of Lichfield and Coventry we object certaine Articles and Interrogatories following concerning your Soules health and reformation of your manners and perticulerly concerning your chideing scolding brawling laying violent hands upon and strikeing of Rebecca Gell
a minor daughter of George Gell, in the parish Church of Wirksworth aforesaid, at the promotion of the said George Gell Guardian lawfully assigned by the authority of this Court to the said Rebecca Gell his daughter And we article and object joyntly and severally and of every thing as followes

First we article and object to you the said Martha Ward that you know beleive or have heard that by the Lawes and Statutes of this Kingdome of great Brittaine, and more particulerly by a Statute made in the 5 and sixth yeares of the Raigne of King Edward the 6th late King of England it is inacted (amongst other things as followeth or the like in effect to wit) That if any person whatsoever shall at any time after the first day of May next comeing, by words only quarrel chide or brawle in any Church or Churchyard, that then it shall and may be lawfull to the Ordinary[12] of the place where the same offence shall be done, and proved by two lawful witnesses, To suspend every person soe offending, that is to say, if he be a Layman *ab ingressu Ecclesiæ* for soe long time as the said Ordinary shall by his discretion thinke meet and convenient according to the fault, and if he be a Clerke from the administration of his Office, And further it is inacted by the authority aforesaid, that if any person or persons after the said first day of May shall smite or lay any violent hands upon any other either in any Church or Churchyard, that then ipso facto every person soe offending shall be decreed excommunicate, and be excluded from the fellowship and company of Christs congregation, as by the said Statute to which we refer our selves, and which we pray to be read and inserted in this place, it does and may more fully appeare, and we article and object joyntly and severally and of every thing

2. Alsoe we article and object to you the said Martha Ward that you well knowing the Premisses in the foregoeing Article to be true, but being unmindfull of your Soules health, and the punishment to be inflicted upon you by Law, in the monthes of October, November, December, January, February and March in the yeare of our Lord 1734 in all some or one of the said monthes and yeare in the parish Church of Wirksworth aforesaid, did scowle Brawle chide and use many opprobrious words to and against the said Rebecca Gell, and at the same time and place did assault beat and strike the said Rebecca Gell with your hands in the said parish Church of Wirksworth contrary to the tenour forme and effect of the said Statute or Act of Parliament in the foregoing Article mentioned, in the sight and presence of several credible Witnesses, thereby incurring the paine and punishment in the foregoing Statute mentioned, in Contempt of the Church, the danger of your owne Soule and the evil Example of other Christian people, and we article and object as above

3. Alsoe that by reason of the premisses you the said Martha Ward have erred and fallen into the penalty of the Law and are worthily to be punished and corrected and soe forth

4. Alsoe that you the said Martha Wạrd were and are of the parish of Wirksworth, in the County of Derby, and Dioces of Lichfield and Coventry and subject to the Jurisdiction of this Court and soe forth

5. Alsoe that all and singuler the premisses aforesaid were and are true publick and notorious and soe forth

The first article of the libel quotes the relevant statute, 5 & 6 Edw.6.c.4, and the punishments for both parishioners and clergy for this offence. Rebecca was aged between 17 and 21 and thus required a guardian to act on her behalf, so her father was elected to speak for her in court. Martha had probably been a little hasty in her actions, in that the ancestors of Rebecca Gell lay in the brightly-coloured splendour of their alabaster tombs in their own chapel in the church, lawyers to a man!

Further verbal abuse could result from disagreements with the clergy in church, leading to causes described as 'scandal to the ministry and its function' at Lichfield, or 'Opprobrious words against the Clergy' in the Salisbury courts. The words in these causes would have primarily related to dissatisfaction with the cleric's performance of his duties and suggest potential personality clashes, social tensions or religious differences within a community. Often dissenters or parishioners finally lost their patience with a less than satisfactory cleric and hurled insults. The vicar of Belton in Leicestershire was described in 1636 as a 'twatling fool'[13] by one of his parishioners, but was shown by witnesses to have been suffering from a 'could palsy', and had been unable to preach for four years. Evidence would suggest that he may in fact have been suffering from Parkinson's disease.[14] Such a public demonstration of disrespect towards the clergy, certainly indicated the necessity for the reformation of manners, if not the health of the souls of those involved.

Church seats

Church seat disputes were often the cause of disturbances and by their nature were more likely than most causes to go as far as the point of producing witnesses and verdicts. These causes took one of three forms. The first would have been the result of a disagreement as to the rights of sitting in the church, which was often linked to the ownership or tenancy of particular properties, occasionally named farms in country parishes, rather than the land that went with them. In some causes the right of sitting was neglected by an individual who had transferred their allegiance to another place of worship, leading to a protracted dispute over a potentially vacant sitting. Many of these causes passed through the courts quickly and simply but others generated considerable disputes as to rights of sitting and how these had accrued over the years. This can be used to trace information about particular houses and their tenants over several generations.

The second type of cause includes petty disputes involved the fitting of locks to pew doors and 'intrusions into sittings' and 'perturbation of sitting', whereby the right of an individual to a peaceful sitting in church was disturbed either by direct intrusion over a period of time, or merely perturbed on a single occasion. The latter type of cause would result from a disturbance in the seat on a Sunday, sometimes involving fisticuffs or the use of pins as a deterrent.

The third type of dispute relates to applications for a faculty for the confirmation of a right to a sitting in the church. The following allegation relates to a disputed seat in Chesterfield church in 1734, when Thomas Wheatley had requested such a faculty for the confirmation of a seat to his own use, which was contested by Joshua Weldon (Fig. 2.4).[15]

Fig. 2.4 (opposite and overleaf) A church seat dispute over the granting of a pew in Chesterfield church in 1734.

Thomas Wheatley against the Minister and Church Wardens of Chesterfield in the County of Derby, Joshua Weldon a parishioner of the said parish intervening for his Interest

The twenty second day of May, in the year of our Lord, One thousand seven hundred and thirty three

Which day Hand the younger as lawful proctor of the aforesaid Joshua Wheldon, as well to prevent the grant of a Licence for the Confirmation of a Seat to the said Thomas Wheatley in the parish Church of Chesterfield, as to all other Intent, and purposes in the Law whatsoever did alledge and propound articulately as follows (to witt)

First That for these ten, twenty, thirty, forty, fifty, and sixty years last past, and time beyond the memory of any man now living, there hath been and now is an antient Seat or Pew situate standing and being in the parish Church of Chesterfield, and on the same Ground where the Seat or Pew described in the Original Citation taken out in this Cause now stands, which said Seat or Pew the said Joshua Wheldon, Hugh Wheldon, Richard Wheldon, and others, Ancestors of the said Joshua Wheldon, Inhabitants and Parishoners of the parish aforesaid, have by themselves, their Wifes, and Familys from time to time for all the time aforesaid, sat in, and enjoyed by sitting, standing, and kneeling therein to hear Divine Service and Sermon read and preached in the said parish Church, without any Lett or hindrance, til of late the said Thomas Wheatley has disturbed them in the Right to or enjoyment of the same, And this was and is true and the party proponent doth alledge every thing in this Article joyntly and severally.

2. Also that the said Joshua Wheldon was and is a parishoner, Master of a Family, and an Housekeeper in the parish of Chesterfield aforesaid, hath a Wife and Family there consisting of eight Children, and two Servants, pays considerable Leveys to the Repairs of the said parish Church, but hath no other Pew, Seat, or Sitting place besides the Seat or Pew in Controversy for himself, Wife, Children, or Servants, or any of them, to sitt in, to hear Divine Service and Sermon read and preached in the said Church, And the party proponent doth alledge and propound as before.

3. Also that the Ancestors of the said Joshua Wheldon who were parishoners residing in the parish of Chesterfield aforesaid, built the Seat or Pew prearticulate, and for all the time in the first Article of this Allegation mentioned have been legally possessed and Intitled to the same, and from time to time the same has been repaired by their Descendants, at their own proper Costs and Charges and particularly by the articulate Richard Wheldon late a parishoner of the said parish, whilst he enjoyed the same, And some short time before the Citation issued out in this Cause, was extracted, the said Seat was also Repaired by the said Joshua Wheldon, the party proponent, at his own expence and Charge, And the Party proponent doth propound and alledge as before.

4. Also that the said Seat or Pew prayed to be Confirmed to the said Thomas Wheatley, is in and by the Citation aforesaid described to be nine foot six Inches long, and four foot wide the party proponent doth alledge that the same ought not to be confirmed to the said Thomas Wheatley, for that the said Thomas Wheatley is not, as is alledged, an Housekeeper within the parish of Chesterfield aforesaid, hath no Child, Servant, or Family, except a Wife, living in the said parish, and pays none at least very small Leveys, Towards the Repairs of the parish Church of Chesterfield aforesaid. And the Party proponent doth propound and alledge as before.

5. Also that the said Thomas Wheatley has not nor ever had any Right in himself, to the Seat or Pew aforesaid, nor were his Ancestors as is alledged, ever possessed thereof, but the said Thomas Wheatley hath several time owned and acknowledged the Party Proponent to be the legal Owner and true Proprietor of the said Seat, And the party Proponent doth propound and alledge as before.

6. Also that all and singular the premisses aforesaid were and are true, and so forth.

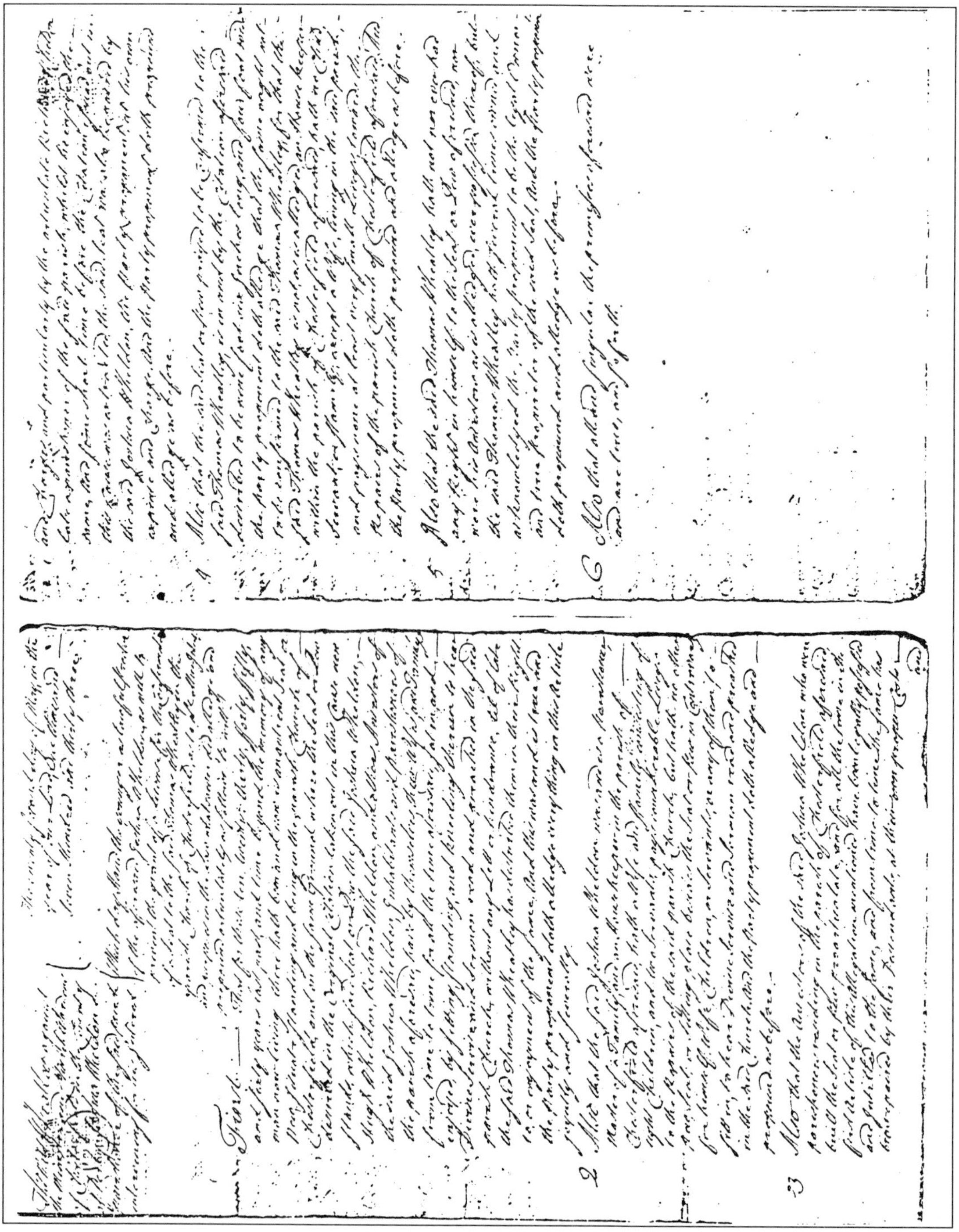

Fig. 2.4 A church seat dispute over the granting of a pew in Chesterfield church in 1734.

Joshua Weldon's opposition to the suggestion that the seat should be confirmed to Thomas can be seen from the phrase 'intervening for his interest'. This could not be heard as an instance cause, because the right of confirmation of church seats lay in the hands of the bishop. In these causes the numbers of individuals in the families of those contesting the right of sitting are often given, as well as the justification of payment of church levies in requesting the right to a seat in church. Note also the appeal to parish custom where, 'for time beyond the memory of man' (usually taken to be sixty years), the Wheldon family had sat in the same place in church, and, what is more, repaired the pew at their own expense. The fact that the Weldon family had paid for the repairs to the pew would have given them a very strong claim to it, which would have been confirmed to them by a faculty and ended the dispute.

Marriage

Another financially rewarding area for the work of the courts was that of clandestine marriage. These causes were heard as office business because it was necessary not only to correct those who had married this way but to admonish the minister who had carried out the ceremony. Marriages were deemed to be clandestine when they had been solemnised outside the diocese wherein the couple lived, in that impediments may not have been revealed. The clergy in peculiars, those areas not under the jurisdiction of the bishop, were often tempted to perform these ceremonies. Other such marriages included those solemnised in places other than a church and during prohibited seasons and at unusual hours, and, on occasion, these were pursued to the point where witnesses to the ceremony were also summoned to appear in court. These are of interest to family historians as the circumstances surrounding the marriage may well be described in some detail. Another type of cause relating to marriage was that of incest, although the term was not used in the strict form that we know it today. Under canon law incest related to marriage within the prohibited degrees of kinship, and most causes were brought to court when a widower had married his deceased wife's sister.

Immorality

The largest proportion of business in this area arose from immorality causes, whereby half of the population had been watching and reporting on the other half of the population who had been guilty of some form of sexual misconduct. This type of business, together with defamation, was responsible for the 'bawdy' epithet attached to the church courts from the medieval period. The causes were brought not only as a reinforcement of christian teaching but for other reasons also. Because the parish was the main provider of relief for the poor from the post-Reformation period down to the 19th century, it was deemed important to control bastardy and thus keep the poor rates as low as possible. A proportion of immorality causes resulted from defamation causes where there was strong evidence to suggest that there was truth in a 'common fame' within the community. Those who were adjudged to be 'too kind to each other' or overfamiliar in any way were immediately suspected of maintaining an illicit relationship. It is interesting to note that almost equal numbers of men and women were cited to appear in this category and the name of their partner was often given. A recent study of a north Nottinghamshire town has shown that these individuals often married other partners at a later date.[16] Incidentally, there were no causes of rape tried in these courts. This act was considered to be a felony and so was tried in the secular courts.

Many of these causes involved statements of witnesses, often in salacious detail. Alongside this, much information can be gleaned about the way of life of the households involved, as well as the names and status of people who had access to the house. The Coventry cause of 1708[17] involving John Critchlow and Anne Orton, the wife of a tailor, brought 27 witnesses into court, the majority of whom were involved in the cloth trade, and whose relationship to the parties concerned was stated, together with the parish in which they lived and their status. The assize courts had recommended the adjudication of the case by the town steward, a barrister by the name of Samuel Wade. He examined some of the witnesses at the Panyer, a Coventry inn, and the case was then taken to the consistory court. This was one of the few causes where political undertones were obviously present, but more examples may well become apparent when other causes are studied in more detail.

Causes were brought by the judge on the churchwardens' presentments following visitations, and could relate to fornication, adultery, and bridal or pre-nuptial pregnancy whereby neighbours counted the months between the wedding and baptism, and eagerly reported any discrepancies. As with defamation, the only punishment, apart from the cause itself, the publicity, and the costs, was that of penance. In these causes, a more impressive form of penance was used than that for defamation where the guilty party simply had to recant in public, in front of the offended party. Those deemed guilty of illicit sexual activity had to be dressed in white sheets, bearing a wand in their hand, without shoes and hair down around the ears when they appeared in church. This, at Lichfield, had to be carried out in three different churches on three consecutive Sundays, each minister signing the schedule of penance which, as with defamation causes, was returned to the registry of the court. The example overleaf relates to penance to be performed by Margaret Sherratt of Biddulph, Staffs. in 1734. (The words in bold type indicate those filled into a pre-existing hand-written form, Fig. 2.5.).[18]

Henry Raynes Doctor of Laws Official Principal of the Bishop's Consistory Court of Lichfield sendeth Greeting To the Ministers of the several parish Churches of **Biddulph Leek and Cheadlton** in the County of **Stafford** and Diocese of Lichfield and Coventry. Whereas Richard Rider Esquire Batchelor of Laws our Surrogate or Deputy hath duly enjoined **Margarett Sherratt** of the parish of **Biddulph** a legal Pennance for having committed the Crime of Fornication with **Thomas Booth** We therefore order and require that each of You call before You the said **Margarett Sherratt** to perform the said Pennance upon the days, in the Places, manner and form underwritten, and that each of You do Certify to Us or our said Surrogate how and in what manner **she** performed the same **on** or **before the Twenty second Day of June next Dated at Cheadle the Ninth Day of May in the Year of our Lord 1734**

W. Buckeridge Deputy to,
Gilbert Walmisley Esquire Registrar

The said **Margarett Sherratt** upon Sunday the **Twelfth** day of **May instant** shall repair to the parish Church of **Biddulph** aforesaid, on Sunday the **nineteenth** day of **May aforesaid** to the parish Church of **Leek** aforesaid, and on Sunday the **Twenty Sixth** day of **May aforesaid** to the parish church of **Cheadleton** aforesaid, and in these your said several parish Churches, upon the respective Sundays before mentioned the said **Margarett Sherratt** during all the Time of divine Service shall stand upon a low Stool placed before the Reading Desk in the Face of the Congregation then assembled, being cloathed in a white Sheet in her Stocken feet, with her hair about her Ears, and having a white Wand in her hand, and immediately after the End of the second Lesson the said **Margarett Sherratt** shall (with an audible voice) make her humble Confession as follows.

Whereas I **Margarett Sherratt** Not having the Fear of God before mine Eyes, but being led by the Instigation of the Devil and my own carnal Concupiscence have committed the grievous Sin of Fornication with **Thomas Booth** To the dishonour of Almighty God, the breach of his most sacred Laws, The Scandal and evil example of others, and the danger of my own Soul without unfeigned Repentance, I do humbly acknowledge, and am heartily Sorry for this my hainous Offence; I ask God Pardon and Forgiveness for the same in Jesus Christ, and pray him to give me his grace, not only to enable me to avoid all such Sin and wickedness but also to live Soberly, Righteously and Godly all the days of my Life, and to that End I desire all You that are here present to joyn with me in Saying the Lord's Prayer Our Father and so forth.

May ye 12th Margaret Sherratt did Pennance in Biddulph Church
before me John Sherratt Vicar of Biddulph
May ye 19 Margaret Sherratt did perform the Pennance enjoyned her
in the Manner & Form herein prescribed, in the Church of Leek
before me Tho Loxdale, Vicar of Leek
May 26th Margaret Sherratt did Penance in Chedleton Church before me
John Slade

Fig. 2.5 The old form of penance in white sheets continued well into the 18th century, this cause relating to fornication.

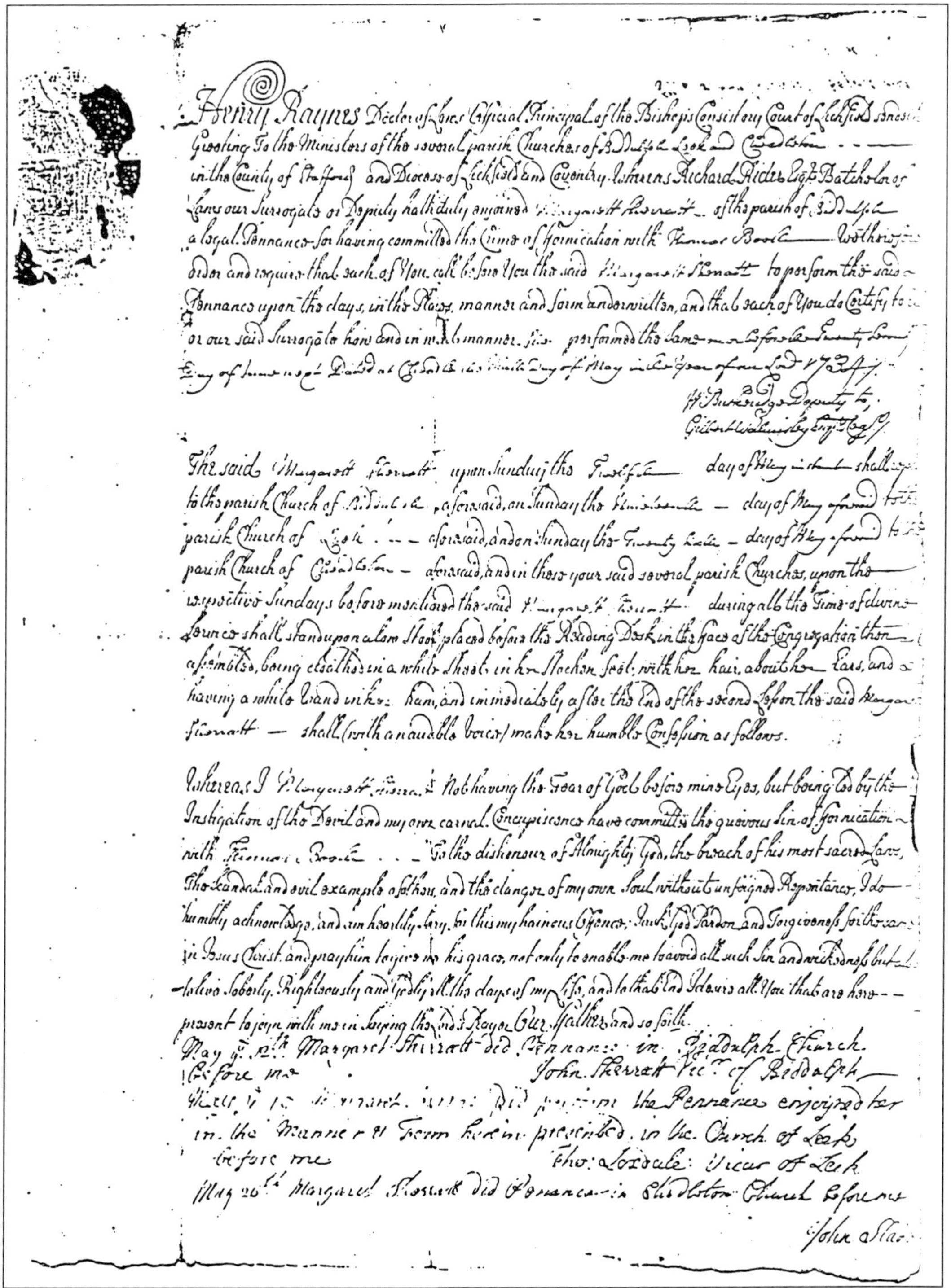

Henry Raynes Doctor of Laws Official Principal of the Bishop's Consistory Court of Lichfield sendeth Greeting To the Ministers of the several parish Churches of Biddulph Leek and Cheddleton in the County of Stafford and Diocess of Lichfield and Coventry. Whereas Richard Rider Esq. Batchelor of Laws our Surrogate or Deputy hath duly enjoined Margarett Stonett of the parish of Biddulph a legal Pennance for having committed the Crime of Fornication with Thomas Brooke We therefore order and require that such of You call before You the said Margarett Stonett to perform the said Pennance upon the days, in the Places, manner and form underwritten, and that each of You do Certify to us or our said Surrogate how and in what manner she performed the same on or before the Twenty [illegible] Day of June next. Dated at Lichfield the [illegible] Day of May in the Year of our Lord 1734.

H Burslem Deputy to
Gilbert Walmisley Esq. Reg.

The said Margarett Stonett upon Sunday the Twelfth day of May instant shall repair to the parish Church of Biddulph aforesaid, on Sunday the Nineteenth day of May aforesaid to the parish Church of Leek aforesaid, and on Sunday the Twenty sixth day of May aforesaid to the parish Church of Cheddleton aforesaid, and in those your said several parish Churches, upon the respective Sundays before mentioned the said Margarett Stonett during all the Time of divine Service shall stand upon a low Stool placed before the Reading Desk in the face of the Congregation then assembled, being clothed in a white Sheet, in her Stocken feet, with her hair about her Ears, and having a white Wand in her hand, and immediately after the End of the second Lesson the said Margarett Stonett shall (with an audible voice) make her humble Confession as follows.

Whereas I Margarett Stonett not having the Fear of God before mine Eyes, but being led by the Instigation of the Devil and my own carnal Concupiscence have committed the grievous Sin of Fornication with Thomas Brooke to the dishonour of Almighty God, the breach of his most sacred Laws, the Scandal and evil example of others, and the danger of my own Soul without unfeigned Repentance, I do humbly acknowledge, and am heartily sorry for this my heinous Offence; I ask God Pardon and Forgiveness for the same in Jesus Christ and pray him to give me his grace, not only to enable me to avoid all such Sin and wickedness but to live Soberly, Righteously and Godly all the days of my Life, and to that End I desire all You that are here present to joyn with me in saying the Lord's Prayer Our Father and so forth.

May ye 12th Margaret Stonett did Pennance in Biddulph Church
Before me John Sherratt Vic.^r of Biddulph

May ye 19 [illegible] did perform the Pennance enjoyned her in the Manner & Form herein prescribed, in the Church of Leek
Before me Tho: Loxdale: Vicar of Leek

May 26th Margaret Stonett did Pennance in Cheddleton Church before me
John [illegible]

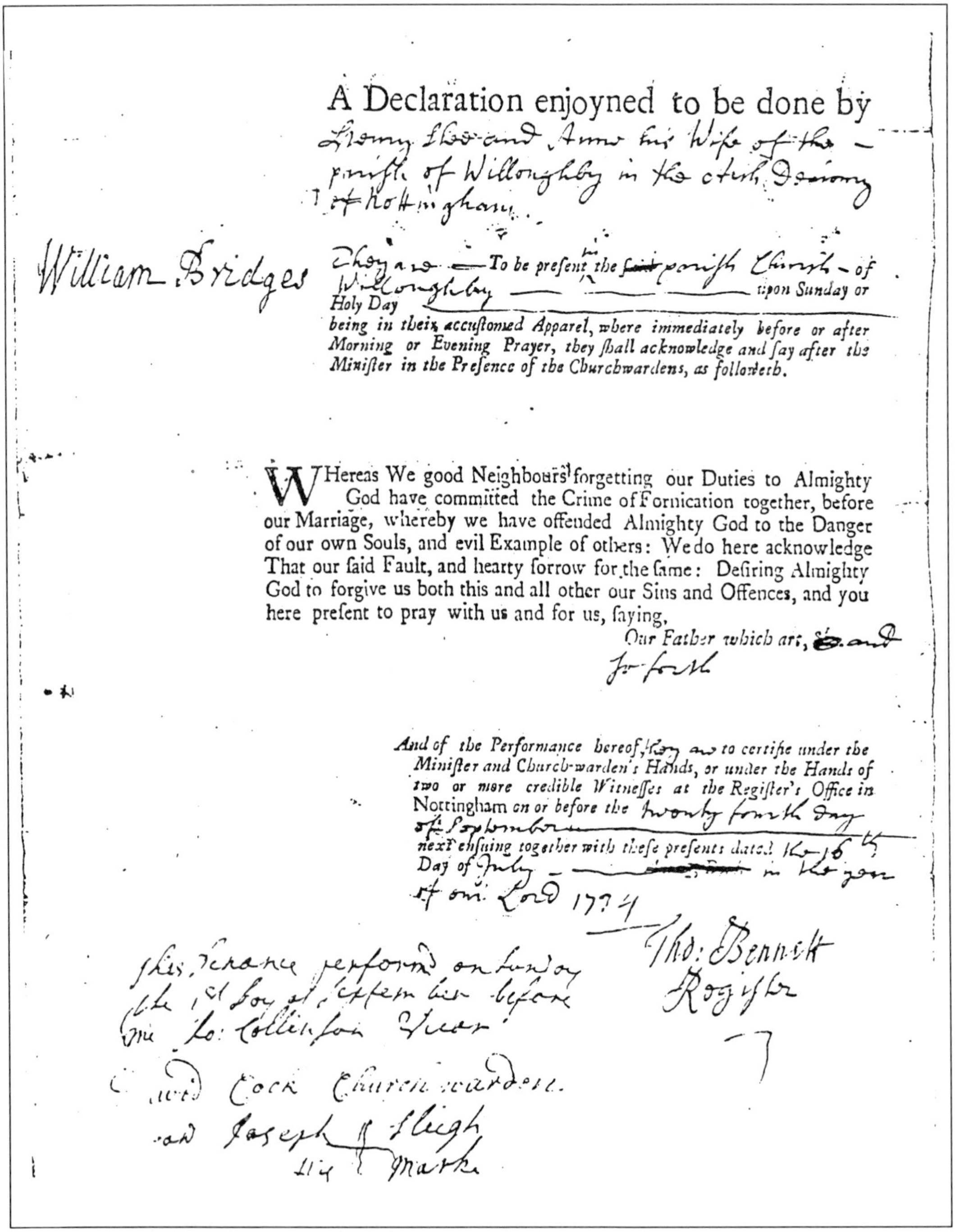

A Declaration enjoyned to be done by Henry Lee and Anne his Wife of the parish of Willoughby in the Arch Deanery of Nottingham.

William Bridges

They are To be present in the said parish Church of Willoughby upon Sunday or Holy Day being in their accustomed Apparel, where immediately before or after Morning or Evening Prayer, they shall acknowledge and say after the Minister in the Presence of the Churchwardens, as followeth.

WHereas We good Neighbours forgetting our Duties to Almighty God have committed the Crime of Fornication together, before our Marriage, whereby we have offended Almighty God to the Danger of our own Souls, and evil Example of others: We do here acknowledge That our said Fault, and hearty sorrow for the same: Desiring Almighty God to forgive us both this and all other our Sins and Offences, and you here present to pray with us and for us, saying,

Our Father which art, and so forth

And of the Performance hereof, they are *to certifie under the Minister and Church-warden's Hands, or under the Hands of two or more credible Witnesses at the Register's Office in* Nottingham *on or before the* twenty fourth Day of September *next ensuing together with these presents dated* the 16th *Day of* July in the year of our Lord 1774

Tho: Bennett Register

This Penance perform'd on Sunday the 1st Day of September before me Jo: Collinson Vicar

David Cock Churchwarden

and Joseph Sleigh his mark

Fig. 2.6 Printed form of penance from the Archdeaconry of Nottingham.

In those causes of pre-nuptial fornication where the couple had later married, it was usual for them only to appear in a single church. The schedules of penance often give the names of both parties involved, whereas the citation usually only gives the name of one of them. This form of penance continued through the 18th century in the Lichfield diocese and probably in many others, but once again local customs were to be observed. In some dioceses penance was enjoined to take place in the market place as well as in church; the permutations were endless.

A slightly different form of penance was used in the Nottingham courts, Fig. 2.6 (see p44), and illustrates the variations in format of documents over time and between dioceses. The word penance is not used but the page begins, 'A Declaration enjoyned to be done by'. An example can be seen from the Nottingham archdeaconry court, where the individual, clad in normal dress, merely appeared before the minister and churchwardens before or after divine service.[19] The use of pre-printed forms for certain documents also varies between dioceses.

Other Office business

Rash administration of wills by executors and administrators who had not obtained a grant of probate, was also part of the business of the office, but will be discussed in the chapter relating to probate and testamentary business.

Perjury, or giving false evidence, and thus breaking an oath, when committed in the church courts was punishable by excommunication, but any damages that were claimed as a result could only be sought in a temporal court. If a member of the clergy committed perjury the seriousness of the offence was such that they could have been deprived of their benefice.

Parish Officers and Professional People

The courts played a major part in the regulation of the professions at a local level by their control of unlicensed curates, schoolmasters, midwives and surgeons. The role of these individuals in supporting the teachings of the church was particularly important between the Reformation and the civil war. From 1559, schoolmasters were not allowed to teach children without a licence from the bishop.

The pursuit of unlicensed midwives may not, on the surface, appear to be of particular importance, but the reasons behind this illustrate the thinking behind so much of canon law. The duties of a midwife included several with important legal associations.[20] Firstly, she was entitled to baptise infants who were not expected to live until a clergyman could arrive; it was her duty to bury those who did not survive secretly, in such a place where they would not be 'disturbed by hog or dog'. She also had to ensure that the child was, where necessary, 'fathered' upon the correct individual in cases where the mother was unmarried. The name of the father was demanded at 'the extremity of labour', whilst the mother held the bible. Midwives were also required to report secret births, those children baptised 'by mass, or latin service', and those practising as midwives without licence. They were also sworn to serve the poor as well as the rich. Similar ground rules applied to surgeons and schoolmasters whose dealings with the community were such that it was important that they conformed to the established church. One unusual survival from Lichfield is a draft of a commission for a surgeon to take his oath before named individuals in place of the vicar general at a place outside the consistory court (Fig. 2.7).[21]

The incompleteness of the document, together with the obliterated words, introduced an unacceptable element of ambiguity into a legal instrument, which would no doubt be the reason why the document was retained with the court papers.

Any dubious legality in the election of parish clerks[22] and churchwardens as well as errors in the 'swearing in' of the churchwardens might occasionally give rise to judicial investigations. The churchwardens fulfilled an important role in the unpoliced community by reporting on those who had committed offences against canon law. If parish officers were found to have been incorrectly sworn, any cause arising from their actions in the church courts would be immediately invalidated, as would any accusations of perjury if they had neglected their duties. The accounts of the churchwardens were sometimes questioned by the incoming officers, and these can survive as exhibits among the cause papers.[23]

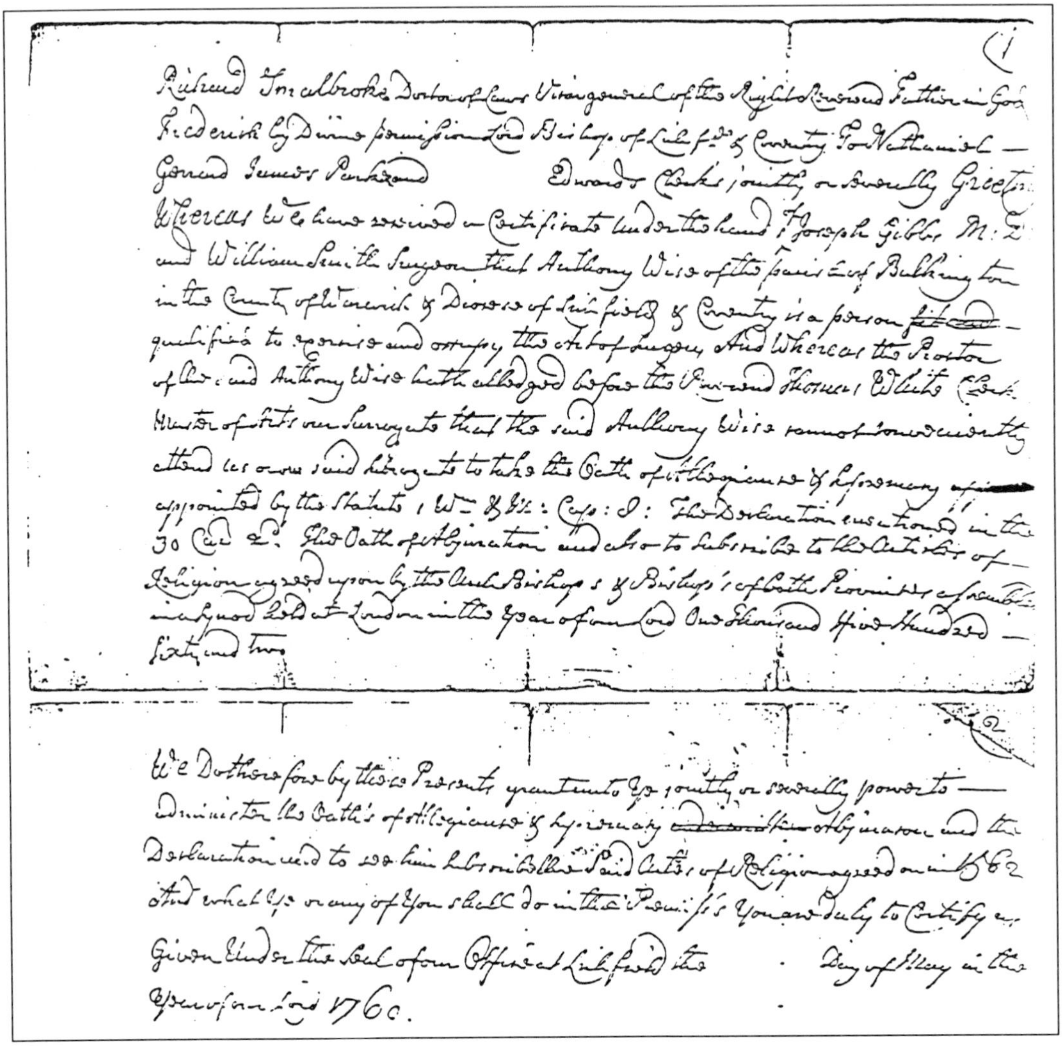

Richard Smalbroke Doctor of Laws Vicar general of the Right Reverend Father in God Frederick by Divine permission Lord Bishop of Lichfield & Coventry To Nathaniel
Gerrard James Parker and [first name ommitted] Edwards Clerks jointly or severally Greeting
Whereas we have received a Certificate under the hands of Joseph Gibbs M:D:
and William Smith Surgeon that Anthony Wise of the parish of Bulkington
in the County of Warwick & Diocese of Lichfield and Coventry is a person
qualified to exercise and occupy the Art of Surgery And Whereas the Proctor
of the said Anthony Wise hath alledged before the Reverend Thomas White Clerk
Master of Arts our Surrogate that the said Anthony Wise cannot conveniently
attend us or our said Surrogate to take to Oath of Allegiance & Supremacy
appointed by the Statute 1 Wm & M:Cap:8: The Declaration mentioned in the
30 Car second The Oath of Abjuration and also to subscribe to the Articles of
Religion agreed upon by the Arch Bishops & Bishop's of both Provinces assembled
in a Synod held at London in the Year of our Lord One Thousand Five Hundred
Sixty and two We do therefore by these Presents grant unto Ye jointly or severally power to
administer the Oath's of Allegiance & supremacy Abjuration and the
Declaration and to see him subscribe the Said Articles of Religion agreed on with Charles the second
And what Ye or any of You shall do in that Premisses You are duly to Certify us
Given under the Seal of our Office at Lichfield the [date ommitted] Day of May in the
Year of our Lord 1760.

Fig. 2.7 Commission for a surgeon to swear an oath, when he was unable to attend the court in Lichfield.

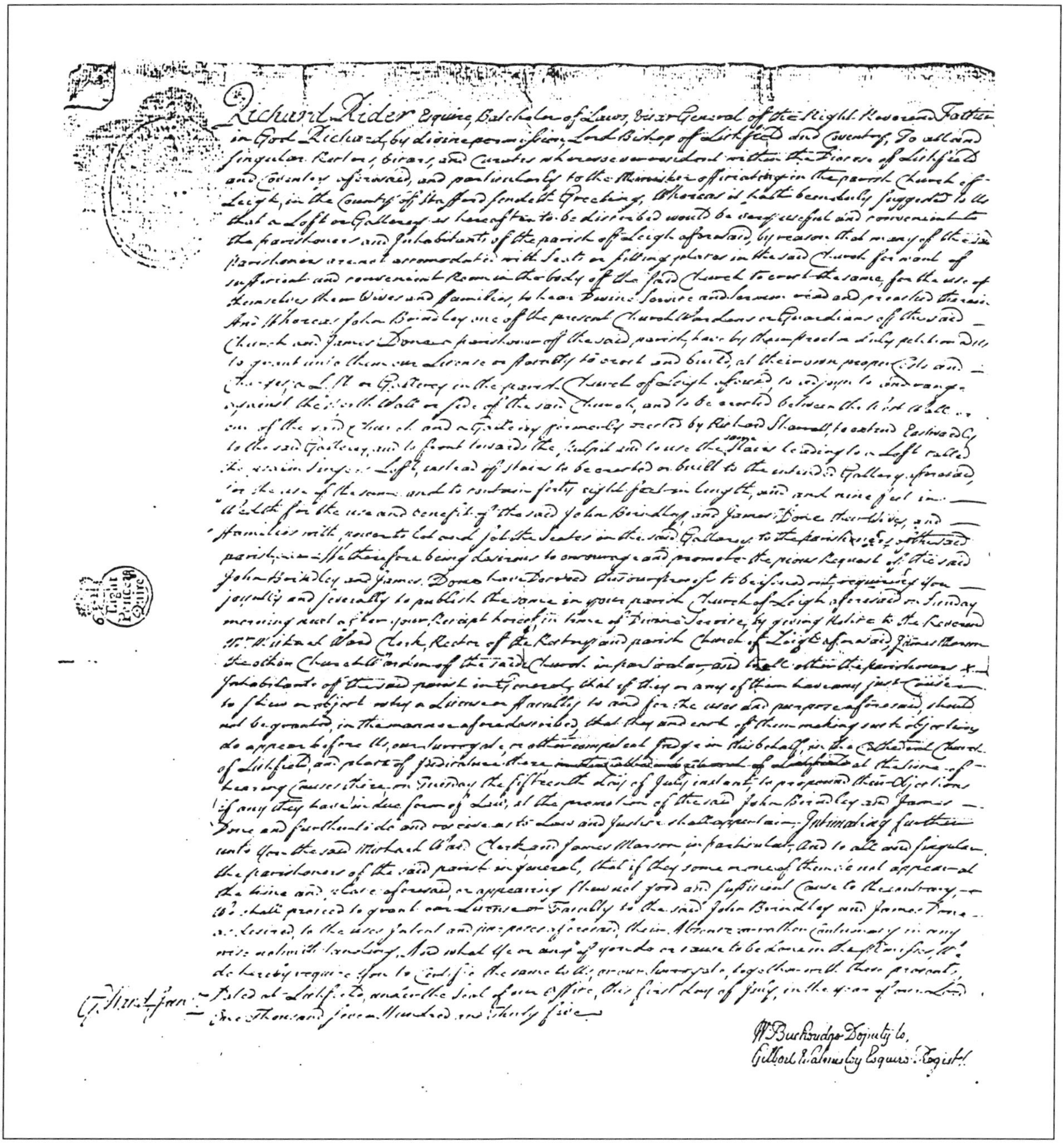

Richard Rider Esquire, Batchelor of Laws, Vicar General of the Right Reverend Father in God Richard, by divine permission, Lord Bishop of Litchfield and Coventry, To all and singular Rectors, Vicars, and Curates whatsoever [illegible] within the Diocese of Litchfield and Coventry aforesaid, and particularly to the Minister officiating in the parish Church of Leigh, in the County of Stafford sendeth Greeting, Whereas it hath been duly suggested to Us that a Loft or Gallery as hereafter to be described would be very useful and convenient to the parishioners and Inhabitants of the parish of Leigh aforesaid, by reason that many of the said parishioners are not accomodated with Seats or sitting places in the said Church for want of sufficient and convenient Room in the body of the said Church to erect the same, for the use of themselves their Wives and families, to hear Divine Service and Sermons read and preached therein. And Whereas John Brindley one of the present Churchwardens or Guardians of the said Church and James Dove a parishioner of the said parish, have by themselves a duly petition'd Us to grant unto them our Licence or faculty to erect and build, at their own proper Costs and Charges, a Loft or Gallery in the parish Church of Leigh aforesaid to adjoyn to and range against the North Wall or side of the said Church, and to be erected between the West Wall [illegible] of the said Church and a Gallery formerly erected by Richard Stannell, to extend Eastwardly to the said Gallery, and to front towards the Pulpit and to use the same Stairs leading to a Loft called the [illegible] Singers Loft, instead of Stairs to be erected or built to the intended Gallery aforesaid for the use of the same, and to contain forty eight feet in length, and [illegible] nine feet in Width for the use and benefit of the said John Brindley and James Dove their Wives and families with power to let and sell the Seats in the said Gallery to the parishioners of the said parish [illegible] We therefore being desirous to encourage and promote the pious Request of the said John Brindley and James Dove have Decreed this our process to be issued out, requiring you jointly and severally to publish the same in your parish Church of Leigh aforesaid on Sunday morning next after your Receipt hereof in time of Divine Service, by giving Notice to the Reverend Mr. Michael Ward Clerk, Rector of the Rectory and parish Church of Leigh aforesaid, James Mason the other Churchwarden of the said Church in particular, and to all other the parishioners & Inhabitants of the said parish in general, that if they or any of them have any just Cause to shew or object why a Licence or faculty to and for the uses and purpose aforesaid should not be granted, in the manner aforedescribed that they and each of them making such objection do appear before Us, our Surrogate, or other competent Judge in this behalf, in the Cathedral Church of Litchfield, and place of Judicature there ~~in the Cathedral Church of Litchfield~~ at the time of hearing Causes there on Tuesday the fifteenth day of July instant to propound their Objections if any they have in due form of Law, at the promotion of the said John Brindley and James Dove and further to do and receive as to Law and Justice shall appertain, Intimating further unto You the said Michael Ward Clerk and James Mason in particular, And to all and singular the parishioners of the said parish in general, that if they some or none of them do not appear at the time and place aforesaid, or appearing shew not good and sufficient Cause to the contrary, We shall proceed to grant our Licence or Faculty to the said John Brindley and James Dove as desired, to the uses intent and purposes aforesaid, their Absence or rather Contumacy in any wise notwithstanding, And what You or any of you do or cause to be done in the premises, We do hereby require You to Certifie the same to Us, or our Surrogate, together with these presents, Dated at Litchfield, under the Seal of our Office, this first day of July, in the year of our Lord One Thousand seven Hundred and thirty five

[illegible]

W. Buckeridge Deputy to
Gilbert Walmesley Esquire Registr.

Fig. 2.8 Citation with intimation for a faculty at Leigh, to build a gallery in the church. This document would be read out in church, so that objections could be raised.

Fabric of the Church and Associated Buildings

The granting of faculties for the physical alterations to a church, or the introduction of new seating and galleries, was one of the duties of the bishop, and this was carried out through the consistory court. All such alterations had to be agreed by the parish and by taking them through the court it was ensured that no disputes could arise at a later date. This business came into the category of an office-promoted cause, which involved the extraction of a citation with intimation from the Registry, against the clergy and churchwardens by the party requesting the alteration, giving details of the dimensions of new seats and galleries and their position in the church in relation to stated sittings, or the location of the seat to be allocated to the promoter of the cause. This document had to be read in church, to allow for discussion, and for any objections to be voiced and accommodated, as can be seen from the following example opposite (Fig. 2.8):[24]

Richard Rider Esquire, Batchelor of Laws, Vicar General of the Right Reverend Father
in God Richard, by divine permission, Lord Bishop of Lichfield and Coventry, To all
and singular Rectors, Vicars and Curates wheresoever resident within the Diocese of Lichfield
and Coventry aforesaid, and particularly to the Minister officiating in the parish Church of
Leigh, in the County of Stafford sendeth Greeting, Whereas it hath been duly suggested to Us
that a Loft or Gallery as hereafter to be discribed would be very useful and convenient to
the parishoners and Inhabitants of the parish of Leigh aforesaid, by reason that many of the said
parishoners are not accomodated with Seats or sitting places in the said Church for want of
sufficient and convenient Room in the body of the saidChurch to erect the same, for the use of
themselves their Wives and Families, to hear Divine Service and Sermon read and preached therein
And Whereas John Brindley one of the present Church Wardens or Guardians of the said
Church and James Done a parishoner of the said parish, have by their proctor duly petitioned Us
to grant unto them our Licence or Faculty to erect and build, at their own proper Costs and
Charges, a Loft or Gallery in the parish Church of Leigh aforesaid, to adjoyn to and range
against the North Wall or side of the said church, and to be erected between the West Wall or
end of the said church and a Gallery formerly erected by Richard Sharratt, to extend Eastwardly
to the said Gallery, and to front towards the pulpit and to use the same Stairs leading to a Loft called
the psalm Singers Loft, instead of stairs to be erected or built to the intended Gallery aforesaid,
for the use of the same and to contain forty eight feet in length, and nine feet in
Width for the use and benefit of the said John Brindley, and James Done their Wives, and
Families with power to let and set the Seates in the said Gallery to the parishoners of the said
parish, We therefore being desirous to encourage and promote the pious Request of the said
John Brindley and James Done have Decreed this our process to be issued out, requiring You
joyntly and severally to publish the same in your parish Church of Leigh aforesaid on Sunday
morning next after your Receipt hereof, in time of Divine Service, by giving Notice to the Reverend
Mr. Michael Ward Clerk, Rector of the Rectory and parish Church of Leigh aforesaid, James Marson
the other Church Warden of the said church in particular, and to all other the parishoners &
Inhabitants of the said parish in General, that if they or any of them have any just Cause
to shew or object why a Licence or Faculty to and for the uses and purpose aforesaid, should
not be granted, in the manner afore described, that they and each of them making such objections
do appear before Us, our Surrogate, or other competent Judge in this behalf, in the Cathedral Church
of Lichfield, and place of Judicature there at the time of hearing Causes there, on Tuesday the fifteenth
day of July instant, to propound their Objections (if any they have) in due form of Law, at the
promotion of the said John Brindley and James Done, and further to do and receive as to Law and
Justice shall appertain, Intimating further unto You the said Michael Ward Clerk and James Marson,
in particular, And to all and singular the parishoners of the said parish in general, that if they some
or one of them do not apear at the time and place aforesaid, or appearing shew not good and sufficient
Cause to the contrary We shall proceed to grant our License or Faculty to the said John Brindley and
Jame Done as desired, to the uses Intent and purposes aforesaid, their Absence or rather Contumacy
in any wise notwithstanding, And what Ye or any of you do or cause to be done in the premises,
We do hereby require You to Certifie the same to Us, or our Surrogate, together with these presents,
Dated at Lichfield, under the Seal of our Office, this first day of July, in the year of our Lord
One Thousand Seven Hundred and Thirty five.

William Buckeridge Deputy to
Gilbert Walmisley Esquire, Registrar

Faculties for the confirmation of seats or the building of new ones, or indeed the re-pewing of entire churches, can give great detail as to the relationship between pews and the names of their occupants in the church, and thus some indication of the social structure of a community. Some faculties, particularly from the later 18th century, had seating plans attached, or small drawings of the proposed work to be done. Many were concerned with the building of galleries during the 18th century, the majority of which have long since disappeared, but whose putlog holes still appear in the unplastered internal walls of churches. Many of these causes relate to urban areas, expanding rapidly in the late 18th century when older, rather haphazard arrangements were replaced by more orderly seating. This repewing also had to be carried out to alleviate the effects of rot and worm on older seating arrangements. In some parishes old medieval churches were totally demolished and replaced, as in the case of the church of Norton in the Moors which was to be completely rebuilt to a different plan, the faculty being approved in 1737 (Fig. 2.9).[25]

The faculty itself is not physically an impressive document by the 18th century, if indeed it ever was. They are not often found in the court papers, having been taken away, but the form can be seen from the following example, relating to the parish of Ashbourne in Derbyshire. Incidentally, note the steps to a gallery leading from the outside of the church (Fig. 2.10).[26]

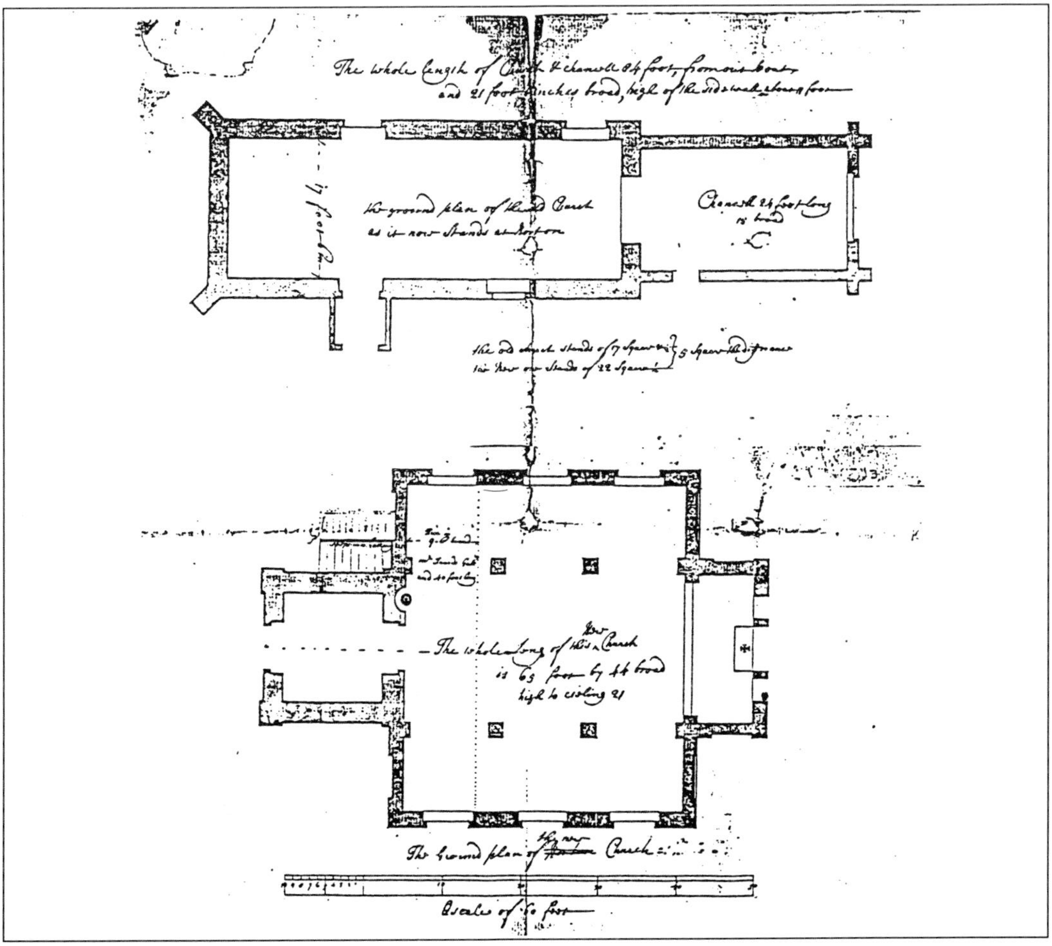

Fig. 2.9 Plan of the rebuilt church at Norton in the Moors, but unfortunately no seating plan has survived.

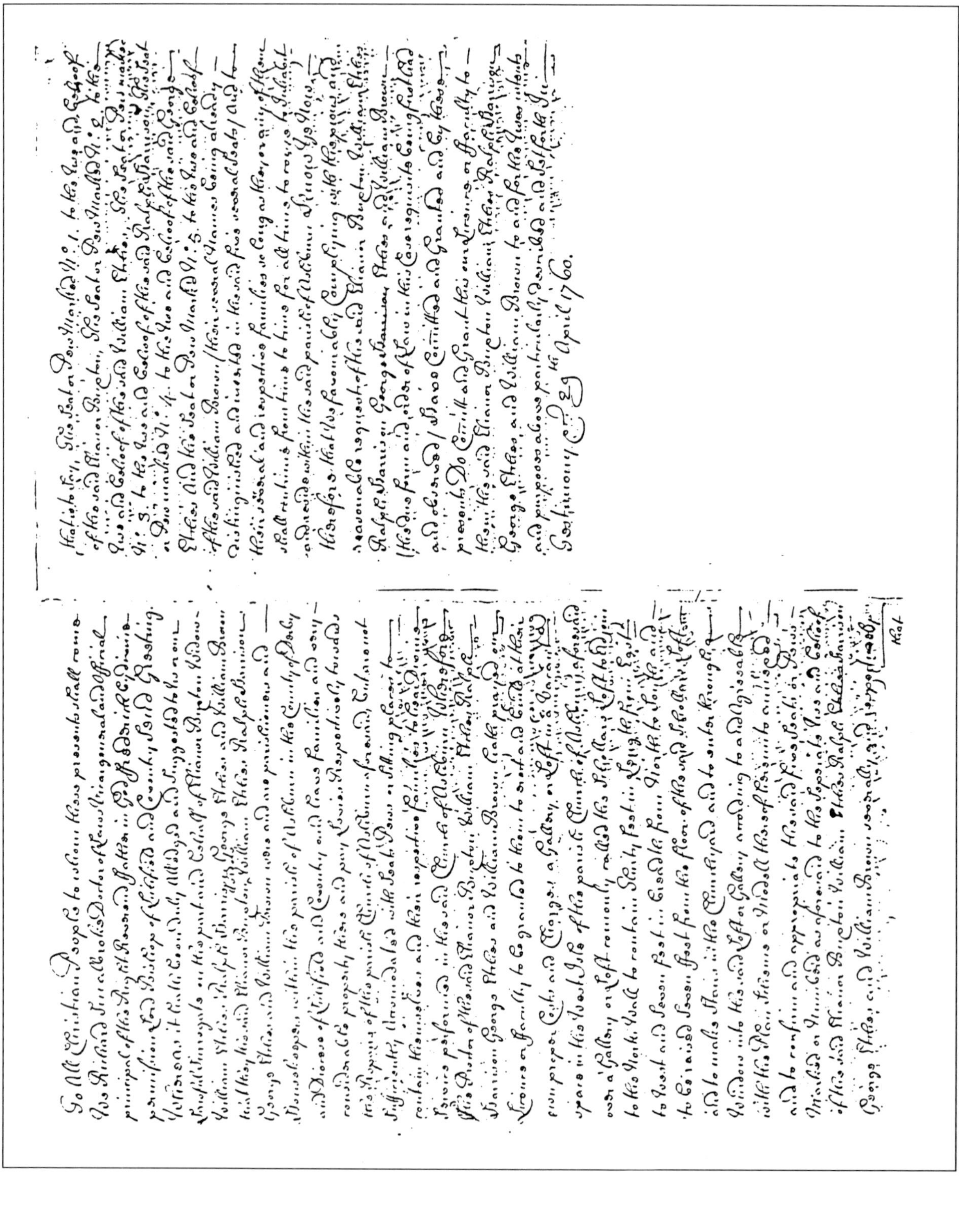

To All Christian People to whom these presents shall come
Wee Richard Smalbroke Doctor of Laws Vicar general and Official
principal of the Right Reverend Father in God Frederick by divine
permission Lord Bishop of Litchfield and Coventry Send Greeting.
Whereas it hath been duly Alledged and Suggested to us or our
lawfull Surrogate on the part and behalf of Elianor Bryton Widow
William Ethles Ralph Harrison George Ethles and William Brown
that they the said Elianor Bryton William Ethles Ralph Harrison
George Ethles and William Brown were and are parishioners and
Housekeepers within the parish of Ashburn in the County of Derby
and Diocese of Litchfield and Coventry and have families and very
considerable property there and pay Levies Respectively towards
the Repairs of the parish Church of Ashburn aforesaid, but are not
sufficiently Accomodated with Seats Pews or Sitting places to
contain themselves and their respective families to hear Divine
Service performed in the said Church of Ashburn Wherefore
the Proctor of the said Elianor Bryton William Ethles Ralph
Harrison George Ethles and William Brown hath prayed our
Licence or faculty to be granted to them to erect and Build at their
own proper Costs and Charges a Gallery or Loft in a Vacant
space in the West Isle of the parish Church of Ashburn aforesaid
over a Gallery or Loft commonly called the Scholars Loft to adjoin
to the North Wall to contain Thirty feet in Length from East
to West and Seven feet in Breadth from North to South and
to be raised Seven feet from the floor of the said Scholars Loft
and to make Stairs in the Churchyard and to enter through a
Window into the said Loft or Gallery according to and agreeable
with the Plan Scheme or Modell thereof hereunto annexed
and to confirm and appropriate the said five Seats or Pews
Marked or Numbered as aforesaid to the Separate Use and behoof
of the said Elianor Bryton William Ethles Ralph ~~Ethles~~ Harrison
George Ethles and William Brown severally and respectively
That

that is to say, The Seat or Pew Marked No. 1. to the Use and behoof
of the said Elianor Bryton, The Seat or Pew Marked No. 2. to the
Use and behoof of the said William Ethles, The Seat or Pew marked
No. 3. to the Use and behoof of the said Ralph Harrison, The Seat
or Pew marked No. 4. to the Use and behoof of the said George
Ethles And the Seat or Pew Marked No. 5. to the Use and behoof
of the said William Brown (their several Names being already
distinguished and inserted in the said five several Seats) And to
their several and respective families so long as they or any of them
shall continue from time to time for all time to come to Inhabit
and reside within the said parish of Ashburn Know Ye Now
therefore that Wee favourably Complying with the pious and
reasonable request of the said Elianor Bryton William Ethles
Ralph Harrison George Ethles and William Brown
(the due form and order of Law in this Case requisite being first had
and observed) Have Committed and Granted and by these
presents Do Commit and Grant this our Licence or faculty to
them the said Elianor Bryton William Ethles Ralph Harrison
George Ethles and William Brown to and for the Uses intents
and purposes above particularly described and set forth In
Testimony &c. 29th April 1760.

Fig. 2.10 Grant of a faculty at Ashbourne, to build a gallery in the west aisle of the church.

To All Christian People to whom these presents shall come We Richard Smalbroke Doctor of Laws Vicar general and Official principal of the Right Reverend Father in God Frederick by divine permission Lord Bishop of Lichfield and Coventry Send Greeting. Whereas it hath been duly Alledged and suggested to Us or our Lawful Surrogate on the part and behalf of Elianor Buxton Widow William Etches Ralph Harrison George Etches and William Brown that they the said Elianor Buxton widow William Etches Ralph Harrison and William Brown were and are parishioners and Housekeepers within the parish of Ashburn in the County of Derby and Diocese of Lichfield and Coventry and have families and very considerable property there and pay Levies Respectively towards the Repairs of the parish Church of Ashburn aforesaid, but are not Sufficiently Accomodated with Seats Pews or Sitting places to contain themselves and their respective families to hear Divine Service performed in the said Church of Ashburn Wherefore the Proctor of the said Elianor Buxton William Etches Ralph Harrison George Etches and William Brown hath prayed our Licence or Faculty to be granted to them to erect and build at their own proper Costs and charges a Gallery or Loft in a Vacant space in the West Isle of the parish Church of Ashburn aforesaid over a Gallery or Loft comonly called the Schollars Loft to Adjoin to the North Wall to contain Thirty feet in Length from East to West and Seven Feet in breadth from North to South and to be raised Seven Feet from the floor of the said Schollars Loft and to make Stairs in the Churchyard and to enter through a Window into the said Loft or Gallery according to and Agreeable with the Plan Scheme or Modell thereof hereunto annexed and to confirm and appropriate the said five Seats or Pews Marked or Number'd as aforesaid to the Seperate Use and behoof of the said Elianor Buxton William Etches Ralph Harrison George Etches and William Brown severally and respectively that is to say, The Seat or Pew Marked No. 1 to the Use and behoof of the said Elianor Buxton, The Seat or Pew Marked No. 2 to the Use and behoof of the said William Etches, The Seat or Pew marked No. 3 to the Use and behoof of the said Ralph Harrison, The Seat or Pew marked No. 4 to the Use and behoof of the said George Etches And the Seat or Pew marked No. 5 to the Use and behoof of the said William Brown/their several Names being already distinguished and inserted in the said five several Seats/And to their several and respective families so long as they or any of them shall continue from time to time for all time to come to Inhabit and reside within the said parish of Ashburn Know Ye Now therefore that We favourably Complying with the pious and reasonable request of the said Elianor Buxton William Etches Ralph Harrison George Etches and William Brown /the due form and order of Law in this Case requisite being first had and observed/Have Comitted and Granted and by these presents Do Comitt and Grant this our Licence or Faculty to them the said Elianor Buxton William Etches Ralph Harrison George Etches and William Brown to and for the Uses intents and purposes above particularly described and Set forth

In Testimony etc 29th. April 1760.

Note that the widow took an active part both legally, socially and financially in the building of a new gallery in the church. The position of the gallery 'raised seven feet from the floor of the said Schollars Loft' with an example of an unusual form of access through a window from the churchyard gives a sense of vertigo, coupled with the implication that the church was well-filled with an assortment of galleries! The presence of the 'Schollars Loft' suggests a local school which may not appear in other sources.

Galleries were built in many churches, for normal seating, for psalm singers, and to be used as organ lofts. A faculty also had to be obtained prior to burial under the floor of the church. A bizarre development during the 18th and 19th centuries was the request from families for the exhumation and removal of bodies from one churchyard to another, as families moved house!

Cases relating to churchyards were relatively rare but one such cause from Lichfield relates to a 'house of ease' or 'necessary house' being built too close to the churchyard at Caldwell in the parish of Stapenhill. The waste material from the toilet was thrown over the wall and this caused considerable offence in some quarters.[27] Other causes involved failure to maintain the churchyard walls and the breaking of the churchyard gates. A most unusual citation refers to the breaking open of the tomb of Anne wife of North Foley by Mary daughter of Thomas King at Aston by Birmingham in 1722, but no other information survives.[28]

Faculties were also needed before alterations to rectories, vicarages and their farm buildings could be carried out. Where the property had been neglected, causes for dilapidations were sometimes brought by new incumbents against their predecessors, their widows or those administering their estates, which can give details of the damages to be repaired and the costs involved. Failure to maintain church property by the incumbent could result in the loss of their benefice.

Revenues Due to the Church

One of the most common, and often long-drawn-out type of case, was that of non-payment of church rates or levies (or leuwans), which could be charged as either real or personal rates. From time immemorial under common law, the rector of the church had been responsible for the maintenance of the chancel and the parishioners were responsible for the repairs to the fabric of the rest of the building, the walls, roof, windows and floor. Not all of the parishioners were involved in paying for these repairs the rates were charged on land farmed in the parish, whether held by the owner (who might have lived in another parish) or a tenant. Richard Morris' work on the history of medieval churches[29] has shown that they were in need of continuous attention, resulting in frequent financial demands. By the 16th century the documentary evidence for this begins to appear in the churchwardens' accounts. Faculties were needed for rebuilding and the costs of this, as well as the workmens' bills, had to be met by the community. In large upland parishes with outlying townships there was often resentment at having to pay for the maintenance of the mother church. Those dissenters who did not use the building also often refused to pay towards its upkeep. Many causes of this type were heard in the Lichfield courts during the last decade of the 18th century, including one large cause from Hayfield in the parish of Glossop in Derbyshire where a levy book was produced in evidence.[30] Repairs of church ornaments including furniture, seats, bells, vestments and books were funded through a personal rate, charged in relation to the personal estate of the parishioners. Both of these rates were levied by the churchwardens.

Occasionally the continuous income to the church from a benefice would be interrupted by the death of the incumbent or during legal disputes as, for instance, in causes relating to the neglect of the cure, or if the incumbent was suspended for being seriously indebted, or living a sinful life. At such a time the living would be sequestered, which was a process by which the revenues of the church were collected by named parties, usually the churchwardens, to 'preserve the profits of vacation' of the benefice on behalf of the bishop, usually for the next incumbent. As we shall see with the collection of tithes, the importance of parish tradition was paramount and any break in their collection could have legal consequences. The results of this process occasionally survive as sequestration accounts in the court records, although they are treated as a separate category in some record collections.

The bill of costs

Every cause would have ended with the payment of the bills, and the following document relates to the cost of the faculty for rebuilding St Alkmund's church in Derby in 1844.[31] It also illustrates the progress of the application through the courts, the abbreviations used, and the costs of each stage of the proceedings (Fig. 2.11).

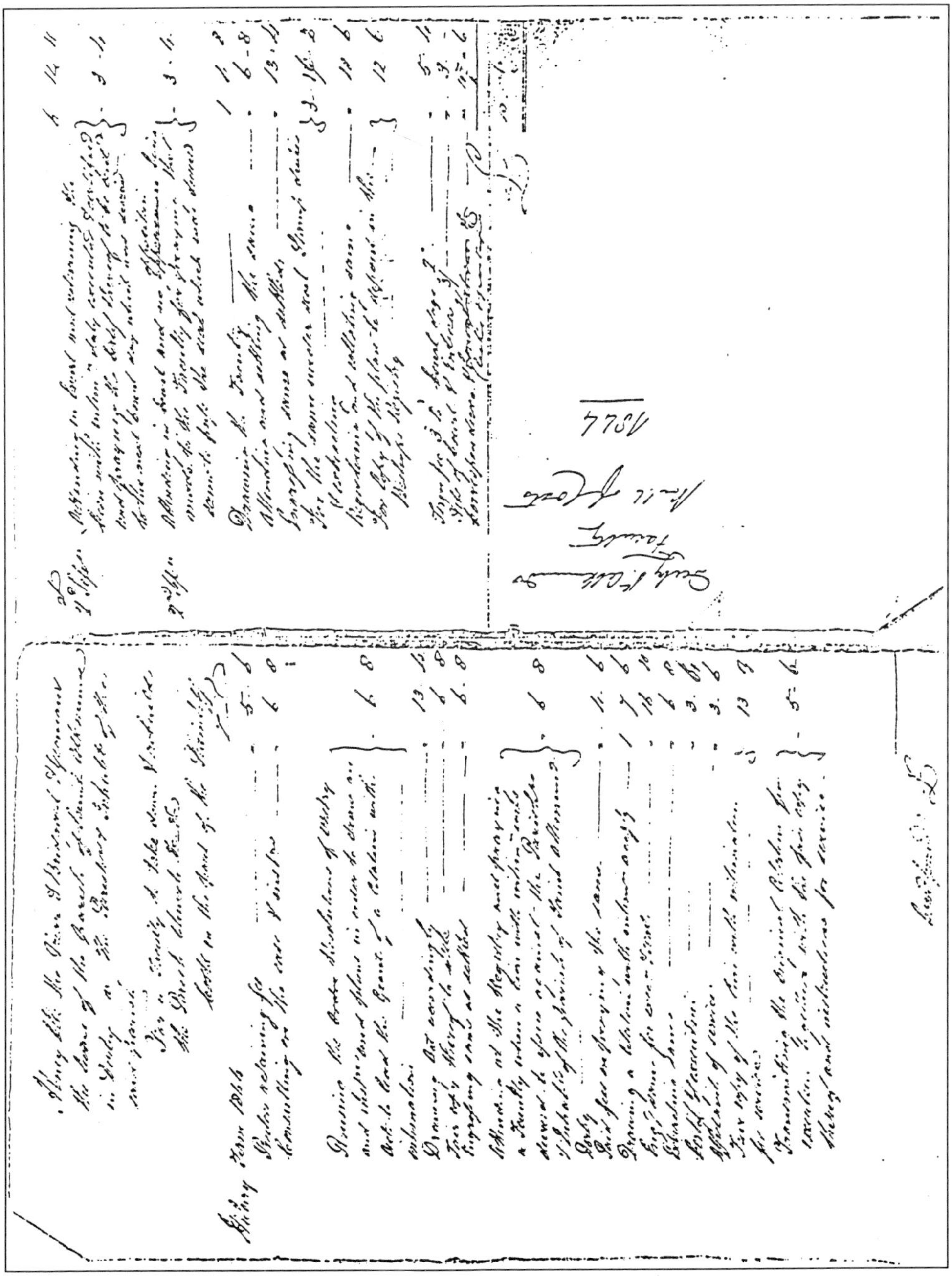

Fig 2.11 Bill of costs for obtaining a faculty, Derby St Alkamund, 1844 giving details of the legal expenses involved.

Abney Clerk the Vicar & Bridgat & Yeomans
the [Church]Wardens of the parish of Saint Alkmund
in Derby v The Parishioners & Inhabitants of the
said parish
For a Faculty to take down & rebuild
the Parish Church etc etc
Costs on the part of the Plaintiff

	£	s	d
Hilary Term 1844			
Proctors retaining fee		5	6
Consulting on the case & instructions		6	8
Perusing the resolutions of Vestry and instructions and plans in order to draw an Act to lead the Grant of a Citation with intimation		6	8
Drawing Act accordingly		13	4
Fair copy thereof to settle		6	8
Engrossing same as settled		6	8
Attending at the Registry and praying a Faculty when a Citation with intimation was decreed to issue against the Parishioners & Inhabitants of the parish of Saint Alkmund Derby		6	8
Paid fees on praying the same		4	6
Drawing a Citation with intimation accordingly	1	7	6
Engrossing same for execution & seal		16	10
Extracting same		6	8
Certificate of execution		3	4
Affidavit of service		3	6
Fair copy of the Citation with intimation for service		13	9
Transmitting the original Citation for execution together with the fair copy thereof and instructions for service		5	6
1st Session			
Attending in Court and returning the Citation with intimation duly executed & certified and praying the certificate thereof to be continued to the next Court day which was decreed		3	4
2nd Session			
Attending in Court and no opposition being made to the Faculty for praying that same to pass the seal which was decreed		3	4
Drawing the Faculty	1	6	8
Attending and settling the same		6	8
Engrossing same as settled		13	4
For the same under seal Stamp duties & extracting	3	17	2*
Registering and collating same		10	6
For Copy of the plan to deposit in the Bishops Registry		12	6
Term fee 3s 4d Court days 2s		5	4
Acts of Court & Entries 3/-		9	
Correspondence & Clerks & postage		10	6
	£15	6	3

* The figures were corrected but not clearly. This, together with other corrections made the document technically ambivalent, and is probably the reason why the document survives in the cause papers.

Then, as now, people were not always willing to pay their bills, and such a failure would have led to a cause relating to fees, stipend and salary. The following citation is in an unusual '*quorum nomina*' style for this business, the usual form only citing a single individual (Fig. 2.12).[32]

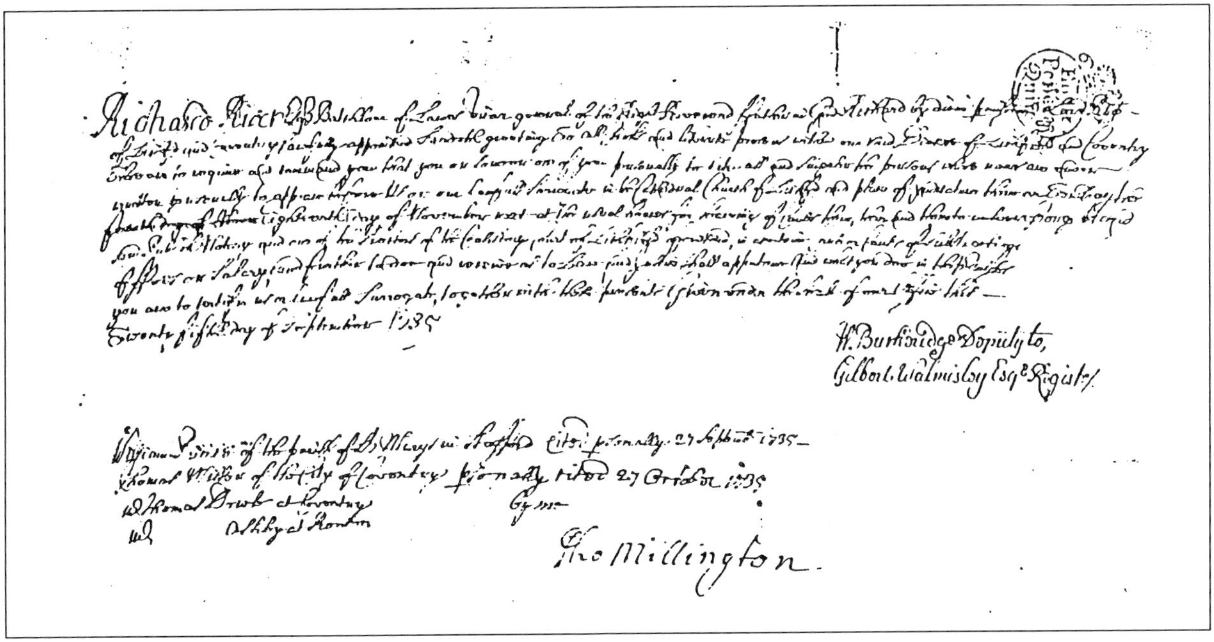

Richard Rider Esquire Batchelor of Laws Vicar general of the Right Reverend Father in God Richard by divine permission Lord Bishop of Lichfield and Coventry lawfully appointed Sendeth greeting To all Clerks and literate persons within our said Diocese of Lichfield and Coventry These are to require and command you that you or some or one of you personally to cite all and singular the persons whose names are under written personally to appear before Us or our lawfull Surrogate in the Cathedral Church of Lichfield and place of Judicature there on Tuesday the Eighteenth day of November next at the usual hours for hearing of Causes there, then and there to answer George Hand senior Publick Notary and one of the proctors of the Consistory Court of Lichfield aforesaid, in a certaine Cause or Causes of Substractings of Fees or Salary, and further to doe and receive as to Law and Justice shall appertaine And what you doe in the premisses you are to certifie us or lawfull Surrogate, together with those present Given under the Seale of our Office this
Twenty fifth day of September 1735

W. Buckeridge Deputy to,
Gilbert Walmisley Esquire Register

Wm Prince of the parish of St. Marys in Stafford cited personally 27 September 1735
Thomas Miller of the City of Coventry personally cited 27 October 1735
Mr. Thomas Dowle at Coventry by me
Mr. [first name omitted] Ashby at Ronton Thomas Millington

Fig. 2.12 Quorum nomina citation in cause for fees brought by George Hand, proctor of Lichfield. The proctors were entitled to use the courts themselves to claim unpaid fees.

A very high proportion of correction causes ceased with the initial citation but, where they were heard in plenary form and continued to the point of bringing witnesses, they include many details of the daily life and attitudes of known social groups for both the family and local historian.

Chapter Three

Probate and Testamentary Business

From the early 13th century the granting of probate for the slowly increasing number of wills being made, and letters of administration of intestate estates, was predominantly the right of ecclesiastical authorities,[1] and the monies collected by the courts for their services remained in their hands, forming an ever-increasing proportion of their revenues. Those areas outside the jurisdiction of the bishop, known as peculiars, could hold their own courts for the granting of probate, as could some manor courts, but these proved only a fraction of the known wills. Their records were often retained in private hands and are generally not well preserved. Ecclesiastical probate was superceded on 11 January 1858 by civil district registries in England and Wales, with the main probate registry established at Somerset House in London. Continuous ecclesiastical jurisdiction was only once over-ruled prior to 1858, during the Commonwealth, when probate was handled by the Court of Civil Commission between 1653 and 1660.

By the 18th century separate probate courts were held twice a year within the diocese of Lichfield, at eight towns, two in each of the archdeaconries, on a regular route; similar arrangements were probably made in other dioceses. Those who had been a little slow in seeking permission elsewhere[2] were summoned by citation to appear.

The granting of probate was merely the legal permission, granted on oath of the executor,[3] to administer the estate of the deceased and was legally confirmed by a written permission also known as a probate act, or fiat. These probate acts were recorded in the act books of the probate courts. The recording of these acts changed over time and the act books ceased in Lichfield in 1638. From this date the fiat took the form of a slip of paper giving the name of the deceased and their chosen executors and was filed with the original will and inventory.[4] This process was known as proving the will;[5] it had to be commenced within four months of the death of the testator although in many cases it was started much sooner. Increasing business led to the use of printed forms by the 18th century. Many died intestate, that is, without leaving a will, and permission to administer their affairs was granted firstly to the surviving spouse (if there was one), then to any children of a marriage, then to a sibling or the next of kin. If none of these survived, administration was granted to a creditor and finally, if there were no creditors, a grant was made at the discretion of the court. The choice of these administrators lay, in theory, with the bishop who had the souls of his flock in his care during their lives, and was thus considered to be a suitable person to have care of their temporal goods, and to ensure their proper administration and distribution after their deaths. Again, an appearance in the probate court was required in order to make application for letters of administration, often known as an admon. The grant of letters of administration sometimes required the named administrators to enter into a bond with the authorities, which can give the occupations of the administrators. In those rare cases where executors and legatees died during a protracted period of settling the deceased's affairs, it may have been necessary for new executors or administrators to seek a second grant of probate.

If a will had been left but no executor named, or a named executor had renounced probate, died, or was otherwise unable to act, then letters of administration were granted 'with will annexed', usually to the next of kin, or an individual named in the will but not specifically as an executor. (An example of this is can be seen in Chapter One where a legatee[6] was called by letters of request to appear at Lichfield.) The widow and next of kin were regarded as lawful friends of the deceased, and thus suitable individuals to carry out this task. The only legal constraints upon executors and administrators was that they should not have been attainted by treason, convicted of a felony or be standing excommunicate by the greater form.

The ecclesiastical courts and those of peculiar jurisdictions were also entitled to hear instance causes which related to disputed wills, legacies and inventories. These causes are described as testamentary business, as distinct from probate business which refers to the simple process of granting of probates. Testamentary causes were only heard in the consistory courts themselves, not in the peripatetic probate courts, although both courts would probably have been manned by the same staff. By the 18th century, testamentary causes provided much of the business generated within the church courts, especially amongst instance causes which usually arose where the validity of the will was questioned, although these courts could not mediate in disputes over real estate. The old tag 'where there's a will there's a relative' was, by the 18th century, extended to a number of very distant relatives, a great many friends and even creditors with an interest in an estate! By their nature, these causes tended to generate depositions of witnesses, usually those involved with the making of the will, as well as a final sentence giving the legal decision. The office could also bring causes to court where legacies had not been paid, or administration had proceeded without the necessary permission, both being contrary to canon law. Throughout the 18th century the rising numbers of attorneys were beginning to conduct private negotiations between individuals in these matters, eroding the instance business of the church courts.

In view of the importance of wills in the activities of the courts it is necessary to consider how they were made and the problems that could arise from them. The making of a will was a solemn and voluntary undertaking and the document would either have been written personally by the testator, a holographic will, by a third party, or, in the last resort, spoken—known as a nuncupative will. The purpose of a will was two-fold, embodied in the phrase 'will and testament'. The will was made to devise land and buildings and the testament to dispose of personal property, including money; both functions have been combined in the single document in England and Wales since the medieval period. The will relating to land empowered the legatee to gain instant access to land and property once the will had been proved which explains the reason for the importance of such documents. The will was also valid from the date of writing but only effective upon the death of the testator and any change in circumstances, the birth of children for instance, would require a new will to be made. Where a will was disputed it had to be proved in 'solemn form' in the spiritual courts.

A holographic will had to be in the handwriting of the testator and witnessed by three credible witnesses,[7] and the evidence of at least two of those present at the time of writing was required for its proof in solemn form. The making of a will by a third party involved an initial visit and discussion between the testator and amanuensis, often a local attorney or schoolmaster who then drew up the document elsewhere. The writer returned at some later date with the will, which was then read over to the testator in the presence of the witnesses, to ensure that the wishes of the testator were recorded accurately and with no opportunity for interference. When the testator was satisfied, hot sealing wax was dropped at the end of the document and impressed, the words 'I publish this my last will and testament' repeated. The document would be signed in the presence of the witnesses who would also sign it. This act also legally confirmed that the testator was 'of sound mind'. The use of a seal on the will was particularly advisable in those wills which devised property, because it was, in effect, a deed and thus required a seal. Occasionally, the time spent drawing up the will or making corrections was too long and the testator died prior to its signature. Under such circumstances the will would have to be taken before the consistory court to be proved in solemn form.

Nuncupative wills were those that were simply spoken and not written down until after the death of the testator. This form of will was generally made by those who had simply left matters until the inevitable was imminent. It was necessary for three witnesses to be present when the words were spoken and for them to be aware of the fact that the testator was making his will. The words were to be written down and signed by the witnesses as soon as possible, often after the death of the testator. In order to prevent fraud, this type of will was not to be proved until

14 days after the testator's death. If there was a widow, still living, she was to be called at the time of probate. Nuncupative wills take many forms relating mainly to the whim of the writer. The following example gives a picture of the comparative simplicity of these statements, although not all began so formally (Fig. 3.1):[8]

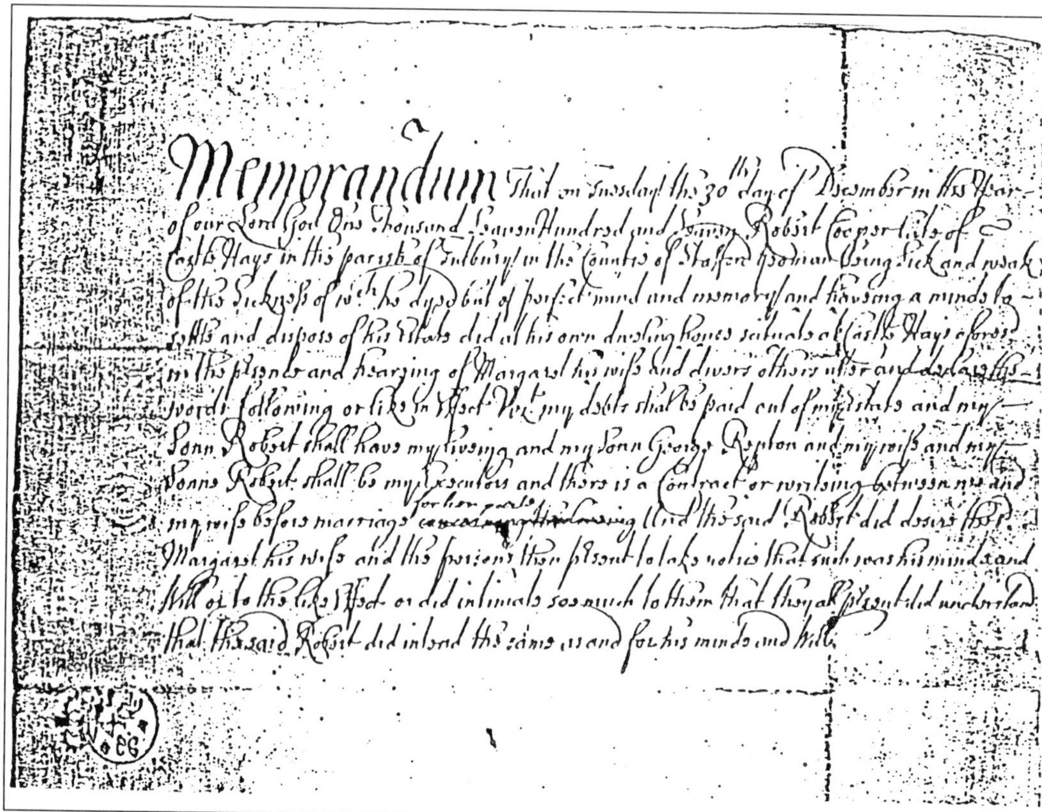

Memorandum That on Tuesday the 30th day of December in the Year
of our Lord God One Thousand Seaven Hundred and Seaven Robert Cooper late of
Castle Hays in the parish of Tutbury in the Countie of Stafford Yeoman being Sick and weak
of the Sickness of which he dyed but of perfect mind and memory and haveing a minde to
settle and dispose of his Estate did at his own dweling house scituate at Castle Hays aforesaid
in the presence and heareing of Margaret his wife and divers others utter and declare the
words following or like in Effect Vizt. my debts shal be paid out of my Estate and my
Sonn Robert shall have my liveing and my sonn George Repton and my wife and my
Sonne Robert shall be my Executors and there is a Contract or writeing between me and
my wife before marriage for her parte And the said Robert did desire the said
Margaret his wife and the persons then present to take notice that such was his mind and
Will or to the like Effect or did intimate soe much to them that they all present did understand
that the said Robert did intend the same as and for his minde and Will.

Fig. 3.1 Nuncupative will of Robert Cooper, 1707. These documents survive where they are disputed, as in this case.

In order to ensure the legality of the document two points had to be made. Firstly, it was important to state that the testator was of sound mind, a vital factor in the validity of any will, and secondly it was also necessary when making a will of this type that those present were 'to take notice that he was making his will'. On this occasion there was a written marriage contract in existence for the wife's part and this was brought to the attention of the executors to ensure that Margaret would be provided for. George Repton was possibly his wife's son by a previous marriage. This document was not signed by the amanuensis, but this was not technically necessary.

Not every member of society was allowed to make a will. Lunatics of course could not do so, not being 'of sound mind'. If the state of mind of the testator gave rise to concern whilst making the will, either by the consumption of alcohol[9] or evident signs of mental illness, the validity of the document would be questioned. The wills of suicides and those under the greater excommunication were declared void. A married woman could only make a will with the consent of her husband and, if he died, a further will had to be made. Children could make wills, a boy from the age of 14 and a girl of 12. These ceased to be valid when they reached their majority—the age of 21, when a new will had to be made.

Disputes relating to wills were usually heard as instance business, between two parties, and the cause began with the usual citation. If no relatives were forthcoming a citation with intimation would be read in the parish church of the deceased to trace someone who would be able to undertake the administration of the estate. Causes then proceeded with an allegation rather than articles of a libel. Witnesses to the will were required to testify to the publishing of it, and were required to give statements in private upon the allegation and to answer the interrogatories of the opposing party, as in the usually plenary form of pleading. Their written depositions were taken down. After deliberation by the vicar general or chancellor, a final decree or 'sententia' was produced. If the will was proved in the absence of interested parties, proof could be requested again some years later, possibly after the witnesses had died, which could prove to be a long and expensive cause. It was, incidentally, possible to question the proof of a will in common form for up to thirty years after the event.

Causes were taken to the consistory courts for a number of reasons. The following were the most common:

1) Proving of a will in common or solemn form where the validity was in doubt by virtue of the conditions under which it was made, or the age and medical condition of the testator.
2) Disputed nuncupative wills.
3) Later additions to wills in the form of codicils and interlined statements.
4) Suppression or concealing of wills.
5) Rash administration, where the process of administration of the estate had commenced without the necessary legal permission.
6) Renunciation of probate.
7) The non-payment, or 'subtraction', of a legacy.
8) Disputed inventories and accounts.
9) Non-payment of tithes.
10) Although not technically a cause, the courts could also legally appoint guardians for those minors who were to inherit goods or sums of money.

These causes are notable for the number of female litigants involved in them. A high proportion of the defendants were widows, who had been slow in their duties in winding up the estates of their departed husbands, and who had since re-married. Incidentally, this gives the family historian a rare opportunity to trace these elusive ladies, and to discover their new circumstances.

The necessity to prove a will in either common or solemn form was one of the most common reasons for a cause in the church courts. Those wills where witnesses had died prior to the proving of the will often came into this category, as did those where an estate had been unadministered due to the death of the executors or administrators. The following interrogatories give an excellent idea of the points that were of legal importance and hence put to the witnesses of a will (Fig. 3.2):[10]

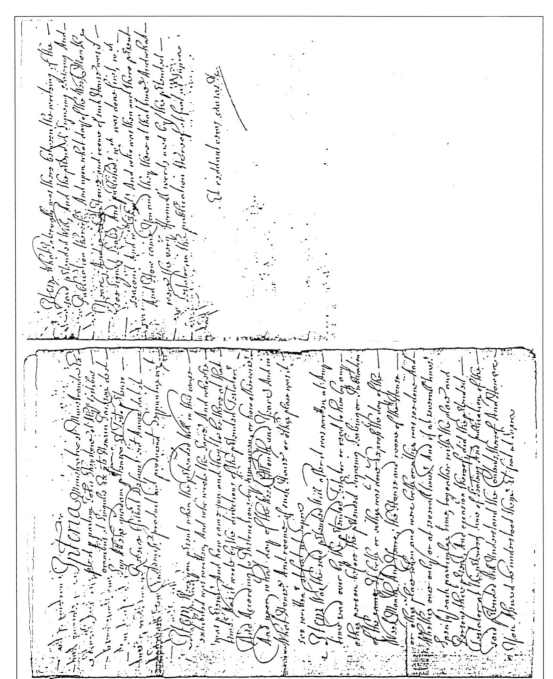

Fig 3.2 *Interrogatories relating to the making of Rebecca Gilbert's will, showing the legal points that had to be proved to ensure the validity of the will.*

Interrogatoria Ministrata et Ministranda Ex
parte per partem Johis Shenstone et Aliis Testibus
omnibus et Singulis Ex parte Henrici Jackson de et
Super Allegacionis quadam pretensa Et Testimento pretenso
Rebecca Gilbert Defuncta eidem Annex dat et
Admissus & productus ant producendus Sequuntur vidilicet

[Interrogatories on the part and behalf of John Shenstone and others to be administered to all and singular the witnesses produced or to be produced and examined on behalf of Henry Jackson of and upon an allegation on the pretended will of Rebecca Gilbert deceased, the same annexed, and are as follows]

1. Item Were you present when the pretended Will in this cause exhibited was written, And who wrote the Same? And who else was present? And how came you and they to be there at that time? Was it wrote by the directions of the pretended Testator? And According to Instructions by him given, or how otherwise? And upon what day of the Week Month and Year? And in What House? And roome of such House or other place was it soe written? *et fiat ut Supra* [and let it be done]
2. Item Was the said pretended Will after it was written at Any time read over by the pretended Testator or read to him by any other person before the pretended Signeing Sealing or Publication of the same, If both or either was done Express the day of the Week Month And Yeare, the House and roome of the House or other place when and were both or either was soe done And Whether once only or at severall times? And if at severall times? Specify each particular time, togeather with the place and Persons there present, And occasion thereof, did the pretended Testator at the pretended time of Sealeing And publication of the said pretended Will Understand the Contents thereof And How are You Assured he understood them? *Et fiat ut Supra* [and let it be done]
3. Item What Intervall was there between the writeing of the said pretended Will, And the pretended Signeing sealeing And Publication thereof? And upon what day of the Week Month & Yeare, And in what House and roome of such House was it soe Signed, Sealed, And published? which was done first, which seacond And which Third? And who was then and there present And How came You and they there at that time? And what were the very Formall words used by the pretended Testator in the publication thereof *et fiat ut Supra* [and let it be done]

Et reddant veras causas etc
[And return the truth of the cause etc]

It was also important to establish that the will, if made by a third party, should be read over to the testator and that they should understand what had been written. The 'very formall words' were probably the usual, 'I publish this my last will and testament'. Due to the fact that these documents were not 'proved' until the final decision had been given, logic demanded that they were to be described as 'pretended'.

Wills made by those of considerable age, suffering from the 'decay of nature', or suspected insanity also tended to be questioned. One cause relating to the health and state of mind of the testatrix comes from Lichfield, where John Bland was being questioned about the validity of his mother's will as follows (Fig. 3.3):[11]

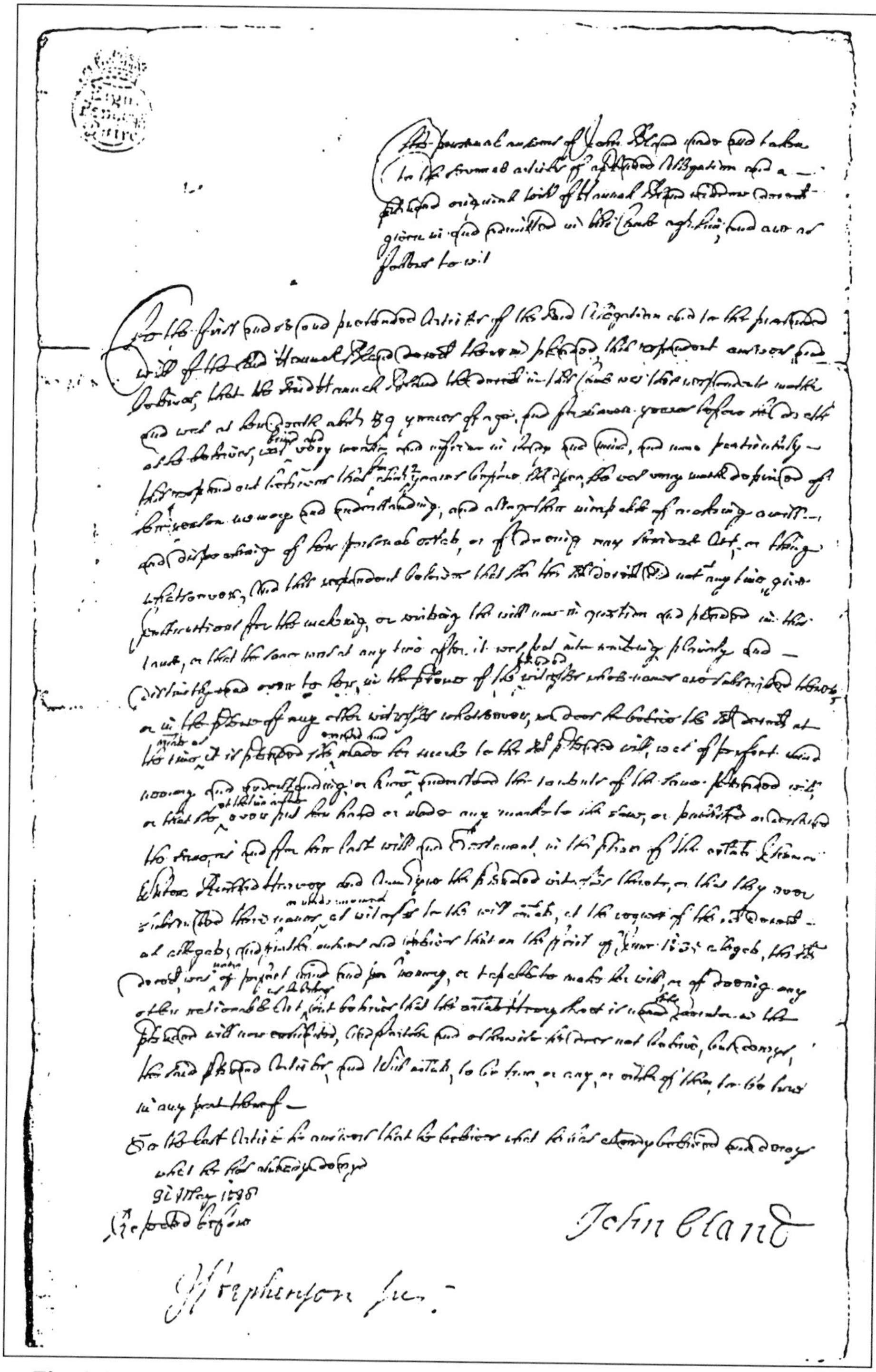
John Bland

J Stephenson Jur.

Fig 3.3 Personal answers relating to the state of mind of an elderly testatrix, giving some details of the age and mental and physical state of the individual.

The personal answers of John Bland made and taken to the several articles of a pretended Allegation and a Pretended original Will of Hannah Bland widdow deceased given in and admitted in this Cause against him, and are as follows to wit

To the first and second pretended Articles of the said Allegation and to the pretended will of the said Hannah Bland deceased therein pleaded, this respondant answers and beleives, that the said Hannah Bland the deceased in this Cause was the respondents mother and was at her death about 89 yeares of age, and for seaven yeares before her death as he believes, was blind and very weake and inferme in body and mind, and more particulerly the respondent beleives that for about 2 yeares before she dyed, she was very much deprived of her reason memory and understanding, and altogether incapable of makeing a will and dispoaseing of her personal estate, or of doeing any Serious Act, or thing whatsoever, And this respondent beleives that she the said deceased did not at any time give Instructions for the makeing, or writeing the will now in question and pleaded in this cause, or that the same was at any time after it was put into writeing, plainely and distinctly read over to her in Presence of the pretended witnesses whose names are subscribed thereto, or in the Presence of any other witnesses whatsoever, nor does he beleive the said deceased at the time articulate as it is pretended she executed and made her marke to the said pretended will, was of perfect mind memory and understanding, or knew or understood the contents of the same pretended will, or that she at the time articulate ever put her hand or made any marke to the same, or published or declared the same, as and for her last will and Testament, in the presence of the articulate Thomas Wilcox Richard Harvey and Ann Eyre the pretended witnesses thereto, or that they ever subscribed their names or made any mark as witnesses to the will articulate, at the request of the said Deceased as allegate, and further answers and beleives that on the first of June 1735 allegate, the said deceased was not of perfect mind and Memory, or capable to make her will, or of doeing any other rationable Act as he beleives but beleives that the articulate Henry Street is named to be Executor in the pretended will now exhibited, And farther and otherwise he does not beleive, but denys, the said pretended Articles, and Will articulate, to be true, or any, or either of them, to be true in any part thereof

To the last Article he answers that he beleives what he has already beleived and denys what he has already denyd

31 May 1736 John bland

Repeated before

J Stephenson Surrogate

Other problems brought to the courts, relating to the wills of the very old and infirm, involved those testators known to have suffered from strokes or paralysis and who could have been subjected to coercion. Proving the will in solemn form would bring witnesses into court whose depositions would sometimes describe the symptoms of those suffering in this way, including blindness, incontinence and what was probably Altzheimer's disease. Other medical problems, including accidents and cases of smallpox, are sometimes described by witnesses.

Nuncupative wills were also open to question in terms of possible collusion between the writer and the witnesses, particularly where the testator had few relatives, or lived some distance from them. Widows, who were often insufficiently literate to produce a will, also tended to speak their wills. This type of cause often produced depositions of witnesses which also described the final illness of the testator.

Codicils, or additions to wills, were also disputed, often because the testator was not aware of the legal necessity for them to be dated and witnessed. Some individuals produced a number of wills and there was confusion as to which was the correct version, particularly where several individuals stood to gain from differing versions. The legal position was, of course, that each succeeding will revoked the previous one.

The suppression or concealment of a will was a moral offence and taken to the church courts, although such causes were comparatively few in the Lichfield courts. The appearance of these causes depended upon reports from other relatives or neighbours.

Rash administration, or the 'intermeddling' in the affairs of the deceased prior to permission being given, was also a moral offence. A flurry of these cases appeared at Lichfield when Archbishop Sancroft was in control of the diocese, *sede plena*,[12] in the late 17th century, during the suspension of Bishop Wood.

Occasionally, executors would be unable to undertake their duties and would renounce probate. This was a serious problem and was generally taken through the consistory court, certainly at Lichfield, where a document called a renunciation would be left in the court papers. Some wills involved more than one renunciation, that of Edward Repington of Tamworth in 1735 involved a total of 10![13] Probate in this case was eventually granted to the unlikely combination of Edward Repington, gent, and John Orme, labourer. The lack of literacy of the executor may well have proved too much for the production of the necessary inventory, as may have been the case in the estate of Henry Fogg, an apothecary from Leek who died in 1750.[14] The executor, his uncle, was unable to read and write and it was an important part of his duties to produce a very long listing of household goods, including 33 books, as well as a list of 200 bad debts. Henry's father, a butcher, undertook the task upon his brother's renunciation. In other cases, an inside knowledge of the financial problems of the testator may have led to the exercise of caution. As with other semi-official documents, the renunciation could take many forms, but the basic structure was as follows (Fig. 3.4):[15]

Know all men by these Presents that I William Atkis of the
town of Shiffnal in the County of Salop Gentleman one of the Executors named
in the last Will and Testament of Richard Horner late of
Shifnall in the said County Gentleman deceased haveing
not intermeddled with or disposed of any part of the Goods Chattels
and Creditts of the said deceased Have Renounced and quitt Claimed
and by the presents Do Renounce and quitt Claim All my right
Title and Interest of in and to the Execution of the said Will of
the said Deceased And to the End that this my Renunciation may
have its due Effect in Law I do hereby Authorize Constitute and
appoint Mr. John Fletcher one of the Proctors of the
Ecclesiastical Court of the Bishop of Litchfield and Coventry
my true and lawful Proctor Giving and Granting unto him full
power and Authority for me in my name place and Stead to
appear before the Judge of the said Ecclisiastical Court and
procure this my Renunciation to be duly admitted and Enacted
and whatsoever my said proctor shall Lawfully do or cause
to be done in the Premisses I hereby promise to ratify and
Confirm In Witnesse whereof I have hereunto set my Hand
and Seal this Eleventh day of October in the
Eleventh Year of his present Majesty King George the Second's
reign over Great Britain France and Ireland and in the Year
of our Lord One thousand seven hundred and thirty seven

Sealed and Delivered in the
presence of
Joshua Piper William Atkis [seal]
Abel Lewis

Fig. 3.4 Renunciation of probate by William Atkis, 1737, executor of Richard Horner of Shifnal, gent.

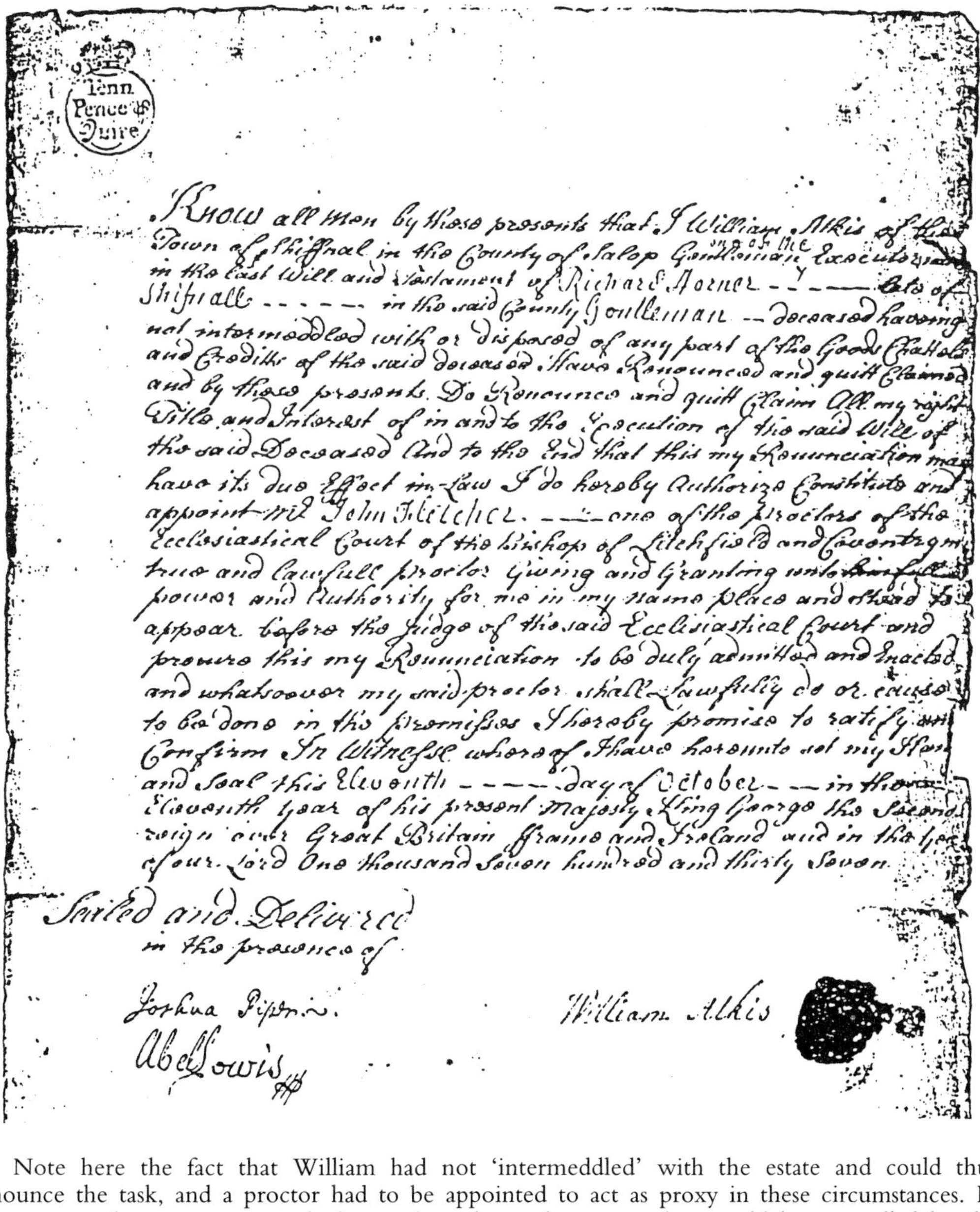

Tenn Pence Quire

Know all Men by these presents that I William Atkis of the Town of Shiffnal in the County of Salop Gentleman one of the Executors in the last Will and Testament of Richard Horner ---- late of Shiffnall ------ in the said County Gentleman -- deceased having not intermeddled with or disposed of any part of the Goods Chattels and Credits of the said deceased Have Renounced and quitt Claimed and by these presents Do Renounce and quitt Claim All my right Title and Interest of in and to the Execution of the said Will of the said Deceased And to the End that this my Renunciation may have its due Effect in Law I do hereby Authorize Constitute and appoint Mr John Fletcher ---- one of the Proctors of the Ecclesiastical Court of the Bishop of Litchfield and Coventry my true and Lawfull Proctor Giving and Granting unto him full power and Authority for me in my name place and stead to appear before the Judge of the said Ecclesiastical Court and procure this my Renunciation to be duly admitted and Enacted and whatsoever my said proctor shall Lawfully do or cause to be done in the Premisses I hereby promise to ratify and Confirm In Witness whereof I have hereunto set my Hand and Seal this Eleventh ---- day of October -- in the Eleventh year of his present Majesty King George the Second reign over Great Britain France and Ireland and in the year of our Lord One thousand Seven hundred and thirty Seven.

Sealed and Delivered in the presence of

Joshua Pipen

Abel Lowis

William Atkis

Note here the fact that William had not 'intermeddled' with the estate and could thus renounce the task, and a proctor had to be appointed to act as proxy in these circumstances. In those cases where an executor had started work on the estate, they could be compelled by the courts to continue with the process.

Withholding of a legacy was a moral sin, though it was often merely the result of the death of an executor or administrator, rather than a deliberate action. In the later 18th century 'probate chains' developed when executors or administrators died before completing their task, perhaps caught up in localised outbreaks of disease. This led to situations where estates were waiting on completion of a previous one for their settlement. Complex citations appear, often from the higher courts where causes had been sent on appeal, and these describe the situation in legal detail which can be daunting to disentangle.

Proving the right to a legacy can reveal vast amounts of information for the family historian. In the following cause, the relationship between the legatees and intestate widow is examined in microscopic detail (Fig. 3.5).[16]

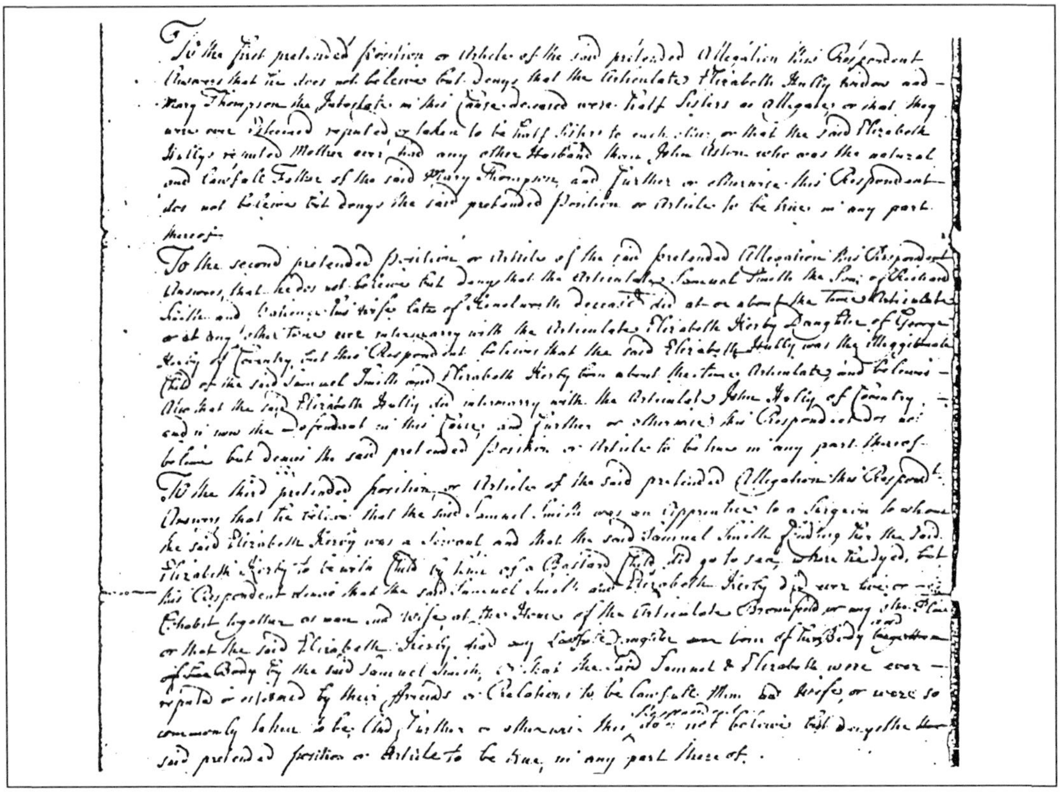

Fig. 3.5 Personal responses in a testamentary dispute giving great detail about the family.

More 'sententia' survive for this type of business than any other, a decision being legally necesary where money was at stake! In the majority of cases where the validity was questioned, the will was upheld; trying to prove otherwise could prove exceedingly difficult, particularly where witnesses had since died.

Inventories and probate accounts were sometimes produced in court at the request of a relative or a creditor, often in cases where the estate was insufficient to meet legacies. Again the death of the executor or administrator may be one of the reasons for this type of cause coming to court. It was necessary under a statute of 21 Hen. VIII c.5 for four honest persons to make an inventory of the goods of the deceased but the numbers of these appraisers declined and inventories generally ceased to be produced by the 1720s and 1730s, when this fascinating source of information all but disappears. Where the management of the estate was called into question through the 18th century and beyond, the law demanded that an inventory should be exhibited in court and, in some cases, a probate account was also produced.

To the first pretended Position or Article of the said pretended Allegation this Respondent Answers that he does not beleive but denys that the Articulate Elizabeth Hully Widow and Mary Thompson the Intestate in this Cause deceased were half Sisters as Allegate, or that they were ever Esteemed reputed or taken to be half sisters to each other, or that the said Elizabeth Hully's reputed Mother ever had any other Husband than John Aston who was the natural and lawfull Father of the said Mary Thompson, and further or otherwise this Respondent does not beleive but denys the said pretended Position or Article to be true in any part thereof
To the second pretended Position or Article of the said pretended Allegation this Respondent answers, that he does not beleive but denys that the Articulate Samuel Smith the Son of Richard Smith and Patience his wife late of Kenelworth deceas'd did at or about the time Articulate or at any other time ever intermarry with the Articulate Elizabeth Kerby Daughter of George Kerby of Coventry, but this Respondent beleives that the said Elizabeth Hully was the illeggitimate Child of the said Samuel Smith and Elizabeth Kerby born about the time Articulate, and beleives Also that the said Elizabeth Hully did intermarry with the Articulate John Hully of Coventry and is now the Defendant in this Cause, and further or otherwise his Respondent does not beleive but denies the said pretended Position or Article to be true in any part thereof
To the third pretended position or Article of the said pretended Allegation this Respondent Answers, that he beleives that the said Samuel Smith was an Apprentice to a Surgeon to whom the said Elizabeth Kerby was a Servant, and that the said Samuel Smith finding her the said Elizabeth Kerby to be with Child by him of a Bastard Child did go to sea, where he dyed, but this Respondent denies that the said Samuel Smith and Elizabeth Kerby did ever live or Cohabit together as man and Wife at the House of the Articulate Bromfield or any other Place, or that the said Elizabeth Kerby had any Lawfull Daughter ever born of her Body and by the said Samuel Smith, Or that the said Samuel & Elizabeth were ever reputed or esteemed by their Friends or Relations to be lawful Man and Wife, or were so commonly taken to be, And further or otherwise this Respondent does not beleive but denys the said pretended position or Article to be true, in any part thereof

These later inventories were often written out by the clerks of the court, in immaculate hands, and signed by the executors. By virtue of their role in these causes, these inventories can include the sale value of the goods, with the contents of a house described in great detail. Some inventories are arranged by named rooms with items individually valued, others show a valuation for the contents of a whole room. During the 18th century it became fashionable to sell household items at auction and some late inventories consist merely of a list of goods sold, often over several days, the prices they fetched and perhaps the name of the auctioneer. However, the prices that the goods realised at auction would relate to the condition of the effects as well as the prevailing market prices. Occasionally some unusual items appear this way. A dispute over the possessions of Joseph Sadler of Wem produced the following responses to the interrogatories by George Bromhall of Whitchurch, a schoolmaster, aged 34 years (Fig. 3.6).[17]

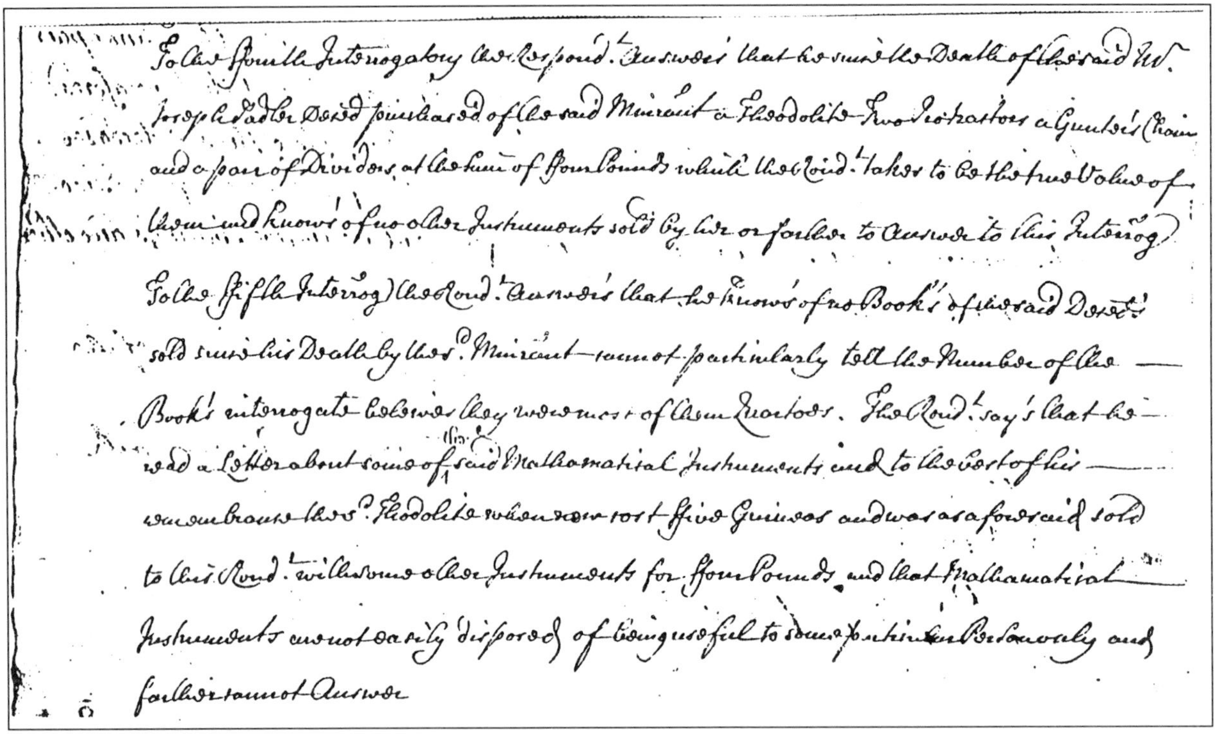

To the Fourth Interrogatory the Respondent Answers that he since the Death of the said Mr. Joseph Sadler Deceased
purchased of the said Ministrant a Theodolite Two Protractors a Gunter's Chain
and a pair of Dividers at the Sum of Four Pounds which the Respondent takes to be the true Value of
them and knows of no other Instruments sold by her or farther to Answer to this Interrogatory
To the Fifth Interrogatory the Respondent Answers that he Knows of no Books of the said Deceased's
sold since his Death by the said Ministrant cannot particularly tell the Number of the
Book's interrogate beleives they were most of them Quartoes. The Respondent say's that he
read a Letter about some of the said Mathamatical Instruments and to the best of his
remembrance the said Theodolite when new cost Five Guineas and was as aforesaid sold
to this Respondent with some other Instruments for Four Pounds and that Mathamatical
Instruments are not easily disposed of being useful to some particular Person only and
farther cannot Answer.

Fig 3.6 Purchase of effects of the deceased. The widow was probably very lucky to find a purchaser for such items.

His answers to the second interrogatory tell us that he paid no taxes to the king, church or poor, and was worth ten pounds and upwards, if his debts were paid. He had been a teacher of writing and accounts for 14 years, and his purchase of the instruments must have represented quite a capital investment, if indeed he was only worth ten pounds.

Some inventories show a lack of possessions which may not simply indicate poverty. Many 'yeomen' 'left off housekeeping' and boarded with their children, who continued to farm the family land. This can often be detected in inventories with a small number of rooms, usually only one or two, containing the most basic items of sleeping and cooking equipment. These individuals were known as boarders, or tablers, and their welfare could be discussed in the courts. Where these individuals lived with members of the family, names and relationships are given. The following is an extract from the deposition of Maria Judd junior of Foleshill in a cause relating to the estate of Jane Wright, widow (John Clifton was the son of Jane) (Fig. 3.7):[18]

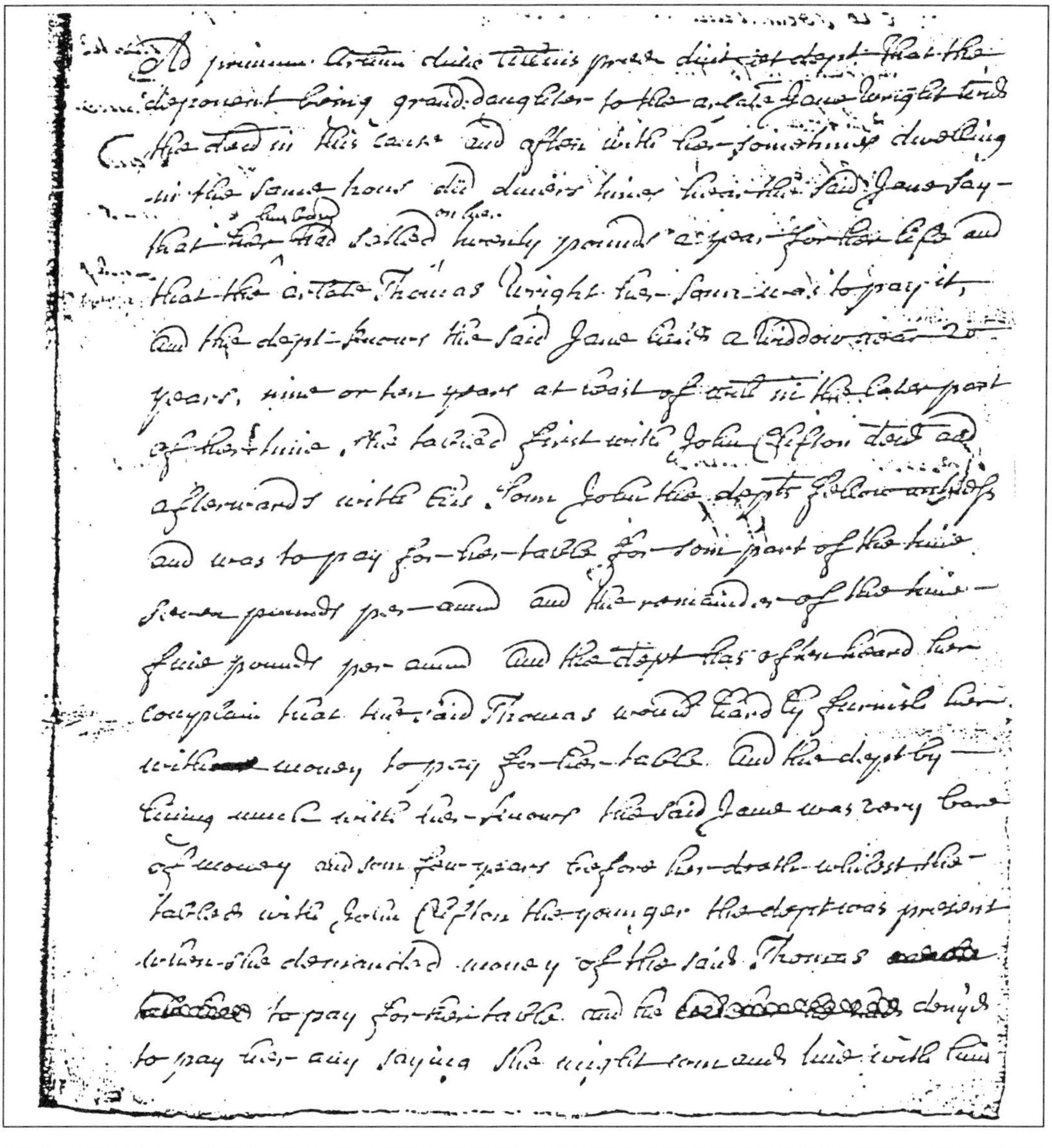

That the deponent being grand-daughter to the articulate Jane Wright widow the deceased in this cause and often with her sometimes dwelling in the same hous did divers times hear the said Jane say that her husband had settled on her twenty pounds a year for her life and that the articulate Thomas Wright her sonn was to pay it, and the deponent knows that said Jane liv'd a Widdow near 20 years, nine or ten years at least of which in the later part of her time she tabled first with John Clifton deceased and afterwards with his Sonn John the deponents fellow witness and was to pay for her table for som part of the time seven pounds per annum and the remainder of the time five pounds per annum And the deponent has often heard her complain that the said Thomas would hardly furnish her with money to pay for her table And the deponent by living much with her knows the said Jane was very bare of money and som few years before her death whilst she
tabled with John Clifton the younger the deponent was present when she demanded money of the said Thomas to pay for her table and he deny'd to pay her any saying she might come and live with him ...

Fig. 3.7 *The elderly did not always live alone, in fact they often 'tabled' with one relative after another, although in this case her financial problems were causing distress.*

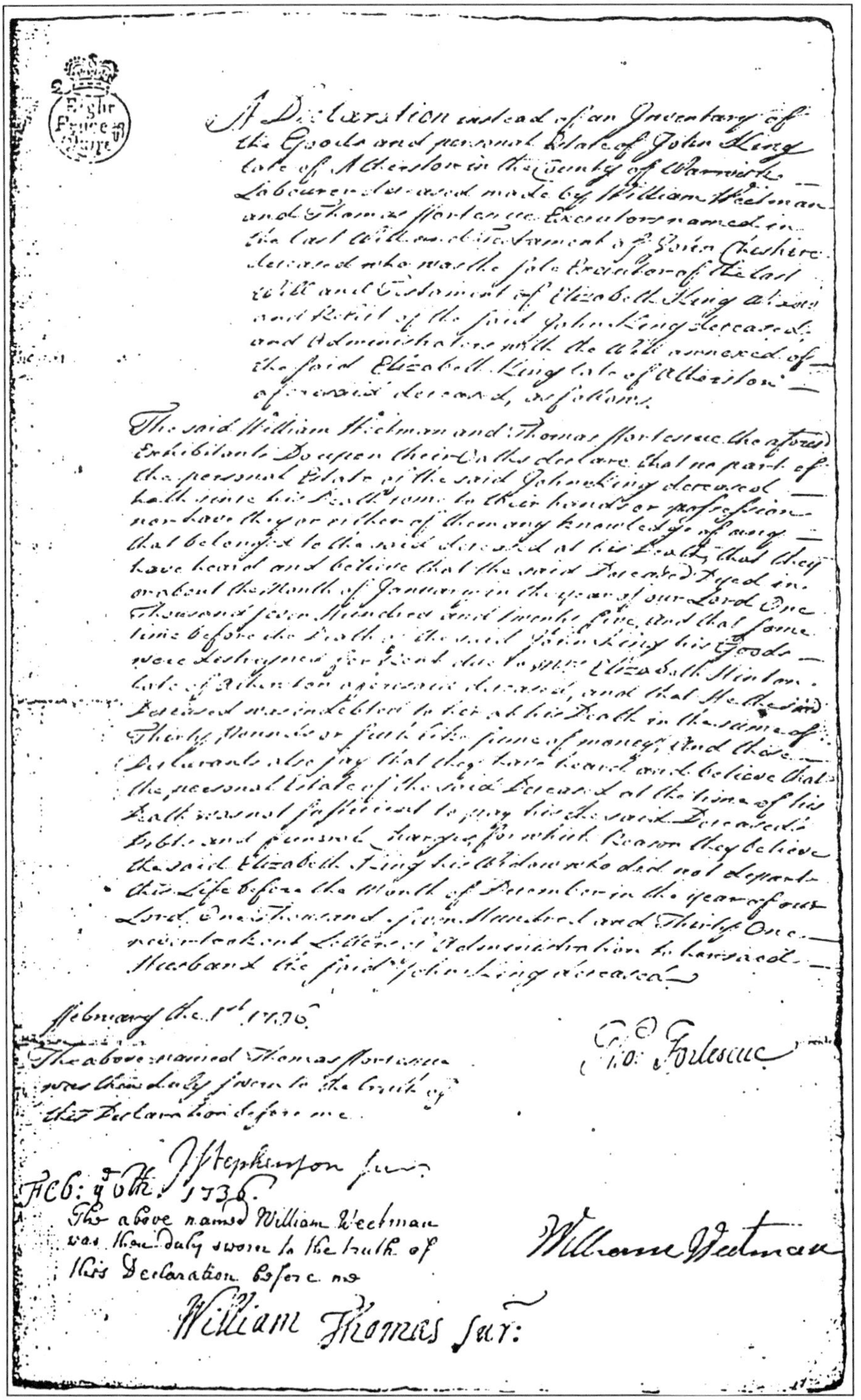

A Declaration instead of an Inventory of the Goods and personal Estate of John King late of Atherston in the County of Warwick Labourer deceased made by William Weetman and Thomas ffortescue Executors named in the last Will and Testament of John Cheshire deceased who was the sole Executor of the last Will and Testament of Elizabeth King alias and Relict of the said John King deceased, and Administratrix with the Will annexed of the said Elizabeth King late of Atherston aforesaid deceased, as follows.

The said William Weetman and Thomas ffortescue the aforesaid Exhibitants Do upon their Oaths declare that no part of the personal Estate of the said John King deceased hath since his Death come to their hands or possession nor have they or either of them any knowledge of any that belonged to the said deceased at his Death, that they have heard and believe that the said Deceased dyed in or about the Month of January in the year of our Lord One Thousand seven Hundred and twenty five, and that some time before the Death of the said John King his Goods were distreyned for Rent due to one Elizabeth Hinton late of Atherston aforesaid deceased, and that the the said deceased was indebted to her at his Death in the sume of Thirty Pounds or such like sume of money, And these Declarants also say that they have heard and believe that the personal Estate of the said deceased at the time of his Death was not sufficient to pay his the said Deceased's Debts and funeral Charges for which Reason they believe the said Elizabeth King his Widow who did not depart this Life before the Month of December in the year of our Lord One Thousand seven Hundred and Thirty One never took out Letters of Administration to her said Husband the said John King deceased.

February the 1st 1736

The above named Thomas ffortescue was then duly sworn to the truth of that Declaration before me.

J Stephenson Sur:

Tho: Fortescue

Feb: y 10th 1736

The above named William Weetman was then duly sworn to the truth of this Declaration before me

William Thomas Sur:

William Weetman

Fig 3.8 It was not always possible to make an inventory and a declaration will throw light on the reasons for this in particular cases.

In some circumstances it was not possible to produce an inventory, so a document called a declaration was produced. This took the form of a sworn statement giving the reasons for the lack of an inventory, which often gives much otherwise unobtainable information relating to the financial affairs of the deceased (Fig. 3.8).[19]

A Declaration instead of an Inventory of
the Goods and personal Estate of John King
late of Atherston in the County of Warwick
Labourer deceased made by William Weetman
and Thomas Fortescue Executors named in
the last Will and Testament of John Cheshire
deceased who was the sole Executor of the last
Will and Testament of Elizabeth King Widow
and Relict of the said John King deceased
and Administrators with the Will annexed of
the said Elizabeth King late of Atherston
aforesaid deceased, as follows.

The said William Weetman and Thomas Fortescue the aforesaid Exhibitants Do upon their Oaths declare that no part of the personal Estate of the said John King deceased hath since his Death come to their hands or possession nor have they or either of them any knowledge of any that belonged to the said deceased at his Death, that they have heard and believe that the said Deceased Dyed in or about the Month of January in the year of our Lord One Thousand seven Hundred and twenty five, And that some time before the Death of the said John King his Goods were destreyned for Rent due to Mrs. Elizabeth Hinton late of Atherstone aforesaid deceased, and that He the said Deceased was indebted to her at his Death in the sum of Thirty Pounds or such like sume of money, And these Declarants also say that they have heard and believe that the personal Estate of the said Deceased at the time of his Death was not sufficient to pay his the said Deceased's Debts and funeral Charges, for which Reason they believe the said Elizabeth King his Widow who did not depart this Life before the Month of December in the year of our Lord, One Thousand Seven Hundred and Thirty One never took out Letters of Administration to her said Husband the said John King deceased.

February the 1st 1736.
The above named Thomas Fortescue was then duly sworn to the truth of this Declaration before me
J. Stephenson Surrogate

Thomas Fortescue

Feb: ye 6th 1736
The above named William Weetman was then duly sworn to the truth of this Declaration before me
William Thomas Surrogate

William Weetman

Also to be found amongst the church court records are the probate accounts which were produced at the demand of a legatee, a relative or a creditor after 1685, when an Act of Parliament deemed this only to be necessary when estates were in dispute. These valuable documents appear when required by causes in the church courts and can give details of the debts of the deceased, which, in many cases considerably reduce the value of the estate. The affairs of the deceased had to be settled in strict order. After the payment of the funeral expenses, debts to the Crown, mortgages, rents, bonds, wages of servants, notes and trade books had to be settled. The remainder of the estate was then available for the disbursement of legacies. The accounts of the payments made by the executors or administrators can give a lot of information where the accountants were diligent; others merely gave total costs for various items and lists of debts, sometimes to named individuals, sometimes merely a global figure. It must be noted, however, that 'sumptuous and delicate expenses' were not be be permitted! The structure of these accounts is very distinctive, as can be seen from this example, relating to the estate of Thomas Hancock of Shrewsbury (Fig. 3.9).[20]

A True and Just Account of Sarah Hancock widow
Relict and Administratrix of Thomas Hancock late
of the town of Shrewsbury in the County of Salop Labourer,
deceased made as well of all her Receipts as of her
Payments and Disbursements out of the said deceased's
Personal Estate by Virtue of her being his
Administratrix And is as followeth, to wit

The Charge[21]

	£	s	d
This Accountant Charges herself with all & singular the Household Goods and other Personal Estate mentioned and Specifyed in an Inventory thereof made & hereunto annexed amounting in all to the sume of	35	13	6

The Discharge

Out of which this Accountant craves the Allowance of the Several & respective Sumes following being paid Disbursed & expended by her as Administratrix to the said deceased (to wit)

	£	s	d
Paid Mr. Williams a Baker for Bread which the Deceased had in his lifetime	00	07	11
Paid to the Milkwoman for Milk which the deceased had in his lifetime	00	05	3
Paid to John Bolton a Shoemaker his Bill for Shoes which was due from the deceased in his lifetime	00	12	6
Paid to Samuel Parker a Tayler his Bill which was due from the deceased in his lifetime	00	17	6
Paid to John Peate for half a yeares Rent due for the Deceased's house, at Michaelmas next after the deceased's death	01	10	0
Paid to Mr. Joseph Mackleston his Bill which was due from the deceased in his lifetime	01	08	0
Paid to Robert Wood his Bill which was due to the Deceased in his lifetime	02	02	0
Paid for the Letters of Administration and other Charges attending thereupon	01	13	0
Paid for Coales which the Deceased had in his lifetime	00	08	9
Paid to Mr. Binnell a Grocer as by his receipt for money & Goods which the Deceased had from him in his lifetime	06	03	11
Paid Thomas Davies for a Peice of Coarse Woollen Cloth which the Deceased had in his lifetime	00	05	0
Paid Anne Gould a Washwoman a Debt due from the Deceased to her for Washing	00	02	0
Paid to Mrs. Mackleston for Goods which she bought for the Deceased in his lifetime	00	13	6

	£	s	d
Paid to Anne Grant a Debt due to her from the Deceased for Shirts	00 :	15 :	0
Paid Edward Pritchard a Keeper for two Bucks Skinns which the Deceased had in his lifetime	01 :	05 :	0
Paid to Mr. Hinks an Attorney as by his Bill & Receipt for Charges in Recovering the Debt which was one from Richard Burley	02 :	18 :	00
Paid the said Mr. Hinks for his fee for attending this Exhibitants Proctor	00 :	03 :	4
Paid the Coroner & other Charges Attending upon takeing the Deceased out of the Water & laying him out	01 :	11 :	01
Paid for a Coffin	00 :	10 :	00
Paid for a Shroud	00 :	10 :	00
Paid for Bran to Putt in the Coffin	00 :	00 :	4
Paid the Parson and Clerk their fees	00 :	02 :	0
Paid for the Grave & tolling	00 :	05 :	6
Paid for the Bier	00 :	00 :	6
Paid for two Bottles of Wine for the funerall	00 :	03 :	4
Paid for Beer for the funerall	00 :	04 :	6
Paid for the Affidavit	00 :	00 :	4
This Accountant Craves the Allowance of the Sume of two pounds seventeen shillings & six pence paid by her for her Mourning Cloaths	02 :	17 :	6
Paid a Man & Horse for going to Enquire after the Deceased who was Missing for Several Dayes before he was found	00 :	05 :	0
Paid Edward Careton his Bill for the Gravestone	00 :	09 :	6
Paid for Cleaning & mending the Deceased's Watch which was in his Pockett when he was drowned	00 :	07 :	6
Paid the Postage of letters from the Plaintiff in this Suite and from her Agent Mr. Williams of Saint Asaph	00 :	00 :	6
This Accountant craves the Allowance of the Sume of three Pounds charged in the said Inventory by her Exhibited, as a Debt due from John Boulton, there being nothing to Shew for it & the same being Desperate & Irrecoverable	03 :	00 :	0
Charges expended in this Court in Passing the Account Proctors Retaining fee Proxy and Stamp	00 :	05 :	6
for Fileing & Drawing the Inventory & Accompt & Copy Stamps and Advice thereupon	01 :	00 :	0
for Informing on the Account	00 :	03 :	4
Paid the Adverse Proctor for his Consent to let this Exhibitant be sworn at Shrewsbury	00 :	05 :	0
Paid the Adverse Proctor for his Consent to stay till the Visitation	00 :	03 :	4
Bill and Taxation	00 :	05 :	10
fifteen Court days	00 :	15 :	0
Fees for four Terms	00 :	13 :	4
Acts of Court & letters	00 :	03 :	9
The Sum total of the Account	£35 :	13 :	01
Sum Total of the Inventory	£35 :	13 :	6
And so Deducting & allowing every thing that by Law ought to be Deducted & allowed there remains in the hands of this Accomptant the sum of	£00 :	00 :	5

The [mark] mark
of Sarah Hancock
24th June 1736,

The above named Sarah Hancock was sworn to the truth of this Accompt by us
R. Rider

Fig. 3.9 A probate account, showing the debts of the deceased. This example is most unusual in that it relates to an individual whose death required a coroner's inquest, the charges of which had to be paid out of the estate.

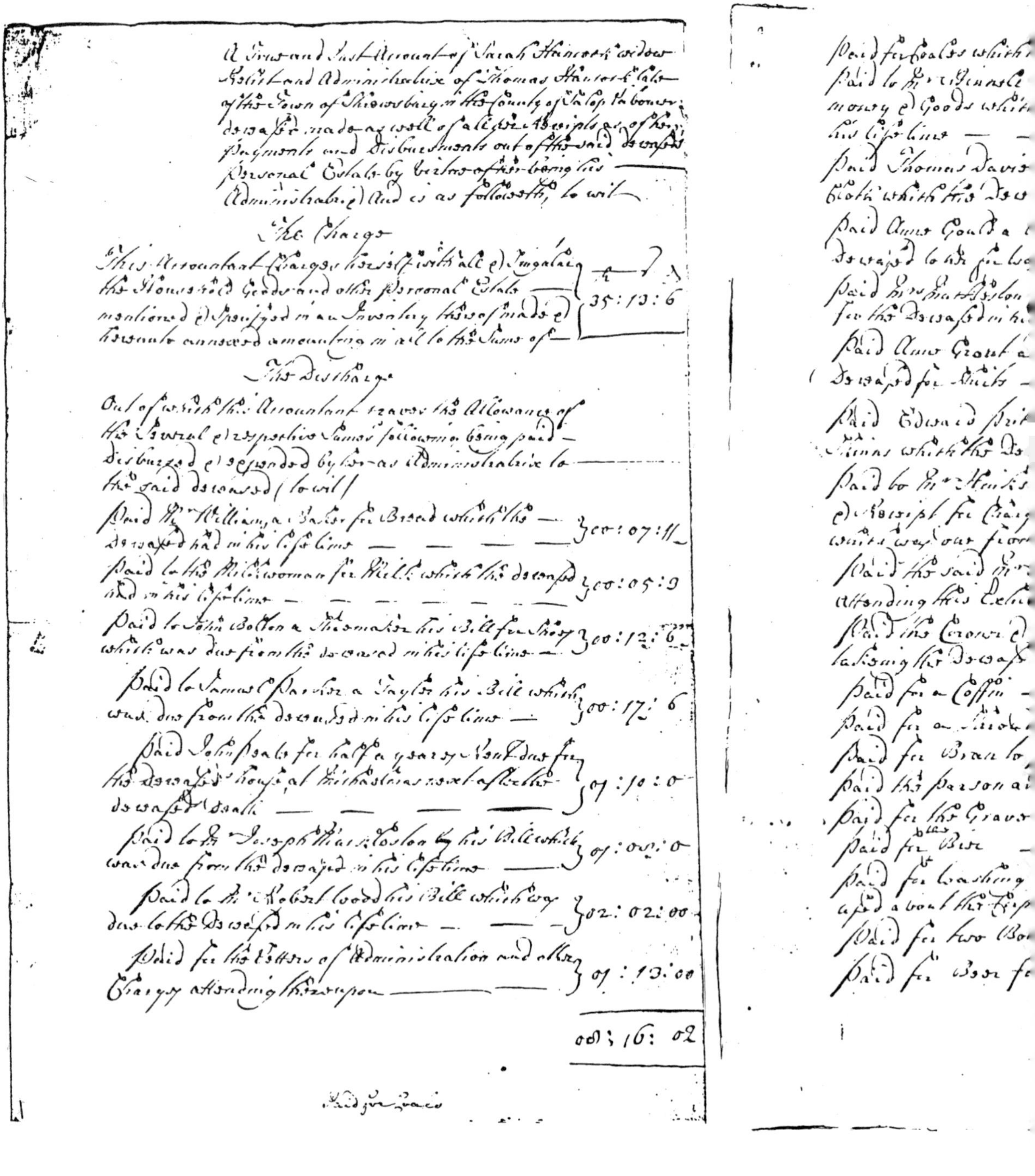

A True and Just Account of Sarah Hancock widow Relict and Administratrix of Thomas Hancock late of the Town of Shrewsbury in the County of Salop Labourer deceased made as well of all the Receipts as of her Payments and Disbursements out of the said deceased's Personal Estate by virtue of her being his Administratrix And is as followeth, to wit

The Charge

This Accountant Chargeth herself with all & singular the Household Goods and other Personal Estate mentioned & specified in an Inventory thereof made & hereunto annexed amounting in all to the Sume of	£ s d 35 : 13 : 6

The Discharge

Out of which this Accountant craves the Allowance of the several & respective Sumes following being paid disbursed & expended by her as Administratrix to the said deceased (to wit)

Paid Mr William a Baker for Bread which the deceased had in his life time	00 : 07 : 11
Paid to the Milkwoman for Milk which the deceased had in his life time	00 : 05 : 9
Paid to John Bolton a Shoemaker his Bill for Shoes which was due from the deceased in his life time	00 : 12 : 6
Paid to Samuel Parker a Taylor his Bill which was due from the deceased in his life time	00 : 17 : 6
Paid John Peale for half a years Rent due for the deceased's house at Michaelmas next after the deceased's death	01 : 10 : 0
Paid to Mr Joseph Marston by his Bill which was due from the deceased in his life time	01 : 00 : 0
Paid to Mr Robert Wood his Bill which was due to the deceased in his life time	02 : 02 : 00
Paid for the Letters of Administration and other Charges attending thereupon	01 : 13 : 00
	08 : 16 : 02

[illegible]

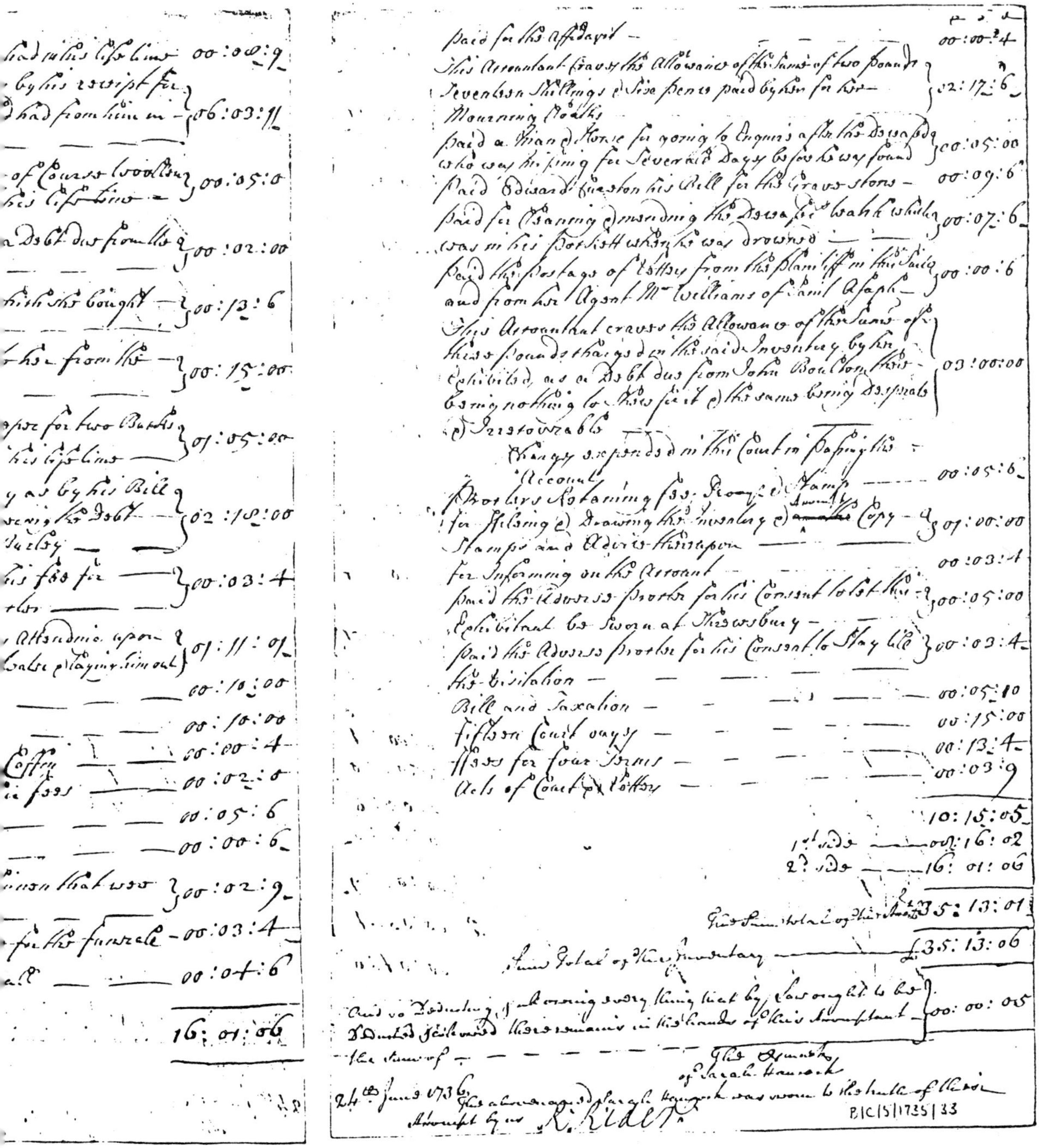

...had in his life time	00:00:9
...by his receipt for ...had from him in	06:03:11
...of Coarse Woollen ...his life time	00:05:0
...a Debt due from the	00:02:00
...which she bought	00:13:6
...the from the	00:15:00
...for two Boxes ...his life time	01:05:00
...as by his Bill ...the Debt ...Jurley	02:18:00
...his fee for	00:03:4
...Attendance upon ...& laying him out	01:11:01
	00:10:00
	00:10:00
...Coffin	00:00:4
...fees	00:02:0
	00:05:6
	00:00:6
...that were	00:02:9
...for the funerall	00:03:4
...all	00:04:6
	16:01:06

	£ s d
Paid for the Affidavit	00:00:4
This Accountant craves the Allowance of the Sume of two Pounds Seventeen Shillings & Sixe pence paid by him for his Mourning Cloaths	02:17:6
Paid a Man & Horse for going to Enquire after the Deceased who was missing for Severall Days before he was found	00:05:00
Paid Edward Preston his Bill for the Grave stone	00:09:6
Paid for Cleaning & mending the Deceased's Watch which was in his Pockett when he was drowned	00:07:6
Paid the Postage of Letters from the Plaintiff in this Cause and from his Agent Mr Williams of Saint Asaph	00:00:6
This Accountant craves the Allowance of the Sume of three Pounds charged in the said Inventory by him Exhibited, as a Debt due from John Boulton there being nothing to be had for it & the same being desperate & Irrecoverable	03:00:00
Charges expended in this Court in Passing this Account	
Proctors Retaining fee Receipt & Stamp	00:05:6
for Filing & Drawing the Inventory & Account & Copy Stamps and Advice thereupon	01:00:00
for Informing on the Account	00:03:4
Paid the Adverse Proctor for his Consent to let the Exhibitant be Sworn at Shrewsbury	00:05:00
Paid the Adverse Proctor for his Consent to Stay till the Visitation	00:03:4
Bill and Taxation	00:05:10
Fifteen Court days	00:15:00
Fees for four Terms	00:13:4
Acts of Court & Letters	00:03:9
	10:15:05
1st side	08:16:02
2d side	16:01:06
The Sum total of the Discharge	£35:13:01
Sum total of the Inventory	£35:13:06
And so Deducting & allowing every thing that by Law ought to be Deducted & allowed there remains in the hands of this Accountant the sume of	00:00:05

The Accompt of Sarah Hancock

24th June 1736 The above named Sarah Hancock was sworn to the truth of this Accompt before me [illegible]

B/C/5/1735/33

It would appear that the coroner had decided that Thomas had been the victim of an accident rather than suicide, and he was buried in the churchyard with due ceremony, with a gravestone set up afterwards. His debts were all for household and personal goods, with only one possible loan of money from the grocer. His financial resources were not great and yet two people owed him money, possibly for work done for them in his capacity as a labourer, there being no security given in the form of Bonds or Notes. Information relating to the financial affairs of individuals of this social class is rare indeed.

Within the court records at Lichfield these documents have been found in a wide variety of formats; the earlier material consisted of single, large, vertical sheets, anything up to fifteen in number, bound together at the top centre with twisted parchment. The most common form was a single small sheet of paper, sometimes folded but again in a vertical form, and later versions produced by the court clerks were also in a vertical format but very much larger. On very rare occasions bundles of receipts, known as vouchers, survive with the accounts and these can give considerable detail of goods purchased and their costs, often with the names of the traders as well as the dates of the transactions.

However, many of the wills questioned in the Lichfield court related to those, both male and female, who had died unmarried, which left them with few relatives to manage their affairs. Throughout the 18th century an increasing number of principal creditors applied for probate of the estates of those who owed them larger sums of money, and their names, and sometimes occupations, are often given on citations in the testamentary business of the consistory courts. Their demands could also be one reason for the production of probate accounts. By the 19th century advertisements would be placed in newspapers seeking the next of kin, and occasionally these papers survive amongst the court records, replacing the earlier citations with intimation read out in church. The following citation relates to the estate of Alice Wagstaff of Madeley, Staffs. (Fig. 3.10).[22]

Henry Raynes Doctor of Laws Vicar General and Official Principal of the right Reverend Father in God Richard by Divine permission Lord Bishop of Lichfield and Coventry To all persons to whom these presents shall come Greeting We do hereby require and command ye joyntly and severally personally to Cite or cause to be cited Thomas Wagstaff Nephew and next of Kindred of Alice Catherine Wagstaff late of the parish of Madeley in the County of Stafford and Diocese of Lichfield and Coventry Widow Deceased to Appear personally before Us our Surrogate or other Competent Judge in this behalf in the Cathedral Church of Lichfield and place of Judicature there on Tuesday the Seventh day of May next ensuing the date hereof at the hours accustom'd for the hearing of causes there then and there to bring in an Exhibit the true Original last Will and Testament of the said Alice Catherine Wagstaff Deceased if she made any And to accept or renounce the execution of the same Or if she died intestate to Accept or renounce Letters of Administration of the Goods Chattels and personal Estate of the said Alice Catherine Wagstaff Deceased And also to bring in and Exhibit a true full plain and particular Inventory of all and Singular the Goods Chattles and personal Estate of the said Deceased which since her Death have come to your hands possession or knowledge by Vertue of Your Corporal Oath Or to shew cause if any you have why Letters of Administration of the Goods and personal Estate of the said deceased with her said last Will and Testament thereto Annexed if she made any or otherwise Simply should not be committed and granted to Charles Sidway principal Creditor of the said Deceased At the promotion of the said Charles Sidway And farther to do and receive as to law and Justice shall Apertain. Intimating further unto you the said Thomas Wagstaff that if you appear not at the time and place aforesaid or appearing shew no good and sufficient Cause to the Contrary The Judge aforesaid or his Lawfull Surrogate doth intend and will proceed to grant Letters of Administration of the Goods and personal estate of the said Alice Catherine Wagstaff Deceas'd with her last Will and Testament Thereto Annexed if she made any or otherwise simply as aforesaid to the said Charles Sidway principal Creditor of the said Deceased as aforesaid And to do all other things necessary and Needfull relating to the Same, Your absence or rather Contumacy (being so Cited as aforesaid) in any wise notwithstanding And what Ye or any of You shall herein lawfully do in or about the premisses or cause to be done herein We do hereby require You to certifye the Same to us or our Surrogate aforesaid together with these presents Dated at Lichfield this Twenty Ninth day of April in the Year of our Lord One Thousand Seven hundred and Thirty four

W Buckeridge Deputy to,
Gilbert Walmisley Esquire Registrar

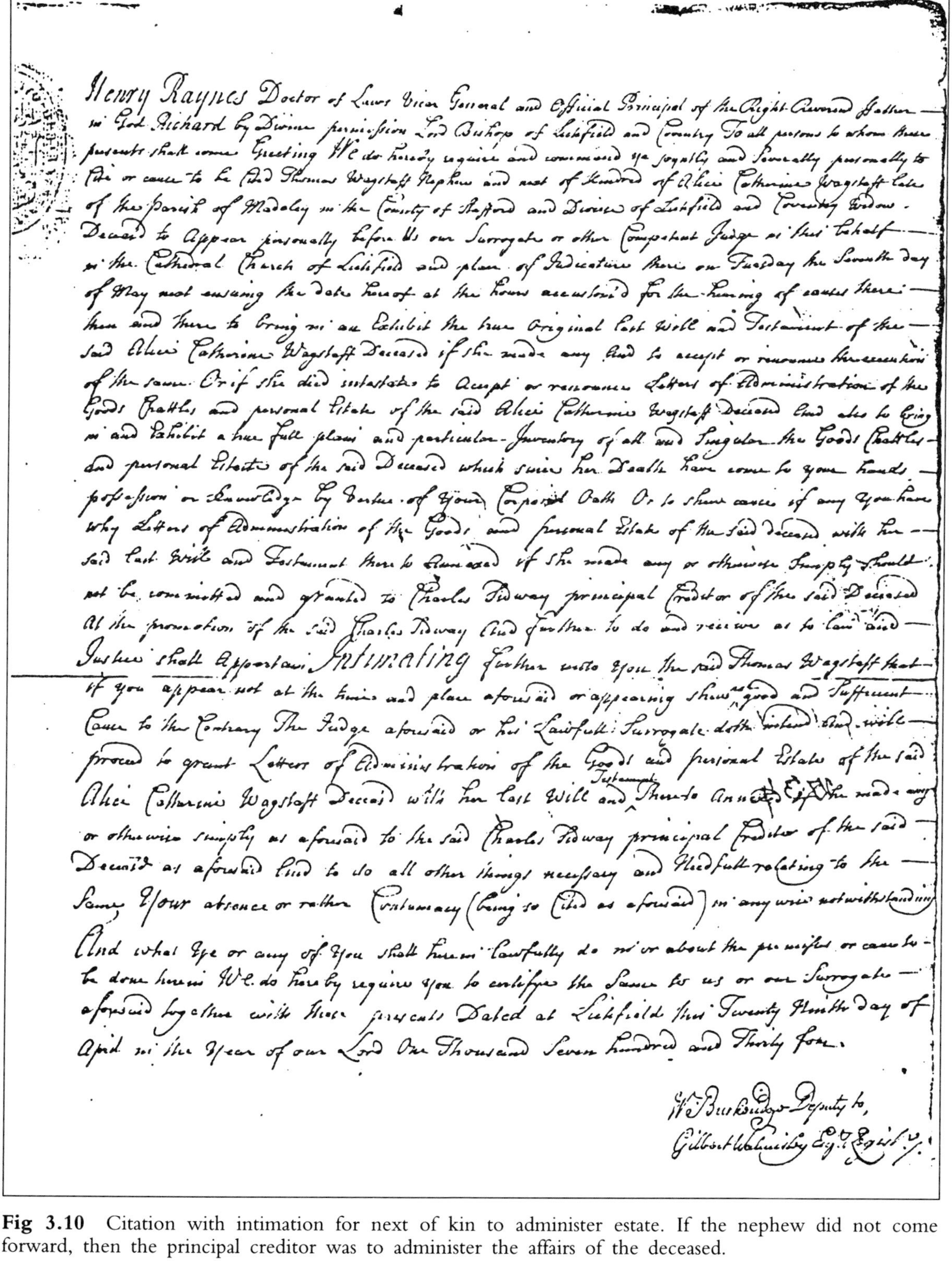

Henry Raynes Doctor of Laws Vicar General and Official Principal of the Right Reverend Father in God Richard by Divine permission Lord Bishop of Litchfield and Coventry To all persons to whom these presents shall come Greeting We do hereby require and command ye jointly and severally personally to Cite or cause to be Cited Thomas Wagstaff Nephew and next of Kindred of Alice Catherine Wagstaff late of the parish of Madeley in the County of Stafford and Diocese of Litchfield and Coventry Widow Deceased to appear personally before Us our Surrogate or other Competent Judge in this behalf in the Cathedral Church of Litchfield and place of Judicature there on Tuesday the Seventh day of May next ensuing the date hereof at the hours accustomed for the hearing of causes there then and there to bring in an Exhibit the true Original Last Will and Testament of the said Alice Catherine Wagstaff Deceased if she made any And to accept or renounce the execution of the same Or if she died intestate to Accept or renounce Letters of Administration of the Goods Chattels and personal Estate of the said Alice Catherine Wagstaff Deceased And also to bring in and Exhibit a true full plain and particular Inventory of all and Singular the Goods Chattles and personal Estate of the said Deceased which since her Death have come to your hands possession or knowledge by Virtue of your Corporal Oath Or to shew cause if any you have why Letters of Administration of the Goods and personal Estate of the said deceased with the said Last Will and Testament thereto Annexed if she made any or otherwise Simply should not be committed and granted to Charles Sidway principal Creditor of the said Deceased At the promotion of the said Charles Sidway And further to do and receive as to Law and Justice shall Appertain Intimating further unto you the said Thomas Wagstaff that if you appear not at the time and place aforesaid or appearing shew not good and Sufficient Cause to the Contrary The Judge aforesaid or his Lawfull Surrogate doth intend and will proceed to grant Letters of Administration of the Goods and personal Estate of the said Alice Catherine Wagstaff Deceased with her Last Will and Testament thereto Annexed if she made any or otherwise simply as aforesaid to the said Charles Sidway principal Creditor of the said Deceased as aforesaid And to do all other things necessary and Needfull relating to the Same Your absence or rather Contumacy (being so Cited as aforesaid) in any wise notwithstanding And what ye or any of You shall herein Lawfully do in or about the premises or cause to be done herein We do hereby require you to certifye the Same to us or our Surrogate aforesaid together with these presents Dated at Litchfield this Twenty Ninth day of April in the Year of our Lord One Thousand Seven hundred and Thirty four.

W. Buckeridge Deputy to,
Gilbert Walmisley Esq. Regist.

Fig 3.10 Citation with intimation for next of kin to administer estate. If the nephew did not come forward, then the principal creditor was to administer the affairs of the deceased.

Testamentary disputes could also arise over unpaid tithes sought by clergy or farmers of tithe who were entitled to sue the estates of the deceased for their unpaid ecclesiastical dues, both in the form of tithes and Easter offerings. Dorothy Howe of Uttoxeter, widow of the farmer of tithes, spent the last years of her life claiming tithes due to her late husband's estate and her executrix also pursued those who owed tithes to Elizabeth.

The election of guardians of orphaned minors takes the form of acts of court and most of these acts are in draft form headed 'Acts had, sped and done' in the 18th century. These elections and assignments often give the status of the proposed guardian, and sometimes a relationship with the minors involved, and their relationship to their parents. These papers sometimes refer to tutors or curators. A tutor was the legal description of a guardian of a minor under the age of 15 in the case of a boy, or 13 for a girl. For boys between the ages of 14 and 21 and girls between 12 and 21 a legal guardian was known as a curator. Legacies left to young children were potentially vulnerable and could, as in some causes, be swallowed up in maintenance charged by relatives for their upbringing. Many causes relating to the subtraction of legacies were brought by minors who had to appoint guardians either for the entire period of their minority or simply to reclaim the legacy due to them. The latter produced a document called a proxy, whereby a relative was deputed to act on the child's behalf in the court proceedings. Longer term arrangements demanded guardians to retain the legacy until the child came of an age to receive it, and were responsible for the production of a pair of documents relating to the election of a guardian and their acceptance. The necessary act of court for the election process often took place out of court hours in the house of one of the proctors in the Cathedral Close at Lichfield. The documents usually occur in pairs, one for the election of the guardian and the other for their acceptance. The following paper was required for the daughter to appoint her uncle to act as administrator of her mother's estate (Fig. 3.11).[23]

Know all men by these presents, that I Ellen Applebey natural and lawful Daughter of Mary Applebey, late of the parish of Alstonfield, in the County of Stafford Widow deceased, being in my Minority, to wit, having attained the age of Seven Years and upwards, but having not yet attained the Age of twenty one years, and being therefore incapable of doing any serious Act in my own Name, or of taking out Letters of Administration of the Goods Chattles and personal Estate of the said Mary Applebey my said late Mother deceased have nominated constituted and appointed and by these presents do nominate and constitute and appoint William Applebey, my Honoured Uncle, to be my Guardian and Curator to all Intents and purposes in the Law whatsoever, but more particularly to take out Letters of Administration of the Goods Chattles Credits and personal Estate of the said Mary Applebey my late Mother deceased, for my Use and behoof, and during my Minority, And to the end this my Election & Choice may the better take effect, I do hereby nominate constitute and appoint George Hand the Elder, and George Hand the Younger, Gentlemen proctors of the Lord Bishops Consistory Court of Lichfield joyntly and severally my true and lawful proctors for me, and in my Name place and stead to appear before the Worshipfull Richard Rider Esquire Batchelor of Laws and Chancellor of the Diocese of Lichfield & Coventry his Surrogate, or other competent Judge in this behalf to pray and procure this my Election & Choice to be admitted and enacted, And what my said proctors shall herein lawfully do or cause severally to be done, I do hereby promise to ratifie and confirm As Witness my hand & Seal this Twenty fifth day of August in the year of our Lord 1735.

Signed & Sealed by the said Ellen Applebey
being first duly stamped in the presence of
John Etches senior
Robert Whiston Junior

Ellen Appleby
Her Mark

[Seal]

Fig. 3.11 A curator had to be appointed by a minor to administer her mother's estate, a duty carried out by the church courts. This can give details of family relationships.

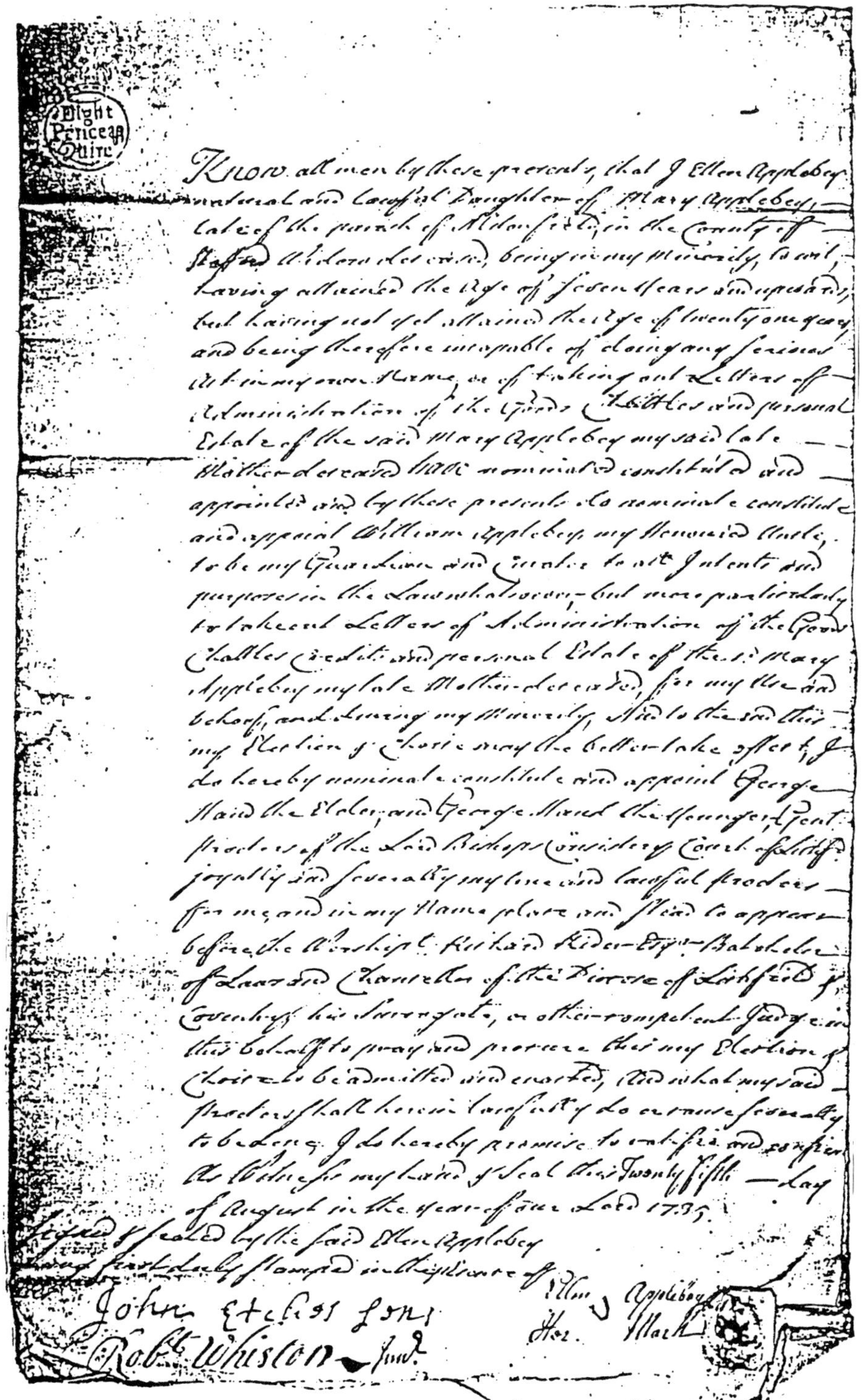

Know all men by these presents, that I Ellen Applebey natural and lawful Daughter of Mary Applebey, late of the parish of [illegible], in the County of Stafford Widow deceased, being in my Minority, to wit, having attained the Age of Seven Years and upwards, but having not yet attained the Age of twenty one years and being therefore incapable of doing any serious Act in my own Name, or of taking out Letters of Administration of the Goods Chattles and personal Estate of the said Mary Applebey my said late Mother deceased have nominated constituted and appointed and by these presents do nominate constitute and appoint William Applebey my [illegible] Uncle, to be my Guardian and Curator to all Intents and purposes in the Law whatsoever but more particularly to take out Letters of Administration of the Goods Chattles Credits and personal Estate of the s.d Mary Applebey my late Mother deceased, for my Use and behoof, and during my Minority, And to the end this my Election & Choice may the better take effect, I do hereby nominate constitute and appoint George Hand the Elder and George Hand the Younger, Gent. Proctors of the Lord Bishops Consistory Court of Litchf. jointly and severally my true and lawful Proctors for me and in my Name place and Stead to appear before the Worship.l Richard Rider Esq.r Batchelor of Laws and Chancellor of the Diocese of Litchfield & Coventry, his Surrogate, or other competent Judge in this behalf to pray and procure this my Election & Choice to be admitted and enacted, And what my said Proctors shall herein lawfully do or cause lawfully to be done, I do hereby promise to ratifie and confirm. As Witness my hand & Seal this Twenty fifth day of August in the year of our Lord 1735.

Signed & sealed by the said Ellen Applebey being first duly stamped in the presence of

John Etchells Jun.

Robt. Whiston Jund.

Ellen Applebey Her Mark

A more unusual form of guardianship would arise where there were reasonable grounds for protecting the interests of the children, as in the following case (Fig. 3.12):[24]

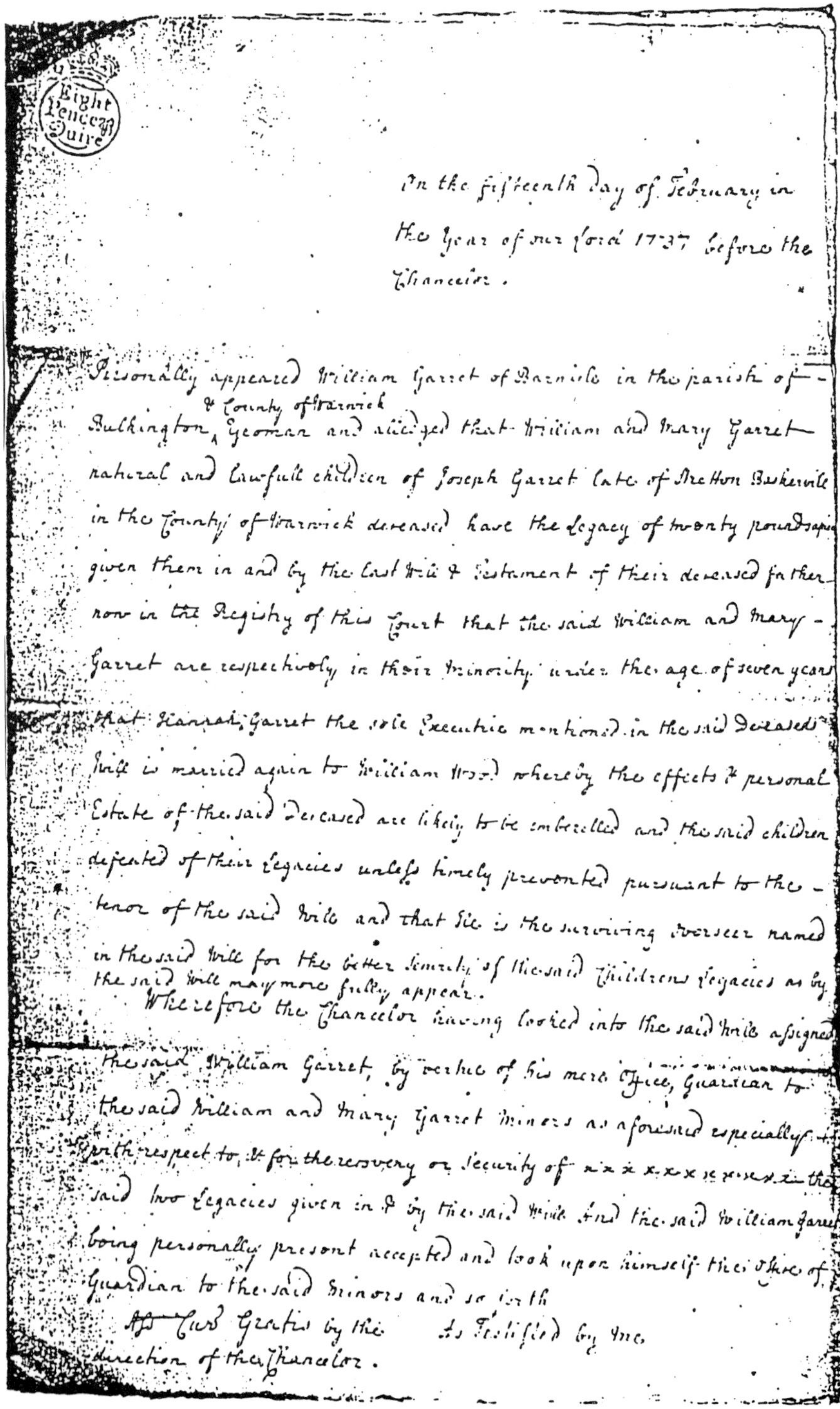
Eight Pence ... Quire

On the fifteenth day of February in the Year of our Lord 1737 before the Chancelor.

Personally appeared William Garret of Barnicle in the parish of Bulkington & County of Warwick Yeoman and alledged that William and Mary Garret natural and lawfull children of Joseph Garret late of Stretton Baskervile in the County of Warwick deceased have the Legacy of twenty pounds apiece given them in and by the last Will & Testament of their deceased father now in the Registry of this Court that the said William and Mary Garret are respectively in their Minority under the age of seven years that Hannah Garret the sole Executrix mentioned in the said Deceased's Will is married again to William Wood whereby the effects & personal Estate of the said Deceased are likely to be embezelled and the said children defeated of their Legacies unless timely prevented pursuant to the tenor of the said Will and that He is the surviving overseer named in the said Will for the better Security of the said Childrens Legacies as by the said Will may more fully appear.

Wherefore the Chancelor having looked into the said Will assigned the said William Garret, by vertue of his mere Office, Guardian to the said William and Mary Garret Minors as aforesaid especially with respect to, & for the recovery or Security of ... the said two Legacies given in & by the said Will. And the said William Garret being personally present accepted and took upon himself the Office of Guardian to the said Minors and so forth

~~Afd~~ Curd Gratis by the direction of the Chancelor.

As Testified by me.

On the fifteenth day of February in
the year of our Lord 1737 before the
Chancelor

Personally appeared William Garret of Barnicle in the parish
of Bulkington & County of Warwick Yeoman and alledged that William and Mary Garret
natural and lawful children of Joseph Garret late of Stretton Basketvill
in the County of Warwick deceased have the Legacy of twenty pounds
apiece given them in and by the last Will & Testament of their deceased father
now in the Registry of this Court that the said William and Mary
Garret are respectively in their Minority under the age of seven years
that Hannah Garret the sole Executrix mentioned in the said Deceaseds
Will is married again to William Wood whereby the effects & personal
Estate of the said Deceased are likely to be embezelled and the said children
defeated of the Legacies unless timely prevented pursuant to the
tenor of the said Will and that He is the surviving Overseer named
in the said Will for the better Security of the said Childrens Legacies as by
the said Will may more fully appear.
Wherefore the Chancelor having looked into the said Will assigned
the said William Garret, by vertue of his mere Office, Guardian to
the said William and Mary Garret Minors as aforesaid especially
and with respect to & for the recovery or security of the
said two Legacies given in & by the said Will And the said William Garret
being personally present accepted and took upon himself the Office of
Guardian to the said Minors and so forth.

Assignatio Curatio Gratis [Assigned Curator free] by the direction of the Chancelor — As Testified by Me

Fig. 3.12 Guardianship of two children granted to the overseer of their father's will, to ensure the security of their legacies following their mother's re-marriage

Occasionally a caveat, written on a small scrap of paper, would be entered into the consistory court requesting notice to be given to individuals with an interest in the estate, who may have been intending to dispute the will of a relative or one who owed them money.[25] The power of a caveat in the spiritual courts was such that, if it was not taken into consideration, a grant of probate could be overturned (Fig. 3.13).

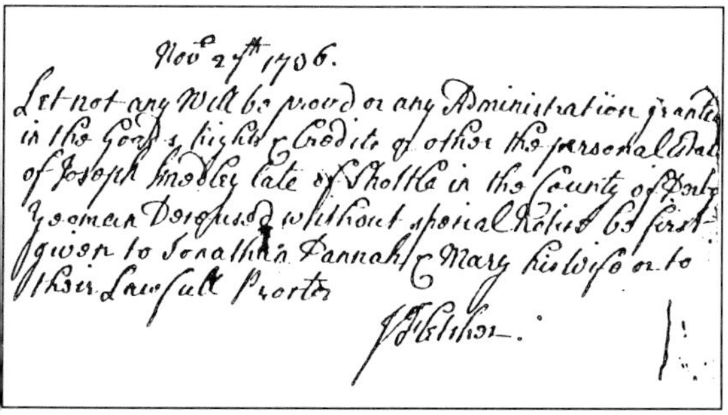

November 27th 1736
Let not any Will be proved or any Administration granted
in the Goods Rights & Credits or other the personal Estate
of Joseph Medley late of Shottle in the County of Derby
Yeoman Deceased without special Notice be first
given to Jonathan Dannah & Mary his Wife or to
their Lawfull Proctor

J Fletcher

Fig. 3.13 Caveat entered into the court at Lichfield, requesting notice of legal action to be taken.

One of the rarest forms of business in the Lichfield courts was that of the revocation of probate, where permission to undertake the administration of an estate was overturned due to the fact that the original permission had been given incorrectly. The care taken in all causes to determine the parish in which those involved resided, to ensure that they were within the jurisdiction of the courts, was also applied to the granting of probate to avoid this situation.

Chapter Four

Marriage

The church courts held the monopoly of marriage litigation until the passing of the Matrimonial Causes Act of 1857. The archdeacon's court was the court of first instance and would probably have been used for this type of business until the civil war. By the late 17th century these causes would probably have been heard in the bishop's courts in most dioceses, and appeals would have been taken to the higher church courts of the provinces. The secular courts would have been used by those seeking financial recompense for breach of promise, although alimony was awarded through the church courts, and claims for the non-payments of dowries were also settled there. Bigamy was considered to be a felony, a secular offence, following the Bigamy Act of 1604, but marriages contracted by the parties following a legal separation could be investigated by the church courts on the grounds that they might have been bigamous.

Matrimonial causes are of increasing interest to social historians, particularly because witnesses often recite the minutiae of household life and inter-personal relations, information not available from any other source. The numbers of matrimonial causes heard in the church courts was very small indeed, but they are of great importance to any family historian fortunate enough to find one relevant to their family.

Most causes coming before the courts concerned the following subjects:

a) making and fulfilling of marriage contracts
b) divorce - separation from bed and board
 - nullity
c) restitution of conjugal rights
d) jactitation, or boasting of marriage

These relate either to the making of the marriage contract and its completion to the satisfaction of all parties, or to attempts to break it if the marriage did not succeed. However, divorce was seen as a suspension of matrimony for an unlimited period of time in the hope of a reconciliation, rather than as the complete dissolution of the contract in the sense that we use it today.

The problems that dominated the courts varied from one diocese to another. Studies in the diocesan courts of Ely and Salisbury[1] have shown that the formation of marriage dominated court business until the mid-17th century, after which time separation came to the fore. In the archdeaconry courts of Nottingham, matrimonial causes relating to marriage formation peaked in the late 16th century.[2] Lichfield saw a continuous trickle of separation causes, which rose in volume through the 18th century. Clandestine marriages were pursued by the office of this diocese up to Hardwicke's Marriage Act of 1754 (discussed in Chapter Two).

Contracts

Problems with contracts provided the courts with the bulk of their business until 1754. This type of agreement originated in the 12th century when a legally binding and indissoluble contract, known as a spousal,[3] could be made simply by the exchange of vows in the present tense, *per verba de praesenti*, by the consenting parties, generally, but not necessarily, in front of witnesses. This pledge could be made anywhere and at any time and a church service as such was not deemed necessary. The only legal requirement was the consent of the parties, and the only reason for its invalidity would be an impediment in the form of a partner from a previous marriage, or because the proposed marriage fell within the prohibited degrees. The tense used in these vows was of critical importance. By using the future tense, *de futuro*, an agreement was made for the couple to marry at a future date, with or without conditions attached. This could become a legally binding marriage at any later date by 'consummation with bodily knowledge' as Burn[4] delicately puts it. Prior to any sexual confirmation, this future contract was tenuous in that it could be invalidated by *de praesenti* vows exchanged with another party, that is to say a contract in the present tense. It could also cease to be binding if both parties agreed to this, or if one of the parties disappeared for any length of time, or if either was unfaithful with a third party. A contract *per verba de futuro* where the conditions had been fulfilled to the letter could be overruled by one made at a later date with or without any conditions specified. Under these circumstances it is not surprising that there was some confusion as to what constituted a valid marriage. Customs such as handfasting and the exchange of gifts continued to be seen as legitimate contracts, in spite of their great potential for misunderstanding on both sides. The complexity of this subject is reflected in the production of a book on spousals in 1686 by Henry Swinburne, a lawyer from the York courts, which ran into many editions and became the standard work on the subject.[5]

Obviously any verbal and unwitnessed contract between two people could lead to legal problems, and by the end of the medieval period the Church was anxious to ensure that such contracts should be made in public. It was also important to establish that there were no obstacles to the contract in the form of extant spouses, or unrevealed relationships by affinity or consanguinity. Certain procedures were laid down before the Reformation to ensure that marriage contracts were enacted correctly. Contracts were to be made in the *de futuro* form, followed by the reading of banns on three consecutive Sundays in the parish churches of both parties, to make their intentions as public as possible and to give ample opportunity to identify any possible impediments. Finally the contract was to be publicly solemnised in the local church, the couple giving their verbal consent and exchanging their vows in the present tense at the church door. The old custom of an exchange of gifts continued with the exchange of rings, as did the requirement for witnesses. However, this procedure was not compulsory until Hardwicke's Marriage Act of 1754 required the publication of banns.

Throughout the medieval period children could be espoused, using the *de futuro* form of contract, at the insistence of their parents. This could take place from the age of seven when infancy was deemed to have ended, until the marriageable ages of 14 for the boy and 12 for the girl. Marriage could then be legally contracted if both parties agreed. One example from Lichfield, dating from 1598, relates to the espousal of Thomas Waterhouse to Sibille Bancrofte. Thomas in his personal answers described their espousal and the resulting problems. In response to the second article of the libel, Thomas said (Fig. 4.1):[6]

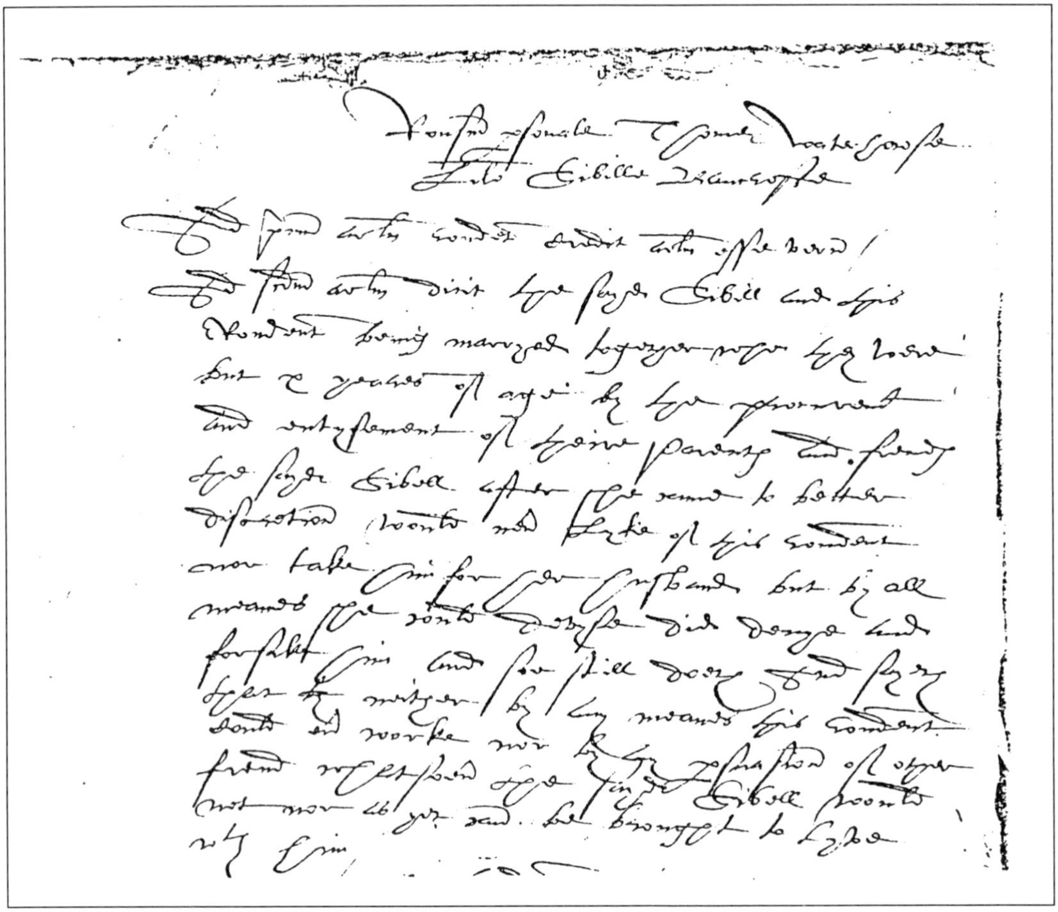

the sayd Sibill and this
Respondent being marryed together when they were
but x [ten] yeares of age by the procurement
and entysement of their parents and frends
the sayd Sibell after she came to better
discretion would never Lyke of this respondent
nor take him for her husband but by all
meanes she could devyse did denye and
forsake him and soe still doeth and sayeth
that neither by any means this respondent
could ever worke nor by any persuasion of other
frend whatsoever the sayd Sibell would
not nor as yet can be brought to lyve
with him ...

... in soe much that he sayeth he many tymes hath byn greatlye afrayd she would have done some mischiefe to herselfe to be ridde of this respondent.

Fig. 4.1 Child espousal cause from the late 16th century at Lichfield, whereby an earlier contract was not fulfilled.

The use of the phrase 'marryed together' in this context presumably refers to a contract because Sibill did not 'take him' for her husband 'after she came to better descretion'. This contract was invalidated by Sibill's failure to give her permission to the marriage.

A few spousals causes have been recorded from the Essex courts by Emmison,[7] as well as a number in the Chester courts.[8] However, they appear comparatively rare at Lichfield, though this may be due to the destruction of many court records during the Civil War.

Although a marriage contract could be made at any time and in any place, there were medieval constraints on the solemnisation of marriage at certain times of the day and at certain times of the year. The three forbidden seasons of marriage were:

a) From Advent Sunday until Twelfth-Tide, or St Hilary's Day
(Sunday nearest 30th November until 13th January)
b) Septuagesima Sunday until Low Sunday
(Third Sunday before Lent until the first Sunday after Easter)
c) Rogation to Trinity Sunday
(Rogation Sunday until Sunday following Whit Sunday)

Until 1886, marriages had to be legally solemnised between 8.00 a.m. and 12 in the forenoon, the marriage service then being followed by communion. These medieval requirements remained in force, despite attempts in 1575 to remove them, and they were included in the canons of 1604, although the wording of the canons is considered to be ambiguous as to whether the time of day or season was to be observed. Grey mentions that these constraints were 'still observed by some' in 1730.[9] A clandestine marriage was one that took place outside these periods, and after the Restoration many couples and the clerics who had conducted the marriage ceremonies were summoned to answer to office causes at Lichfield. (See Chapter Two, page 36.) Attempts were probably being made to clear up the confusion about what constituted a legal marriage, following the Commonwealth period when marriages could be contracted before the justices of the peace, obviously outside the church, and at any hour.

The position was further complicated by the fact that clandestine marriages were perfectly valid in law, a contract having been exchanged in front of witnesses and intercourse having followed. The following citation was issued by Richard Rider as vicar general in his role of correction, requiring several people to prove the validity of their marriages.[10] There had obviously been a 'common fame' in each case, and to quell local gossip it was necessary to ensure that a legal marriage had taken place (Fig. 4.2).

Richard Rider Esquire Batchelor of Lawes Vicar general of the Reverend Father in God Richard by divine permission Lord Bishop of Lichfield and Coventry and Official principal of the said Lord Bishop's Consistory Court at Lichfield aforesaid sendeth greeting To all Clerks and literate persons within our said Diocese of Lichfield and Coventry These are to will and command you or some or one of you personally to cite John Fox and Hannah his pretended wife Thomas Furnis and Mary his pretended wife, Ralph Frost and Mary his pretended wife, Myles Wilkin and Ellen his pretended wife Thomas Ibbotson and Sarah his pretended wife and Abraham Cowper of the parish of Hathersage in the County of Derby and Thomas Wilcoxson of the parish of Dronfield in the said County of Derby, to appear in the Cathedral Church of Lichfield and place of Judicature there, on tewsday the Thirtyeth day of March instant between the houres of nine and twelve in the forenoon of the same day, then and there to prove your respective marriages, to answer to Articles for your liveing and cohabiting together; in scandalous and clandestine manner, which will be then and there objected against you and each and every of you, and further to doe and receive as to Law and Justice shall appertaine And what you doe in the premisses you are to certifie Us our Surrogate or some other competent Judge in this behalfe, together with these presents Given under the seale of our Office this eight day of March 1735 (english Style)

W. Buckeridge Deputy Registrar

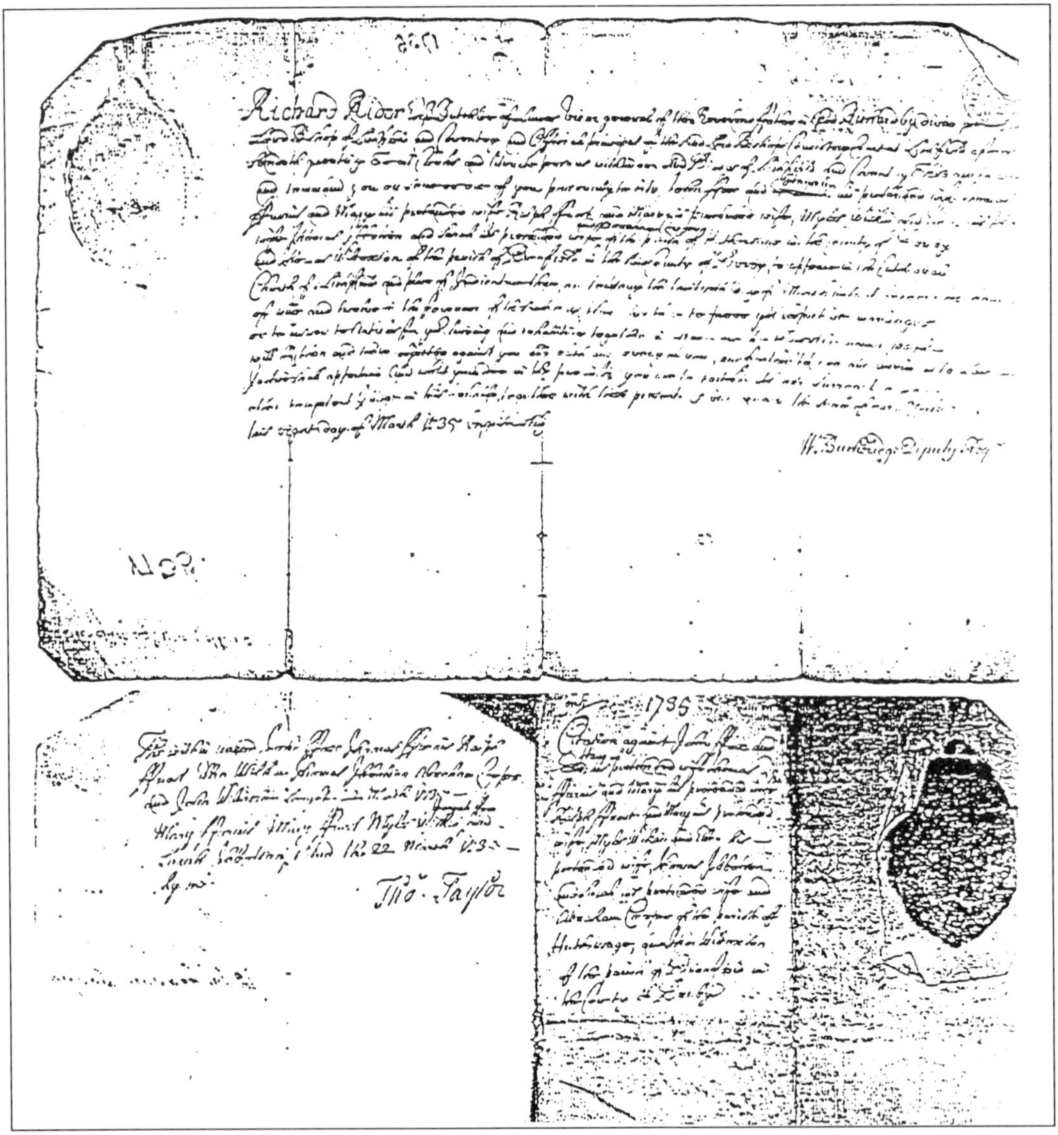

Fig. 4.2 Citation form to prove marriages, showing endorsement of folded document. Thomas Taylor was the apparitor here.

The couples in question may have been presented by the churchwardens following complaints from within the community that their marriages had not been publicly solemnised. This type of cause can occasionally leave exhibits amongst the papers, including extracts from parish registers, signed by the incumbent or curate, confirming a marriage.

The old ways were not easily forgotten and it was still considered perfectly acceptable, well into the 17th century, to marry by a legal contract, so long as there were witnesses present. The example below, from articles of libel introduced in 1624 at Lichfield, gives an interesting account of the events leading up to the making of a contract by repeating the marriage vows in the present tense whilst holding hands, in front of a number of friends (Fig. 4.3):[11]

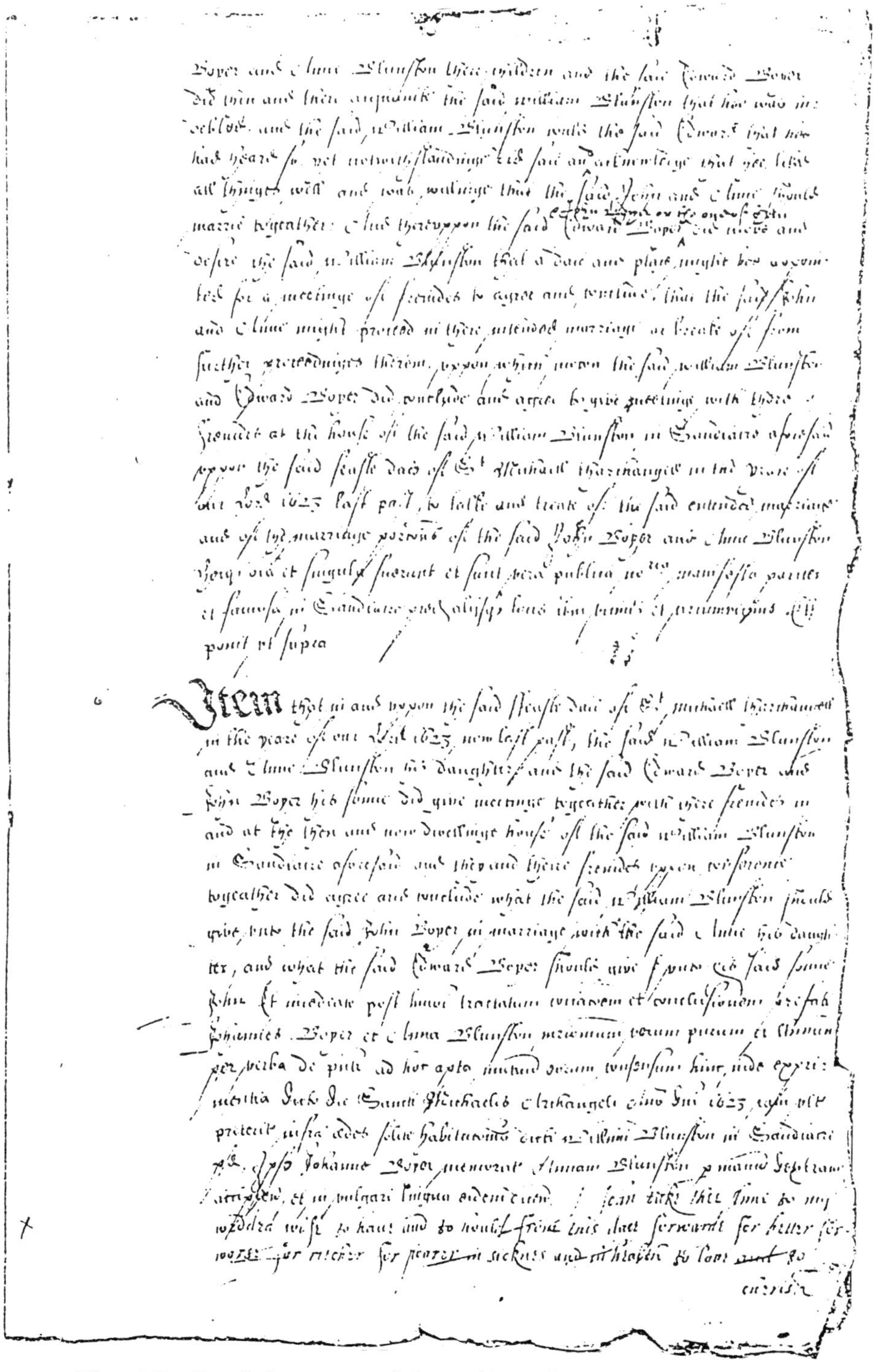

Fig. 4.3 Detailed account of the making of a marriage in 1623.

2. Item that about the feaste of St. James the Apostle in the yeare of our Lord 1623 last past Robert Maunsfeild of Lockington in the Countie of Lecester being a workeman for the said William Blunston father of the said Anne Blunston, and beinge of acquaintance with the said John Boyer, and Edward Boyer father of the said John, did make a motion unto the said William Blunston and Anne Blunston, for and conserninge a marriage to bee made betwixt the said John Boyer and Anne Blunston And the said William Blunston and Anne Blunston or the one of them did like of the said motion, and said, the said John should for that purpose bee welcome unto them, or used words to the like effect. *Et ponit ut supra* [And deposes as above].

3. Item that after the said motion, and uppon a Satterdaie which was a market daie in Nottingham about the said feaste daie of St. James in Apostle, the said William Blunston and Anne Blunston his daughter, and the said John Boyer did meete togeather in Nottingham aforesaid and had conference togeather touching the said marriage to bee had betwixt the said John Boyer and Anne Blunston and then and there, theie shewed and acknowledged one to another a good likeing of the said motion of marriage, and the said William Blunston and Anne Blunston or the one of them wished the said John Boyer to come unto the said William Blunston at his house in Sandiacre aforesaid, and tould him hee should bee welcome, or used words to the like effect, and thereupon they parted in greate kindness, and likeinge one of another. *Et ponit et supra* [And deposes as above]

4. Item that after the said meetinge at Nottingham, and betweene the said feaste daie of St. James the Apostle in the yeare of our Lord 1623 and the next daie before the feaste of St. Michaell tharchangell[12] then next following the said John Boyer did verie often viz 1.2.3.4.5.6 or 7 severall tymes repaire and go unto the house of the said William Blunston in Sandiacre aforesaid as a suytor unto the said Anne Blunston in waie of marriage and was verie kindlie and lovinglie enterteyned of the said William and Anne, and the said Anne did at all tymes lovinglie and kindlie behave and carried herselfe towardes the said John Boyer and did shew herselfe verie contented and willinge to have the said John Boyer to bee her husband and to bee marryed unto him and bee his wife *Haecquaeque omnia et singula fuerunt et sunt vera publica notorita manifesta pariter et famosa in Sandiacre predicto aliisque locis ibidem vicinis et circum vicinis Et ponit et supra* [All of these things were and are true public and notorious and equally manifest and famous in Sandiacre aforesaid and other places near there and in surrounding places And deposes as above]

5. Item that uppon the premisses and betweene the said feaste daie of St. James the Apostle in the yeare of our lord 1623 and the next daie before the said feaste of St. Michaell tharchangell then next followinge the said John Boyer findinge the love and kindnes of the said William and Anne Blunston to bee greate towardes him, did move the said William Blunston to enquire of the estate carriage and behavior of him the said John and of his father and mother And the said William answeared that hee had inquired of them, and that hee heard that they were honest people And then the said John Boyer did intice the said William Blunston to come unto the said Edward Boyer his fathers house in Hathorn aforesaid, and to see his said father and mother and there [their] house and meanes and the said William Blunston accordingley came to the said house and had conference with the said Edward Boyer touchinge the said marriage intended to bee had betwixt the said John Boyer and Anne Blunston there children, and the said Edward Boyer did then and there acquainte the said William Blunston that hee was in debted, and the said William Blunston tould the said Edward that hee had heard so, yet notwithstandinge did saie and acknowledge that hee liked all thinges well and was willinge that the said John and Anne should marrie togeather: And thereuppon the said Edward Boyer and John Boyer or the one of them did move and desire the said William Blunston that a daie and place might bee appointed for a meetinge of freindes to agree and conclude, that the said John and Anne might proceed in there intended marriage, or break off from further proceedinges therein uppon which motion the said William Blunston and Edward Boyer did conclude and agree to give meetinge with there freindes at the house of the said William Blunston in Sandiacre aforesaid uppon the said feaste daie of St. Michaell tharchangell in the yeare of our Lord 1623 last past, to talke and treate of the said entended marriage and of the marriage portions of the said John Boyer and Anne

continued ...

Blunston *Haecquaeque omnia et singula fuerunt et sunt vera publica notorita manifesta pariter et famosa in Sandiacre predicto aliisque locis ibidem vicinis et circum vicinis Et ponit et supra* [All of these things were and are true public and notorious and equally manifest and famous in Sandiacre aforesaid and other places near there and in surrounding places And deposes as above]

6. Item that in and uppon the said ffeaste daie of St. Michaell tharchangell in the yeare of our Lord 1623 now last past, the said William Blunston and Anne Blunston his daughter and the said Edward Boyer and John Boyer his sonne did give meetinge togeather with there freindes in and at the then and now dwellinge house of the said William Blunston in Sandiacre aforesaid and they and theire freindes uppon conference togeather did agree and conclude what the said William Blunston should give unto the said John Boyer in marriage with the said Anne his daughter, and what the said Edward Boyer should give unto his said sonne John. *Et imediate post hujusmodi tractatum communicationem et conclusionem prefati Johnnes Boyer et Anna Blunston matrimonium verum purum et legitimum per verba de presenti ad hoc apta mutuum eorum consensum hinc inde exprimentia dicto die Sancti Michaelis Archangeli Anno domini 1623 Iam ultimo preterito infra aedes solitae habitacionis dicti Willimi Blunston in Sandiacre predicto, Ipso Johanne Boyer mencorat*[13] *Annam Blunston per manum dextram accippiens, et in vulgari lingui eiusdem dictum* [And immediately after such discussion, consultation and conclusion, the true, proper and legal matrimony of the aforesaid John Boyer and Anne Blunston was verbally established for the present with an appropriate expression of otheir mutual consent on the said day of St. Michael the Archangel in the year of the Lord 1623 now last past in the building which was the accustomed dwelling place of William Blunston in Sandiacre aforesaid, John Boyer [married?] Anna Blunston, taking her by the right hand and saying in his own common language] I John take thee Anne to my wedded wife to have and to hould from this daie forwarde for better for worse for ritcher for poorer in sicknes and in health to love and to cherish

A further seven articles show that six heifers had already been given to Edward and suggest that there were some problems with the completion of the financial element of the contract.

This statement reveals several interesting features. Firstly, that a journeyman, or workman, of the bride's father was acting as go-between; secondly that events moved fairly swiftly from the Feast of St James the Apostle on 25 July to the quarter day just over eight weeks later. Thirdly, Edward Boyer's confession to being indebted was probably seen by him as a potential impediment to the contract. That William 'had heard so', indicates that he had made enquiries in the neighbourhood, although he had also been informed of Boyer's honesty. Finally, the contract was agreed in front of friends in a private house. It is important to note the use of the present tense in this ceremony. This, followed by intercourse, would become a binding marriage and automatically nullify any previous contracts. The parties may well have intended to ratify the marriage with a church service, after the reading of banns, or after a licence had been obtained from the bishop. The documents in this cause would probably have been endorsed with the Latin phrase '*contractum matrioniali fuit sponsalitica*'.[13]

Hardwicke's long overdue Marriage Act of 1754 finally clarified the legal position relating to marriage, although it was only valid in England and Wales. The main points were that the publication of banns in the parish churches of both parties became a legal necessity; marriage had to be performed by the Anglican clergy, although Jews and Quakers were exempt from this. Most importantly, those under the age of 21 could only marry with the consent of their parents, the medieval marriageable age still being valid in law. A further Marriage Act of 1823 restored the validity of clandestine marriages without banns or licence but ensured that the clergy could be prosecuted for their part in such events. Finally, in 1836, marriages were permitted in the office of a registrar or solemnised by non-conformist clergy.

Licences

Not all marriages were celebrated after the publication of banns. Bishops had been empowered to grant licences for marriage from the early 16th century, and the procedure was set out in the canons of 1603, that the licence had to be obtained from the bishop within whose diocese the marriage was to be solemnised. In Lichfield, after the Restoration, licences were available through local surrogates, acting as deputies for the chancellor. Incidentally, they were obliged to give security in the form of a bond to the bishop for the privilege of doing this work, as a precaution against the abuse of their authority. The court fee books, where they are available, give lists of the numbers of licences issued to surrogates, and also the names of parties to whom they were issued, although they only identify the deanery, and not the exact parish where they lived. The marriage bonds give full names and details of the parties (but these are not technically part of the records of the church courts).

Few marriages were solemnised by licence by comparison with the numbers using banns, probably for financial reasons (Grey quotes a fee of 5s. in 1730). The same information was required from applicants for a licence as from those seeking marriage by banns. No impediment should exist in the form of an existing contract with another party, or of a pending law suit involving either party in matrimony with a third party. The usual questions were asked as to consanguinity and affinity, and parental consent was required. However, where a surrogate was known to be relaxed in his attitude towards the accuracy of information required, or a 'common fame' arose, his bond could be forfeited and he could also be prosecuted by the bishop.

Divorce

Marriage was seen as a legally binding contract and divorce was not possible for the majority of the population until 1857. Prior to this the only legal form was by Act of Parliament, which restricted its use to the upper social reaches of society. The marriage contract was only terminated by the death of one of the partners, and breaking the marriage contract whilst both parties were alive was not possible. What was described as divorce was not a total break in the legal contract, but involved separation *a thoro et mensa*, from bed and board. This was seen as the temporary suspension of matrimony for an unlimited period with the hope that the partners would be reconciled. Acceptable grounds for separation were adultery, impotence, cruelty, infidelity, and also for the relief of unnatural practices.

The success of separation causes was usually dependent upon the proof of either cruelty or adultery on the part of one of the partners. Fortunately for the local historian, confession alone for adultery was not valid due to the possibility of collusion, and witnesses were always required. If one is to believe their testimony, servants with intimate knowledge of the household were often to be found gazing intently through cracks in doors, or minutely examining the bed linen of a morning in households where all was not well.

The seriousness of the cause required the parties to attend the consistory court, but at Lichfield in the 18th century the number of causes was generally less than five per year, more often two or three. On other occasions when life became intolerable, private negotiations may have taken place, or one party simply departed, leaving no evidence in the church court records. It was a legal offence for a married couple to live apart without good reason, but any prosecutions for such offences would have been in the secular courts.

In those causes where cruelty was involved, the descriptions can be harrowing, involving beatings, threats with knives or hot coals and less direct assaults like 'cutting the bedcords' and, during the 18th century, 'smashing the teapots'. As Rogers pointed out[15] 'mere austerity of manners, petulance of temper, rudeness of language, a want of civil attention, even occasional sallies, if they do not threaten bodily harm, do not amount to legal cruelty'. A realistic definition of cruelty was taken to be 'a peril from which the wife ought to be protected, because it is unsafe for her to continue in the discharge of her conjugal duties'.[16]

This type of cause, by virtue of the intimacy of the details of household life tended to bring servants into court to act as witnesses. From their evidence we can learn of their age and length of service within the household. The following deposition of Cordelia Ball, a servant and a spinster, aged 25 of Birmingham, describes the cruelty involved in one such cause (Fig. 4.4):[17]

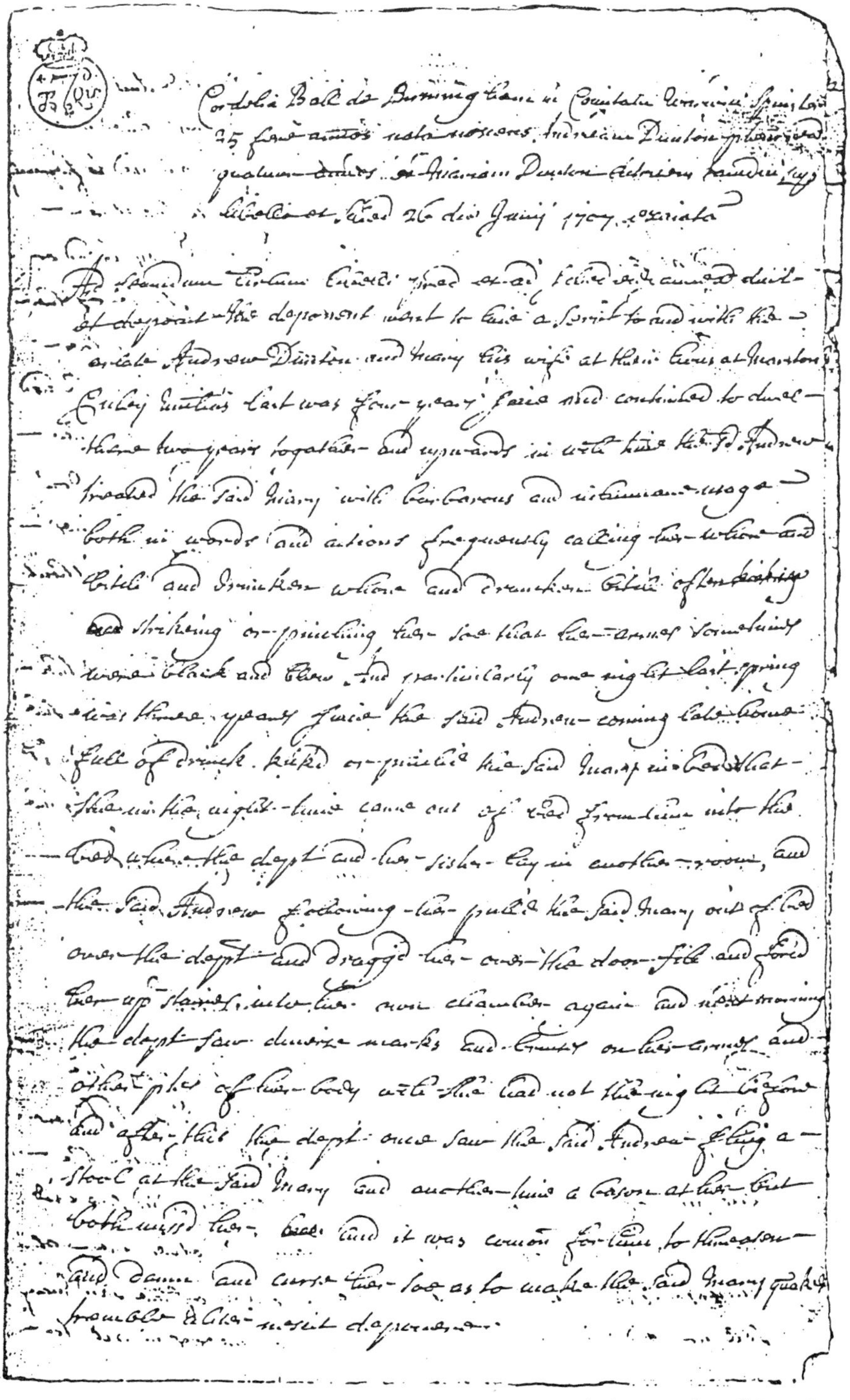

the deponent went to live a servant with the articulate Andrew Dunton and Mary his wife at their house at Marston Culey Michaelmas last was four years since and continued to dwell there two years together and upwards in which time the sd Andrew treated the said Mary with barbarous and inhumane usage both in words and actions frequently calling her whore and bitch and drunken whore and drunken bitch often beating and strikeing or pinching her soe that her armes sometimes were black and blew. And particularly one night last spring was three years since the said Andrew coming late home full of drink kick'd or pinch'd the said Mary in bed that she in the night time came out of bed from him into the bed where the dept and her sister lay in another room, and the said Andrew following her pull'd the said Mary out of bed over the dept and dragg'd her over the door sill and forc'd her up staires into her own chamber again and next morning the dept saw divers marks and bruises on her armes and other parts of her body which she had not the night before and after this the dept once saw the said Andrew fling a stool at the said Mary and another time a bason at her but both miss'd her. And it was common for him to threaten and damn and curse her soe as to make the said Mary quake & tremble

Fig. 4.4 Deposition of Cordelia Ball in matrimonial dispute describing the alleged cruelty inflicted by Andrew Dunton upon his wife.

Ad secundum Articulum libelli predicti et ad seled[18] *eadem annexus dicit et deponit* [To the second article of the aforesaid libel and to the same chosen the attached says and deposes] The deponent went to live a servant to and with the articulate Andrew Dunton and Mary his wife at their hous at Marston Culey Michaelmas last was four years since and continued to dwel there two years together and upwards in which time the said Andrew treated the said Mary with barbarous and inhumane usage both in words and actions frequently calling her whore and bitch and drunken whore and drunken bitch often strikeing or pinching her so that her armes sometimes were black and blew And particularly one night last spring was three yeares since the said Andrew coming late home full of drinck kicked or pinched the said Mary in bed that she in the night time came out of bed from him into the bed where the deponent and her sister lay in another room, and the said Andrew following her pull'd the said Mary out of bed over the deponent and dragg'd her over the door sill and forc'd her upstairs into her own chamber again and next morning the deponent saw diverse marks and bruises on her armes and other partes of her body which she had not the night before and after this the deponent once saw the said Andrew fling a stool at the said Mary and another time a bason at her but both miss'd her, and it was common for him to threaten and damn and curse her soe as to make the said Mary quake and tremble *aliter nescit deponere* [and further knows not how to depose]

The malt and corn were 'locked from Mary' whilst Andrew was 'away three or four days together'. Andrew also brought a counter cause against Mary (daughter of the minister of Churchill in Worcestershire), accusing her of drunkenness.

A range of tradesmen were involved in Lichfield separation causes in the late 18th century and early 19th century including a plumber and glazier, a spoonmaker, two clergymen and a labourer. Most were being sued by their wives for separation on the grounds of cruelty and/or adultery. For a husband to sue his wife for cruelty would show him not to have been master in his own house and would have reduced him to a laughing stock. Adultery, however, was another matter. Some of these causes involved the 'middling sort' of people who, whilst not rich, were able to afford small marriage settlements. In those causes alimony was also sought and discussed by the courts, with statements of the financial status of husbands. Here again, caution must be exercised in that the sums of money, particularly assets, may not be entirely accurate.

If the cause was successful and the couple were legally allowed to live apart, with alimony paid in some circumstances, they would be forbidden from re-marriage, until the death of one of the partners. The wife would not be barred from her dower and any children of the marriage would still be considered legitimate.

The collection of alimony was not always easy as Elizabeth Ensor of Tamworth found, after suing her husband William for separation from bed and board on the grounds of 'severity and other evil usage'. The couple had married in 1741 and by 1763 the situation had become intolerable. William had been legally discharged at the Quarter Sessions on a charge of cruelty, but the day labourer on his farm, Thomas Ditchfield, reported that William was drunk on some occasions. Ellen Bird, spinster and servant to William Ensor, reported that he had been cruel to his wife. Ellen, incidentally, only worked for William for three months. Elizabeth was awarded her separation and requested alimony, which was granted. William was asked for £2 16s. 0d. in July and absolved from excommunication for an unspecified fault. In December, a further request for alimony arrived. The sentence was announced the following 27 March, the day after William had entered into a bond for £100, John Paviour, yeoman (and William's son-in-law) acting as a witness, to guarantee that he would not re-marry. In May, William received a bill for £8 for alimony. Whether or not this was paid we shall never know.

An example of a bond in a separation cause is (Fig. 4.5).[19] The bond was for £500, a considerable sum for the period, and would have been forfeit if Richard had married again. Alimony was paid to Sarah at 15s. per week. William Buckeridge and Edward Burslem Sudell were proctors in the Lichfield consistory court. This cause revolved around Sarah's adultery between 1727 and 1729 with John Southam, an ironmonger. Richard and Sarah had married in 1724, Richard coming from Yardley and Sarah from Aston near Birmingham, and they had lived in Birmingham for four years after their marriage. Richard was a gentleman, with real estate worth £210 per annum. The cause tells us that Sarah had a brother, Joseph, who was an innholder, and a sister by the name of Mary Ruston. It would appear that Sarah's lover John Southam had been found guilty of adultery at Warwick Assize prior to his appearance in the Lichfield courts. Mary Orme, wife of a cutler by the name of Greathay, was one of the servants who gave evidence on Richard's behalf, noting Sarah's tendency to leave the shutters open at night!

Know all Men by these Presents that I Richard Eaves late of the Town of Birmingham in the County of Warwick but now of Sarehole in the County of Worcester Gentleman am held and firmly bound unto Richard Smalbroke Esquire Vicar General and Official principal of the Right Reverend Father in God Richard by divine permission Lord Bishop of Lichfield and Coventry in the sum of Five Hundred Pounds of good and lawful money of Great Britain to be paid to the said Richard Smalbroke or his certain Attorney his Executors Administrators or Assigns which payment well and truly to be made I oblige myself my Heirs Executors & Administrators firmly by these presents sealed with my Seal Dated the ninth day of October in the nineteenth Year of the Reign of our Sovereign Lord George the second by the grace of God of Great Britain France and Ireland King Defender of the Faith and so forth and in the Year of our Lord 1745.

Whereas the above bounden Richard Eaves hath commenced an Action in the Lord Bishop's Consistory Court of Lichfield against Sarah Eaves his now Wife and hath charged her with committing the Crime of Adultery and hath therefore prayed that he may be divorced and Seperated from the Bed and Board and mutual Cohabitation with the said Sarah Eaves, Now the Condition of this Obligation is such that if the above bounden Richard Eaves shall not during the Life time of the said Sarah Eaves contract Matrimony with any other Woman then this Obligation to be void or else to remain in full Force and Vertue.

Sealed and Delivered in the presence of Us
W. Buckeridge,
Public Notary.
Edward Burslem Sudell

Richard Eaves Seal

Fig. 4.5 overleaf

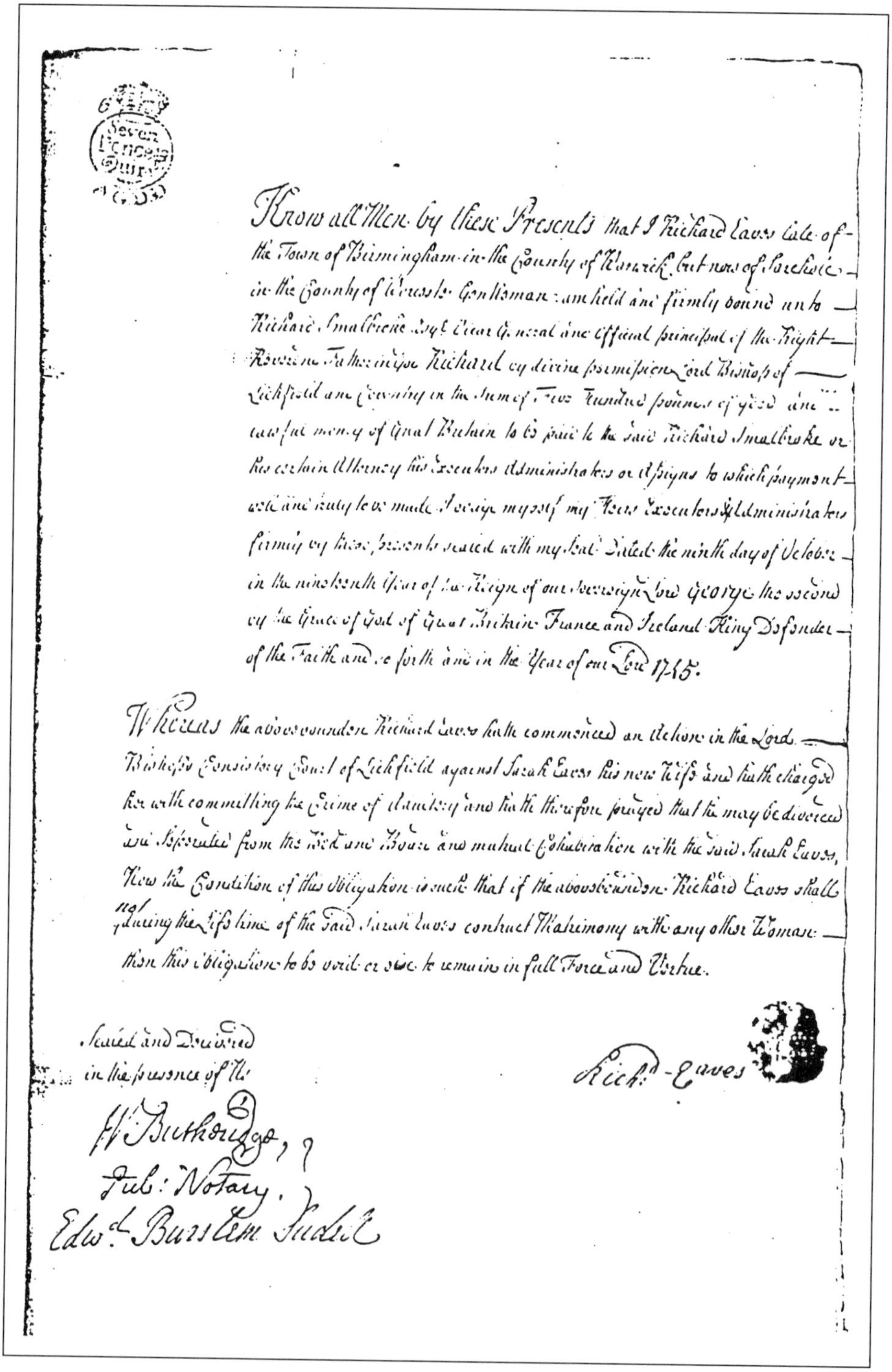

Know all Men by these Presents that I Richard Eaves late of the Town of Birmingham in the County of Warwick but now of [illegible] in the County of Worcester Gentleman am held and firmly bound unto Richard Smalbroke Esq. Vicar General and Official principal of the Right Reverend Father in God Richard by divine permission Lord Bishop of Lichfield and Coventry in the Sum of Five hundred pounds of good and lawful money of Great Britain to be paid to the said Richard Smalbroke or his certain Attorney his Executors Administrators or Assigns to which payment well and truly to be made I oblige myself my Heirs Executors & Administrators firmly by these presents sealed with my Seal Dated the ninth day of October in the nineteenth Year of the Reign of our Sovereign Lord George the second by the Grace of God of Great Britain France and Ireland King Defender of the Faith and so forth and in the Year of our Lord 1745.

Whereas the abovebounden Richard Eaves hath commenced an Action in the Lord Bishops Consistory Court of Lichfield against Sarah Eaves his now Wife and hath charged her with committing the Crime of Adultery and hath therefore prayed that he may be divorced and separated from the Bed and Board and mutual Cohabitation with the said Sarah Eaves, Now the Condition of this Obligation is such that if the abovebounden Richard Eaves shall not during the Life time of the said Sarah Eaves contract Matrimony with any other Woman then this Obligation to be void or else to remain in full Force and Virtue.

Sealed and Delivered in the presence of Us

H. Buckeridge, Pub: Notary.

Edwd. Burslem Pudet

Richd. Eaves

Fig. 4.5 Bond entered into by Richard Eaves upon his separation from his wife.

Some causes related to events that had happened some considerable distance away from the marital home, adultery by its nature being a secret affair. Hepsibah Sley, also Slee, of Uttoxeter in Staffordshire, sued her husband Thomas, a shoemaker, for adultery in 1753.[20] Hepsibah was the daughter of James Rush, a deputy corn meeter,[21] and she had married Thomas in October 1739. Six years later, a son of Thomas was baptised in London, another child the following year, and twin girls, Jane and Sarah in 1748. Witnesses from London were called in this cause and it was decided that they were to be examined in London in the Consistory Court of St Paul's Cathedral. Due to the distance involved a proxy was appointed to act on Hepsibah's behalf. It would appear that Thomas had been lodging at the house of Margaret Young, a widow, at Castle Court, Castle Lane in Southwark for four years. A fellow shoemaker, Thomas Allen, knew Thomas during that time and he lodged in a house owned by Sley's uncle, Richard Blaylock. A midwife by the name of Hannah Chattin, wife of a lighterman by the name of William, remembered delivering a child to a stranger living at Margaret Young's house. The bond in this cause was for £100, given by Bowyer Walker, a goldsmith and Jonathan Neal, a gun stock maker of the parish of St Botolph in Aldgate. As usual, the parties were forbidden from remarriage.

The clergy were not immune from this type of problem. In 1739 Saint John Haynes had married Mary Clerke at Willoughby, and lived there until a few months before the cause began in 1754.[22] Mary had had an affair with Joseph Berrington, also known as Dr. Berrington, the main events of which had taken place in a 'little parlour next to the kitchen'. The story was relayed back to Saint John by the servants and Mary was sent to a lodging house in Cheltenham with her servant Mary Webb in an attempt to stop the affair. However, Mary Webb's rigorous inspection of her mistress's bed every morning revealed incriminating evidence in the form of black hairs, which did not belong to her obviously fair-haired mistress. Shortly after this she confessed to her sins in 1755, at the house of Theophilus Holebrook, a clerk at Church Aston. Her confession to her husband seemed easy 'when repentence would offer forgiveness', but this did not keep her out of the courts. Saint John was granted a separation upon a bond for £100, and both parties were forbidden from re-marriage within the lifetime of the other.

Cases of under-age marriage were more common. As Burn wryly pointed out, when 'sons and daughters arrive at a competent age, and are endowed with the use of strong reason, they may of themselves contract marriage without ... consent'.[23] This was the basis of several causes at Lichfield when parents attempted to annul such marriages; a number of them date from the first decades of the 19th century, in spite of Hardwicke's Act fifty years earlier. Parents could also prohibit the publication of banns by those under the age of consent and canon 100 forbade any form of espousal without parental consent.

Marriage within the prohibited degrees was judged to be incestuous and therefore invalid. Many causes described as incest are, in fact, the result of this problem, the most common type of cause being second marriages when the widower married his dead wife's sister. Some causes where extra-marital affairs had taken place with relatives of the husband or wife were technically described as incest and were dealt with as immorality in an office cause. One such heard at Lichfield in 1742 involved the marriage of William Rolley, a husbandman from Glossop in Derbyshire. He had married a widow, Ellen Platt, in 1723. Following the death of Ellen he had, at the age of 53, remarried in 1734, his bride being a girl of 18. The young girl perhaps reminded William of his former wife, and after the birth of two children, it was revealed that his second wife was the daughter of his first wife by a previous husband. This marriage was declared null and void.[24] This was described as separation *a vinculo*, or an annulment of the bond of marriage. The result was that the very bond of marriage was dissolved by virtue of the fact that it had never existed. Any children of the marriage would become illegitimate, but the parents were permitted to re-marry. If either of them had been previously contracted to another potential partner, then they would have to honour the earlier arrangement, if this was still possible. As we have seen, annulment could result from marriage within the prohibited degrees of consanguinity and affinity. Nullity could also be claimed on the grounds of impuberty where the partners were under the necessary ages of consent, or from impotence after three years of marriage, but causes on the grounds of sexual impotence were very rare in the Lichfield court between 1680 and 1860, embarrassment perhaps leading to reticence.

One cause of an unusual type heard at Lichfield in 1754 contained overtones of blackmail.[25] William Wolseley, Baronet, was suing Ann Wolseley his wife for separation from bed and board. Ann had married William on 23 September 1752, describing herself as a widow in the copy of the parish register. By October she had left William. Her last known abode was the house of John Robins, Esquire in the borough of Stafford and investigation revealed that she had in fact married a bachelor by the name of John Robins in June 1752 at Castle Church in Stafford St Mary. A witness to the first marriage was Richard Wolseley, a Lieutenant in General Bland's Regiment. Before he could appear in court, he had to be absolved from excommunication resulting from his presence at a clandestine marriage. Sir William was in a very embarrassing situation, which could have involved him in a bigamy case in the secular courts. The final document in the cause papers requested all the documents to be sent to Doctors Commons[26] in London, where an appeal was to be heard. Ann may well have been trying to blackmail Sir William, with or without the collusion of her husband, and there is at least a hint of political events in the background.

Jactitation of marriage

Jactitation of marriage is the legal term used when one party claims to be either contracted to or married to another, when in fact there has been neither contract nor ceremony. This situation was obviously more common when spousals and clandestine marriages still occurred. The church courts saw jactitation as an act of malice and a falsehood, damaging to the good name of the other party which, as we shall see in defamation causes, was an important principle of canon law. Such causes were never common, but most occurred during the period of irregular marriage prior to Hardwicke's Marriage Act of 1754. This procedure could be used to determine the validity of a marriage in the courts, by the depositions of witnesses who had been present proving that the marriage had taken place. If a marriage could not be proved, the plaintiff would be ordered to 'forever hold his peace', and was generally charged with the costs of the cause.

Restitution of conjugal rights

Many matrimonial causes were brought by wives for restitution of conjugal rights, but unfortunately most of the surviving papers are simply citations, implying either that those failing in their duties had either returned, or more likely had fled beyond the reach of the officials of the diocese. Under such circumstances, letters of request (sometimes known as letters requisitional) could be sent to the appropriate bishop if the individual's whereabouts were known, but this would have involved more expense for those who probably could least afford it. The call for restitution was not simply a request for the missing partner to return to the marital bed but to a state of cohabitation in, and therefore maintenance of, the domestic home which had been left for no lawful reason. The individual concerned was to 'return and treat the complainant with conjugal affection', which did not necessarily involve the bedroom. Failure to return could result in a cause for nullity if the partner had fled and the validity of the marriage was in doubt. Such causes could be brought by someone who had been turned out of house and home, like Mary Taylor in 1737 (Fig. 4.6):[27]

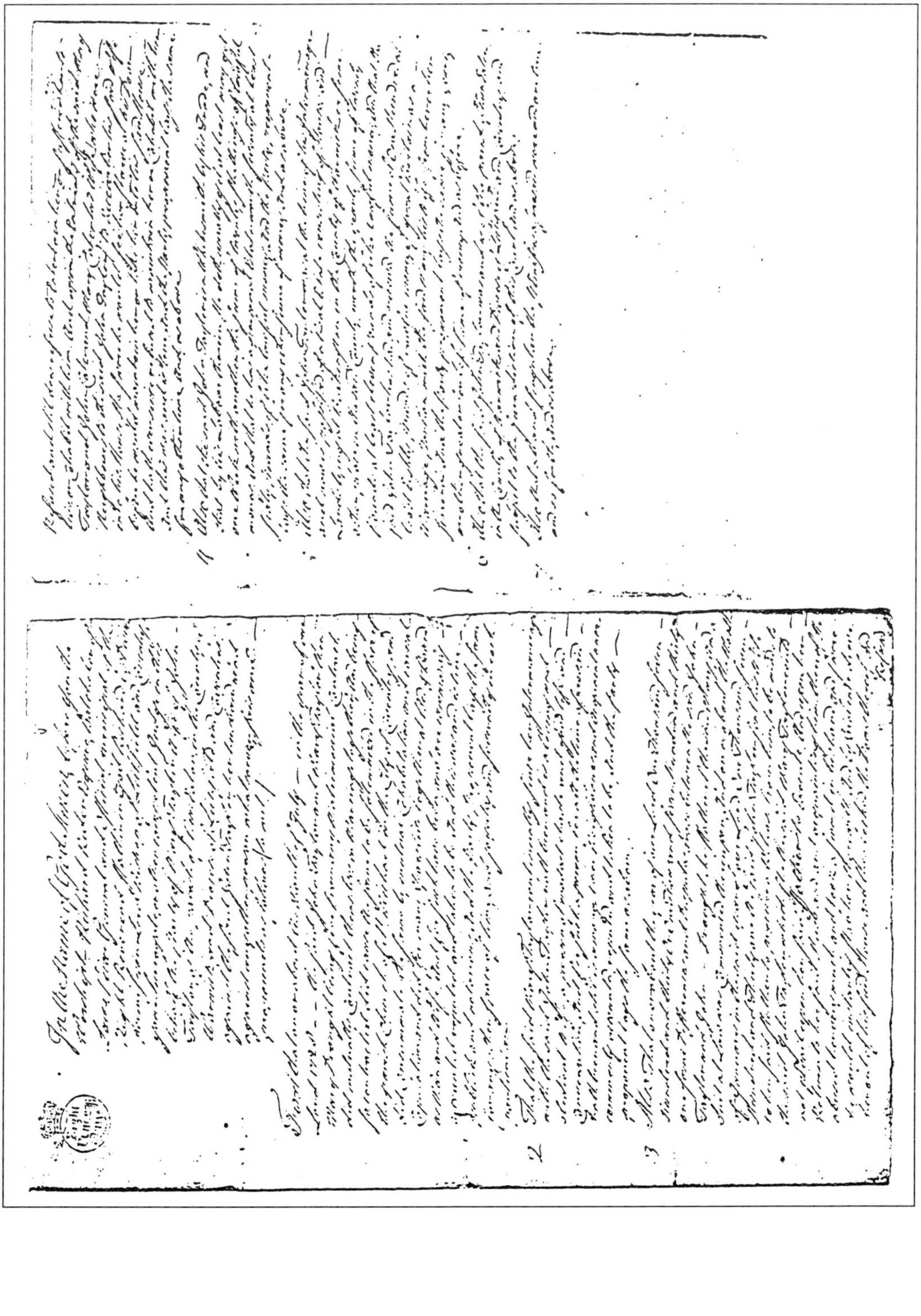

Fig. 4.6 Restitution of conjugal rights, Mary Taylor trying to get back into her house.

In the Name of God Amen, before You the Worshipful Richard Rider Esquire, Batchelor of Laws, Vicar General and Official principal of the Right Reverend Father in God, Richard by Divine permission Lord Bishop of Lichfield and Coventry, your Surrogate, or other competent Judge in this behalf the Party of Mary Taylor Wife of John Taylor, of the parish of Nun Eaton, in the County of Warwick, and Diocese of Lichfield and Coventry, against the said John Taylor her husband, and against any other person whatsoever, sais and propounds as follows (to wit)

For that on or about the Month of July in the year of our Lord 1728 the said John Taylor and Mary Taylor then Mary Drought being free from any Matrimonial Contract, did mutually Contract themselves in Marriage together, And being so contracted did cause the same to be solemnized in the Face of the parish Church of St. Michael in the City of Coventry, and did Consummate the same by mutual Cohabitation and carnal Copulation and did for many Years live together at Bed & Board as Man and Wife, And for such have been, and are commonly accounted reputed and taken to be And this was and is true publick and notorious, And the party Proponent lays the same for any other space of time, and joyntly and severally in each particular.

2. That the said Mary Taylor continually since her Intermarriage with the said John Taylor hath been and is a loving and obedient Wife, a person of modest, chaste and good life and Conversation, And for such a person for all the time aforesaid been and still is amongst her Neighbours and Acquaintances commonly accounted, reputed and taken to be, And the party proponent lays the same as above.

3. Also That on or about the year of our Lord One Thousand Seven Hundred and thirty Or One Thousand seven Hundred and thirty one some Differences and Disputes arose between the said John Taylor and John Drought the Father of the said Mary, And a Suit at Law was Commenced thereupon, And on or about the Month of January in the said year of our Lord One Thousand Seven Hundred and Thirty one the said John Taylor sent his Wife to her said Father to procure a Release from him, to be made to the said John Taylor, which the said Mary Taylor could not prevail upon her said Father to Execute. And upon her Return to her said Husband and acquainting him thereof He abused her very much and took a sword in his hand and swore he would instantly stab her therewith, And by violence drove her out of his said House and then locked the Doors thereof and Refused and still does Refuse to Entertain her or sufferer her to live or Cohabit with him. And upon the Entreaty of the said Mary Taylor and John Cater and Mary Cater his Wife (who were Neighbours to the said John Taylor) to Receive her his said Wife into his House, He swore he would see her starve at his Door before he would maintain her or take her into his said House, And hath ever since refused to maintain her or Cohabit with her And this was and is true And the Party proponent lays the same for any other time, And as above

4. Also that the said John Taylor is a Whitesmith by his Trade, and that by his Labour therein, He doth usually get at least may get one Week/with another, the sume of twenty shillings of lawful money, And that he has a personal Estate worth seventy at least sixty pounds, of like lawful money, And the party proponent lays the same for any other sum of money And as above

5. Also that the said John Taylor was at the time of his Intermarriage and now is possessed of a Real Estate consisting of Houses and Lands lying at Bulkington in the County of Warwick or some other place in the said County, worth the yearly sume of twenty Pounds at least eleven pounds of like lawful money, And that the said John Taylor has had and received the sume of One Hundred, at least Eighty pounds of lawful money of great Britain as a Marriage Portion with the said Mary his Wife from her or her Friends, And the Party proponent lays the same for any yearly or other greater or lesser sume of money And as before

6. Also that the said John Taylor was and is of the parish of Nun Eaton, in the County of Warwick, and Diocese of Lichfield and Coventry, and subject to the Jurisdiction of this Court And as above

7. Also that all and singular the Premisses aforesaid were and are true and so forth, And as above.

Mary had, at least, had a home. Ann, wife of George Morley, sued for restitution of conjugal rights at Lichfield in 1743. As Ann Marshall of Abbots Bromley, she had married George in 1730 but he had not always provided a house for her. Thirteen years later she was living at Brailsford in Derbyshire and her husband was in Derby Gaol for an unspecified offence. His occupation was not given but his brother was a blacksmith, whose wife denied that George was ever cruel to Ann.[28] The outcome of this cause is not known.

In all these causes it was technically necessary for the courts to produce a judgment, but the causes reflected complex domestic situations and some were also strongly contested which rendered judgment difficult. These factors would result in a long-drawn out cause which could prove to be extremely expensive, and many causes vanish from the records, either due to lack of money, success by family or friends acting as mediators, or one of the partners in the dispute simply disappearing.

The church courts finally lost their jurisdiction over the hearing of divorce causes in 1857 following the Matrimonial Causes Act, and the Court of Divorce and Matrimonial Causes was established solely for the hearing of divorce cases, staffed by civil lawyers.

Chapter Five

Tithes and Easter Offerings

Tithes were the tenth part of the agricultural crops and garden produce grown by every parishioner that was to be given to the church, described by Burn[1] as the 'yearly increase by Act of God'. The concept of yearly increase was central to tithes, which could only be collected once a year from each category of produce, although payments were made throughout the year to accommodate the harvest times of different crops.

Tithes were technically divided into those arising directly from the soil and those deriving indirectly—known as predial and mixed tithes respectively, but generally referred to as great tithes and small tithes. The great tithes consisted of the tenth part of crops harvested directly from the soil, that is grain, hay and timber. The right to collect these valuable tithes lay with the rector of a parish who was also entitled to gather the small tithes. The grains included wheat, barley, oats, rye, and maslin, as well as pulses—peas and beans. There were many regional combinations and variations of mixed grain crops. Maslin or blendcorn was a mixture of rye and wheat grown and harvested together in the Midlands and used in breadmaking, and dredge was a mixture of oats and barley. Trees of oak, elm, ash and beech over the age of twenty years were exempt from tithe, whereas coppice wood that was harvested was tithable on the grounds that it renewed itself, albeit more slowly than other crops.

The small tithes resulted indirectly from cultivation and included the young of livestock—lambs, calves, foals, piglets, poultry and their eggs, and also wool. Lambs and wool were the most valuable and sought after of these small tithes. Although it arose directly from the soil, garden produce was also deemed to be a small tithe, on the grounds that the value of the items that could be collected was so small and the problems of collection very great. These tithes were due to the vicar of a parish. Curates were normally paid a stipend for their services and were not, in theory, allowed to claim tithes. Areas that were extra-parochial, that is not within any parish, paid their tithes to the monarch, as head of the Church of England.

Corn mills, although not involved with the growing of crops, were subject to personal tithe if they were not considered to be ancient, the critical date for their existence being 9 Edw. II, or 1315. The construction of mill races and leats was not a task to be undertaken lightly and water mills tended to utilise specific reaches of rivers and streams for centuries. However, windmills were introduced during the 13th century and, due to the fire risk involved in this form of milling, they were frequently rebuilt. The due tithe was a tenth part of the pure profit of the mill, be it powered by wind or water. Naturally, this was extremely difficult to assess. Disputes were not common but, where they do occur, can give the names of millers from the surrounding area who often acted as witnesses.

Personal tithes could also be demanded from those craftsmen not engaged in agriculture, at the rate of one tenth part of their pure profits (after the deduction of expenses), by the statute of 2 & 3 Edw.VIc.13. This again was a notoriously difficult assessment and by the turn of the 17th century it was often reduced to a modus payment for 'hands' included in payments for Easter offerings.

From time immemorial it had been the custom to collect tithes of crops and animals in kind, which involved gathering the tenth part of the crops as they were harvested, as well as the tenth lamb and fleece. In law the tithe remained the property of the grower until the time of separation of the tenth at harvest time. At this point the parson or his tithe-gatherer had to witness the separation of the tithes. Once separated from the main part of the crop, the grain or livestock became the personal property of the parson who could either store it for his own use or sell it for cash. If he chose to leave his grain crops on the ground for collection later and they were ruined by rain, or the rats had a feast, then that was his responsibility.

This source of income was proof against inflation, although it could be seriously affected by harvest failure and murrain.[2] However, some parsons were either elderly or absentees and unable to spend the vast amount of time necessary to collect their dues this way, and opted to accept a modus payment, or *modus decimandi*. This was an agreed amount of money in lieu of tithes in kind—much sought after by parishioners. There were two types of modus, the customary and the prescriptive. The customary modus was used, by custom, over the whole parish and related to a particular item, the hearth penny is a good example being a modus payment in lieu of tithes on firewood. A prescriptive modus related either to some particular part of the parish or for a certain item for example, a payment of 2d a yardland for hay in the late 16th century at Claybrooke in Leicester in 1579.[3] Individual parishioners also made their own agreements with the clergy, which were described as compositions.

In order to separate the tenth part of the crop it was necessary to establish a unit of measurement for tithe purposes. For grain this was generally the sheaf, the shock (a stook of 12 sheaves), or the thrave (2 shocks), but there were many regional variations of both units of measurement and their names. Peas and beans were tithed by the cock in the Midlands as was hay, but the methods used varied between parishes, some using the windrow or the windlath for hay. Hemp and flax were the exceptions to this and these were tithed after retting. Occasionally the term *decimae garbarum* appears and this simply refers to crops bound or garbed into sheaves, particularly wheat, due to the importance of the straw. Failure to bind the corn together into sheaves would negate the tithing process, as the villagers of Stoney Stanton in Leicestershire well knew when they refused to bind their sheaves in the summer of 1579. When Edmund Messenger became rector of the parish in the previous autumn he had refused to follow the putative custom of the parish by providing a Christmas party, and his parishioners doubtless enjoyed their brief revenge at harvest time before being taken to court.[4]

During the medieval period, the growth of large monastic estates led to extensive areas of tithe income being placed beyond the reach of individual clergy, when large areas of land were donated to religious houses. The great tithes of these estates were collected by the monasteries and stored in vast tithe barns built to contain them. In such parishes, tithes were said to have been appropriated. After the Reformation, these monastic tithes were sold to the highest bidders, and afterwards described as impropriate. Those who held the right to collect such tithes were known as impropriators. These individuals either collected the tithes for their own use or rented the right to collect them to others, either individually or occasionally to a group of two or three people. They were known as farmers of tithes, and would undertake their collection and hope to make a profit. With crops ripening all through the summer this could be a long task, especially in a densely populated parish. In parishes where enclosure had not taken place and holdings were fragmented in the medieval open fields, tithe-gatherers had to know their parish intimately, both the people and their land holdings. One of the most complex yet encountered lay in Leicestershire in the parish of Congerstone where one man's holdings lay in four parishes[5] due to the complexity of the parish boundaries. In theory this individual could have been pursued by up to 12 tithe-gatherers or more!

The right of collection of tithes by the clergy was also occasionally rented out to avoid the sensitive problems of inspection of crops and the labour of their eventual collection, particularly by absentee clerics or in those parishes with a high proportion of non-conformists. Those who rented tithes from the clergy were also known as farmers of tithes and they were responsible for bringing many causes to the courts. It was always tempting to the clergy to let the tithes and leave the other party to collect them, but not always profitable as a Leicestershire parson discovered to his cost. In 1629, the parson of Appleby, who had previously farmed the tithes from the rector of Seale for four houses in the village, thought that he had a hard bargain and chose to sublet the tithes to one Mr. Ralph Woolley. This gentleman then collected the tithes in kind, paid his rent of 40 shillings to the parson and 'gained well thereby'. Needless to say, the following year the parson of Appleby reverted to collecting the tithes himself.[6]

From the Reformation to the Commutation of Tithes Act in 1836, the question of collection of this produce became one of continual aggravation. Tithes causes varied over time in terms of goods or money sought and also in terms of the court used—being heard in both the church and secular courts. Causes ranged from disputes brought by individuals before the local justice of the peace, where small tithes of less than 40s in value could be sought[7] up to the Westminster courts, using the proliferating services of attorneys and solicitors whose numbers increased during the second half of the 18th century.

Individual crops

Individual crops and livestock presented their own problems and potential for disputes. Tithe hay was much prized and due not only from meadows but from headlands and baulks in the open fields, and the question of tithing of the aftermath[8] was a vexed one, as this could often provide grazing of good quality. Although technically one of the great tithes, the hay was sometimes claimed as a small tithe by the vicar of a parish.

Hemp and flax were difficult to tithe and were often the source of problems, but they seem generally to have been tithed by the burden,[9] bundle or handful, after retting. Hops were tithed by the tenth measure, when they were harvested, and before drying. Wool, of course, was tithed by the fleece but even this brought its problems, in that not every flock produced fleeces in tens. The tithing times for wool and lambs were comparatively close and often some compromise would be reached with those farmers whose lambs and fleeces did not reach ten. In some places 'odds' were paid, in other words one halfpenny for each lamb or fleece 'wanting of ten' but, as always, the custom of the parish had to be maintained.

With certain animals, tithing was particularly difficult and was one of the main subjects for the introduction of a modus into a parish. Very few farmers had sufficient horses to produce ten foals per year, generating one for tithe and the same was often true for calves. These items were often charged at a nominal rate of one penny per year, and added to the payments for Easter offerings. The use of a modus was further encouraged by the fact that cattle for 'plough and pail' were not tithed, and neither were animals killed for domestic consumption, which further reduced the numbers of tithable animals. The question of tithe milk was one that was solved in most parishes by a modus payment but it continued to be collected in kind in some parishes into the 17th century. However, when surplus milk was converted into cheese which was tithed, no tithe was paid for milk and, where milk was tithed, nothing was paid for cheese. Old milk cattle, known as strappers, were usually charged at a nominal annual rate alongside Easter offerings.

Lambs were the most easily tithed farm stock in view of the numbers of sheep kept, and most of the small tithes causes in the Midlands tend to revolve around the tithes of wool and lamb. The process of tithing had to be seen to be a fair one and consequently became quite complex. The lambs would be penned and the farmer and tithe man would each take two, and one would be selected for the tithe payment from the remainder. This ensured that the farmer did not lose his best animals and that the tithe-gatherer did not have to accept the worst.

Another problem with animals was their mobility and, in the case of sheep, controls operated in almost every parish, regarding the payment of tithes on sheep in a parish at particular times of year. This was to prevent what can only be described as 'sheep shunting', whereby sheep were moved from parish to parish to avoid payment of tithes. With the spread of enclosure and the fattening of stock for market rather than maintenance of breeding flocks, the income from small tithes dropped. A tithe for agistment[10] or depasturing (grazing) was levied at one tenth of the rent for pasture land and was payable on cattle 'that do otherwise yeild [*sic*] no profit to the parson'. In effect it was a tithe on the grass that could have been cut if it had been allowed to grow, because it was due from the owner of the grass rather than the cattle owner. This also produced a tithe income from horses, including those used to draw coaches, but not for saddle horses kept by their owners permanently in the parish.

By the 18th century, some areas of land could pay up to four tithe payments each year, for different uses. Hay could be cropped in June (hay tithe), the aftermath grazed by cattle (agistment), grazed in the winter by barren cattle (agistment) and finally cattle grazed on the early spring 'eatage' (agistment). In spite of the dominance of the custom of the parish, interpretation of tithe law did change, albeit slowly through constant negotiation and, when reading these disputes, this must be borne in mind.

Claims were made for a wide variety of produce, down to potherbs from the garden—in a cause from Cossington in Leicestershire in 1634-5 tithes were demanded on handfuls of herbs and nuts.[11] In this cause one is led to wonder about the relationship between the parson and his community, although the picture is clarified a little by his tombstone in the parish church. He was trying to support 11 children on his comparatively meagre income, but again, there may be other motives yet to be discovered. Small amounts of items from gardens, and the fact that cropping of them was continuous, rendered tithing extremely difficult, particularly when the recipient had to be present at the separation, and even in a small settlement this could be endlessly time-consuming. By the Reformation a common modus of a penny had been introduced, which was known as a garden penny. This, together with a hearth penny in lieu of tithes on firewood, came to be paid with Easter offerings, although technically these payments were not linked in any way. Later citations at Lichfield (from around 1700 onwards) quote ecclesiastical dues and tithes together, and it can be difficult to separate these two areas of contention at the citation stage; although all is revealed if the cause progressed to the articles of a libel.

Technically tithes were only payable on items that were the result of man's activities and not on *ferae naturae* or wild things, but this was subject to a broad local interpretation. One universal and major exception was that of bees. Although they were technically wild, their honey and wax were such vital items in the local economy that these products were deemed tithable. Honey was tithed by the tenth measure, usually the pint, and wax by the tenth weight, but this subject for tithes had disappeared by the 18th century in most areas, with mounting imports of sugar and larger scale manufacture of candles from tallow. Pigeons presented a similar problem, and dovecotes and their occupants provided endless hours of discussion for clergy and parishioners, and an excellent source of revenue for the courts. These birds were technically wild and comparatively worthless in fiscal terms, and not subject to tithe when used for the table, but became a matter of some importance in times of economic stress when their sale could raise much needed revenue.

During the later 18th and 19th centuries crops that had formerly been grown as garden produce, such as potatoes and turnips, were farmed extensively. These continued to be tithed as small tithes, although in temporal law the major crops of a parish could encourage claims for great tithes. This was hotly contested by canon lawyers, who felt that this would create a precedent by undermining the principle of continuity. The same thing happened in parishes where hops were the major product of the parish, which also remained a small tithe. On one occasion matters were taken to their legal limit in that the bark on the hop poles was the subject of a tithe dispute. Bark, particularly from oak trees, was tithable because of its use in the tanning process.

Occasionally, items were tithed which were not technically growing things. For instance, lead in Derbyshire was conveniently thought to 'grow' in the veins or grooves, and was thus subject to tithe, as was tin in Devon and Cornwall. In riverside parishes, flags, or irises, were tithed, although they may not have been deliberately planted crops. In inland parishes, fish were tithable only by custom, and as most were for domestic consumption tithing could have been invalid.

Tithing customs

An eloquent picture of the complexity of tithing customs comes from Fleckney in Leicestershire, where 23 of the elders of the community, aged between 53 and 87, committed their customs to paper during a prolonged dispute in 1638,[12] which began with a parishioner grazing his sheep in Billesdon parish seven miles away. This is a rare illustration of the customs in use at a known date not derived from a glebe terrier (where these things were sometimes listed).

Imprimis, we have accustomed to pay at Easter for every Communicant one penny
Item, for the corn and grain of all sorts the tenth in kind
Item, for apples, plums and pears, the tenth in kind
Item, for every child that is there baptised if it live until the mother be churched either four pence or a Chrisome[13]

Item, for young pigs if the sow have farrowed seven, one, and that first to suck a month, we first choosing two and the tytheman other two, whereto taking one

Item, on Good Friday the tytheman coming to demand for every cock three eggs, every drake three eggs, every hen two and every duck two.

LAMMAS TYTHES[14]

Item, at Lammas we pay the tythe of wool in kind of such sheep as depastured and went in the Sheep Commons of Fleckney at New Years Day before we first taking two fleeces and then the tytheman take other two out of which they choose one

Item, we pay a tythe fleece at seven the tytheman allowing a halfpenny for every fleece

Item, we pay tythe of lambs in kind

Item, we pay a lamb at seven the tytheman allowing a halfpenny for every lamb wanting of ten

Item, if we have four odd fleeces and three odd lambs or if we can make seven of both the tythe men are to take either a lamb or a fleece he allowing us a penny for every one wanting of ten

Item, if the sheep that went and despastured in the fields and Sheep Commons of Fleckney upon New Years Day be sold and others bought in their stead before shear time then those sheep which were so bought being shorn here are tytheable in kind, but if there be none bought in their stead nor shorn in their wool then we pay for every sheep so sold an halfpenny either ewe or lamb and for every one that dies before Martinmas an halfpenny

Item, we are not to join the wool and lambs together if they be over ten either of wool or lamb.

MARTLEMAS TYTHES[15]

Item, at Martlemas in lieu of tithe hay of every yard land in Fleckney we pay four pence or according to the proportion of a yard land either half yard land or quarter

Item, for every new milk cow which has had a calf since Martlemas next before for the milk three half pence

Item, we pay for every old milk cow which formerly had a calf but none since Martlemas next before for the milk one penny

Item, for every hundred sheep that come into the field of Fleckney after New Years Day four pence for every month and so after that rate proportionally either more or less which said sheep there do go upon the Common and not else, and no tythe in kind though they be shorn there

Item, for every cow and calf sold since Martlemas next before two pence

Item, calves we pay in kind and one at seven, the tytheman allowing for every one that wanteth of ten a penny and every one which wanteth of seven if we wean or kill them we pay to the tytheman a halfpenny and if we sell them we pay the tenth penny so sold for

Item, every tythe calf is to suck a month

Item, we pay for every foal whether we weane it or sell it a penny

Item, for every hive of bees we sell the tenth penny

Item, for all wood and fuel which we have cut or used since Martlemas next before every dwelling house a hearth penny

Item, for every garden a penny

This list would have been well known to every member of the community. It represents an amalgam of true tithes, modus payments and Easter offerings, and serves to illustrate the accretion of custom through the centuries.

Tithe causes

Causes were brought by the clergy, either the rector or vicar of a parish, or by a member of the laity, described as the impropriator, lessee, or farmer of tithes. Fig. 5.1 shows the available sources of income of the parsonage illustrating the importance of tithes to the clergy. Easter offerings and dues of passage contributed a very small proportion of the total income when compared with that from tithes or glebe land. However, not all parsonages were well endowed with glebe and in such parishes tithes formed the major source of income. The income of those clergy who were left with only the small tithes and glebe land for their subsistence eventually became very vulnerable to periods of poor harvests and murrain.

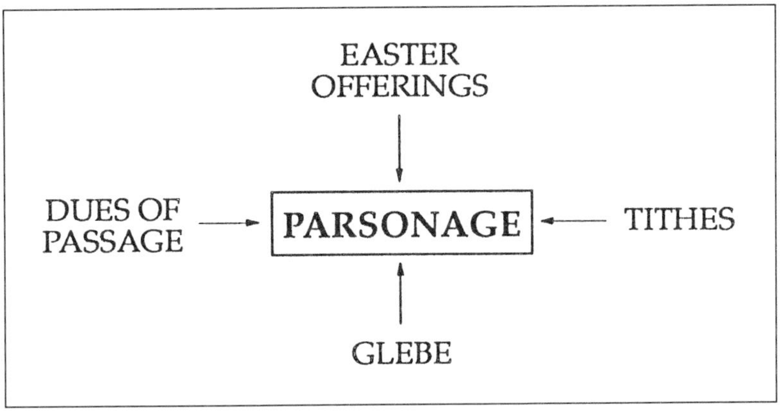

Fig. 5.1 Sources of clerical income.

These disputes form an excellent source of information for parish historians, giving many names of parishioners—possibly identifying those reluctant to pay for doctrinal reasons—locations of disputed land, crops grown, and the state of enclosure within a parish. However, many of these causes are simply represented by citations, either singly or in *quorum nomina* form. But even so, one must ask why those individuals who refused to pay took such action, and whether they appeared in any other causes in the church courts. Were they Dissenters, did they object to those who collected this bounty, or were they simply tight-fisted? The Quakers certainly had strong moral objections to the payment of tithes and Easter offerings. Many of these disputes probably never reached the courts, settlements being negotiated privately through lawyers.

Disputes arose over tithes obviously as a result of non-payment both of tithes in kind and moduses, but it must be remembered that these causes were not always simple affairs. Legal definitions were sometimes sought as well as clarification of various points of law. One of the most important elements in the tithing process was that the custom of the parish should be followed precisely and failure to do this was one of the most common reasons for plaintiffs to come to court, because this could lead to an award of double or triple value of the tithes detained. By the statute of 2 & 3 Edw. VI c.13, notice had to be given to the holder of the tithes when the separation was going to take place, so that they could be present. If the rector, vicar or farmer of tithes was not informed of the separation of the tithes or was unable to be present, or if the crops were taken away without separating the tenth part, then the grower could be sued for double value. If the tithe holder's route away with the tithes was deliberately blocked, then triple value could be sought. The range of potential disputes was endless with both clergy and laity able to collect tithes from all, or part of the parish.

If a custom became established it was almost impossible to break and some new incumbents began their careers in a parish by trying to break existing moduses negotiated by their often ageing predecessors, who had neither the energy to collect their just dues nor the wish to aggravate their parishioners. Once a modus had been used in a parish it was difficult to return to the principle of payment in kind, and the ecclesiastical income would fall over a period of time. This was felt very strongly from the Reformation down to the end of the 16th century, a period of high inflation and bad harvests; when these problems were compounded by the fact that clergy could marry and raise families straining their meagre financial resources. The evidence it has left in the court papers is considerable with many causes related to efforts to reverse these arrangements.

A number of disputes related to the enclosure of the open fields and the use of the Act of 2 & 3 Edw. VI c.13, concerning the bringing of barren land into cultivation. Many Leicestershire parishes were enclosed piecemeal during the late 16th and early 17th centuries, using the excuse that 'Barren Heath and Waste grounds, which have heretofore paid no tithes by reasons of barrenness thereof but be now improved and converted to arable Ground or Meadow, shall at the end of seven years next after such improvement pay Tithes'.[16] In spite of the fact that the newly enclosed land was often taken from the medieval open fields, claims were made for tithe exemption following the 'improvement' of enclosure. The given dates of enclosure should be treated with some circumspection, due to a degree of elasticity created in order to obtain the maximum benefit from exemption.

In causes which passed through the spiritual courts, tithe causes were instance in form and conducted by plenary pleading. The prolific cause papers which were produced were stored in the usual manner, endorsed with the names of plaintiff and defendant and the phrase *csa Xma - causa decima*, or tithe cause. The process through the courts is a familiar one, beginning with the normal citation, followed by the articles of libel. Sometimes, the plaintiff sought to sue a number of people from the same parish and the citation was drawn in the *quorum nomina* form, whereby a number of names appeared at the bottom of the normal citation, instead of a single name in the text. The endorsements by the apparitor on these documents show the problems that this form could bring in terms of catching up with the parties concerned; the phrase 'sought for' telling all. The example illustrated from Chesterfield,[17] shown in Fig. 5.2, lists defaulters by township within this large parish. Presumably those whose names were crossed through had paid their dues to avoid the problems of travelling to the court at Lichfield, a distance of over forty miles (as the crow flies).

Tithe causes were often brought by wealthier individuals, or those with a greater than average knowledge of the law, and causes might be strongly contested when the defendant could afford to do so. The plaintiffs occasionally took large numbers of farmers from a single parish to court with each duplicate cause running parallel to each other, using the same witnesses. Such a series of very similar causes generated a daunting pile of documents.

Following the issue of the citation, the articles of the libel were prepared. The initial preamble gives the names and status of the parties concerned, the parish involved usually being that of the plaintiff, described as either cleric, farmer of tithes or impropriator. By the early 19th century the lay plaintiff is described as the lessee or proprietor or farmer of tithes. Sometimes the occupation of the defendant is given, but by the nature of the dispute, they are usually farmers, although some tradesmen continued to farm land as an additional source of income. The defendants did not necessarily come from the same parish as the plaintiff, and there was a reluctance to pay tithes in more than one parish.

The first article of the libel established the rights of the plaintiff either rector, vicar, impropietor or farmer of tithes in the parish concerned, and also to any specific items in dispute. The second article stated that from time immemorial, or 'beyond the memory of man' (a figure of 60 years is often quoted), the tithes of the particular parish have been paid to either the rector, vicar, or farmers of tithe, whichever was appropriate. The third article listed the types of crops which the defendants were growing in the parish in the years in which the tithes were unpaid; the years where loss of revenue had been incurred were also given. In some courts, a schedule of the tithes due was given at the end of the initial libels, as in the Leicester archdeaconry, but this has not been found in post-Restoration documents at Lichfield. In a large cause the next articles comprised one paragraph for each type of tithe withheld.

Following this, the articles of the libel gave the value of the tithes unpaid, again one article for the tithe of each crop demanded. This was then followed by an article which gave the value of the tithes being sought, whether it was the true value or double or even triple value, followed by a statement that the defendants had failed to pay their tithes to the plaintiff. The penultimate article summarised the plaintiff's cause and stated that it was public knowledge that the tithes were due to them.

The final articles followed the usual pattern, stating that the parish and diocese or archdeaconry in which the defendants live wais located within the jurisdiction of the court.

Fig. 5.2 (opposite) Quorum nomina citation from Chesterfield, showing the problems of contracting the defendants—56 in this case—within the 12 days between the issue of the citation and the date of their appearance at Lichfield.

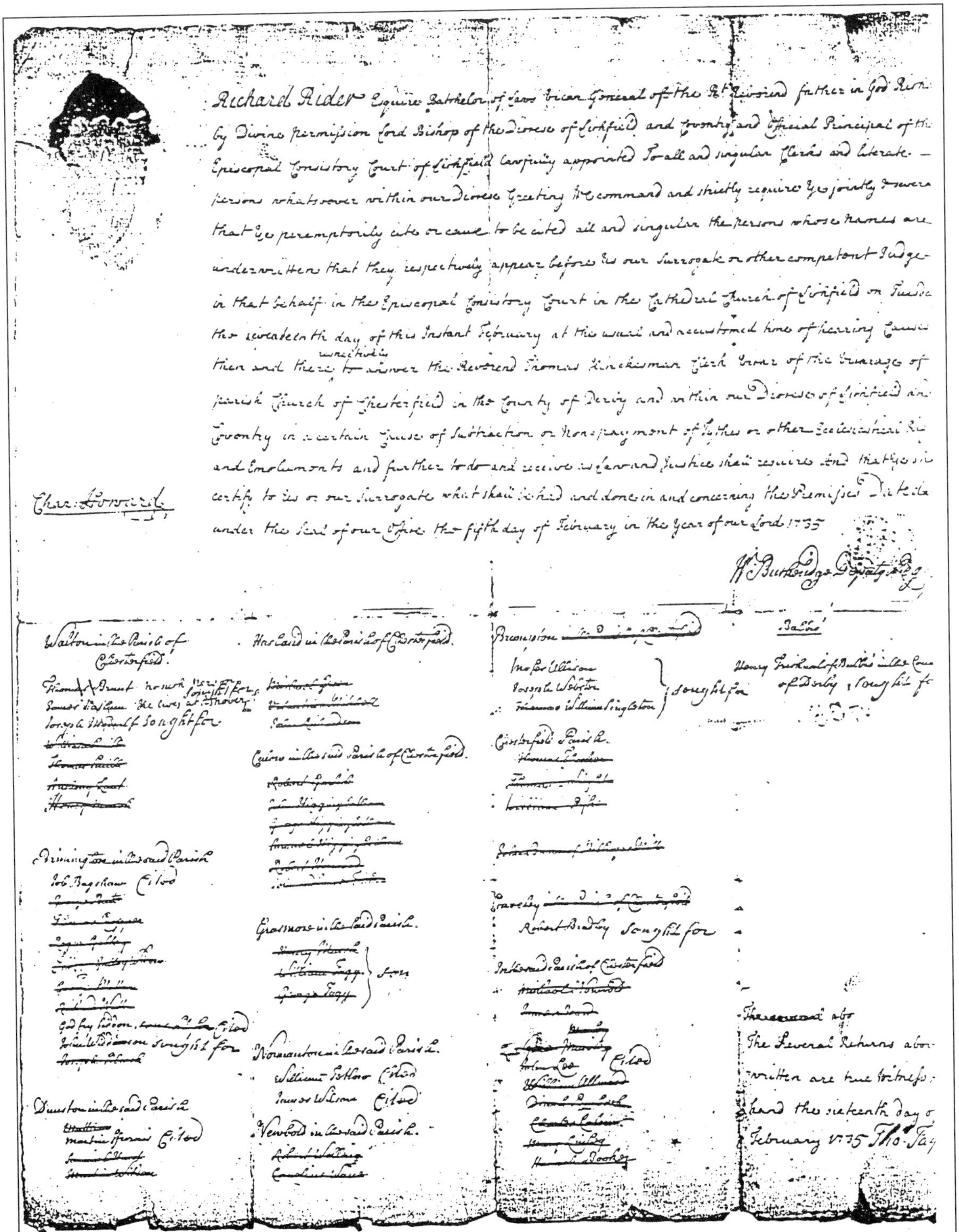

Richard Rider Esquire Batchelor of Laws Vicar General of the Rt Reverend father in God Rich[illegible] by Divine permission Lord Bishop of the Diocese of Lichfield and Coventry and Official Principal of the Episcopal Consistory Court of Lichfield lawfully appointed To all and singular Clerks and Literate persons whatsoever within our Diocese Greeting We command and strictly require You jointly & severa[illegible] that You peremptorily cite or cause to be cited all and singular the persons whose names are underwritten that they respectively appear before Us our Surrogate or other competent Judge in that behalf in the Episcopal Consistory Court in the Cathedral Church of Lichfield on Tuesda[illegible] the seventeenth day of this Instant February at the usual and accustomed time of hearing Causes then and there respectively to answer the Reverend Thomas Hinckesman Clerk Vicar of the Vicarage of parish Church of Chesterfield in the County of Derby and within our Diocese of Lichfield and Coventry in a certain Cause of Subtraction or Non-payment of Tythes or other Ecclesiastical Ri[illegible] and Emoluments and further to do and receive as Law and Justice shall require And that You certify to Us or our Surrogate what shall be had and done in and concerning the Premises Dated under the Seal of our Office the fifth day of February in the Year of our Lord 1735

Chas. Howard

Wm Burbidge Deputy Reg[illegible]

Walton in the Parish of Chesterfield.
[illegible] he works [illegible] Sought for
[illegible] He lives at [illegible]
Joseph [illegible] Sought for
[illegible]

Brimington in the said Parish
Job Bagshaw Cited
[illegible]
[illegible] Cited
[illegible] Sought for

Dunston in the said Parish
[illegible] Cited
[illegible]

Hasland in the Parish of Chesterfield.
[illegible]

Calow in the said Parish of Chesterfield.
[illegible]

Grassmore in the said Parish.
[illegible] Sons

Normanton in the said Parish.
William [illegible] Cited
Thomas Wilson Cited

Newbold in the said Parish.
[illegible]

Brampton [illegible]
Moses Allison
Joseph Webster
Thomas William Singleton } Sought for

Chesterfield Parish.
[illegible]

Tapton [illegible]
Robert Bradley Sought for

In the said Parish of Chesterfield
[illegible]
John Lee Cited
[illegible]

Barlow
Henry Trickett of Barlow in the County of Derby, Sought for

The several Returns above written are true Witness hand the sixteenth day of February 1735 Tho. Tay

An unusual but informative schedule was drawn up by Edward Blunt, vicar of St Margaret's church in Leicester in 1634, when he took Robert Coates, Gent of St Martin's parish to court for his tithes, dating back to 1616.[18] He was suing for the following items:

Item fortie Oxen the pasturage of each weekelie worth one week with an other	ijs
Item fortie milch kine and of them fortie Calves each Calfe one with an other worth	xiijs ivd
Item the milke of everie of the said Cows worth weeklie one week with an other	iijs iiijd
Item one hundred cart or waine loades of hay each Loade worth	xxs
Item one hundred barren kine the weeklie despasturage of each worth one weeke with another	ijs
Item two hundred young beasts *scilicet*[19] stirkes steeres heifers and twinters respectivelie which were fed and depastured within the said parishe and which brought noe profitt to the church the depasturinge of each of the respectivelie worth weeklie one weeke with another	ijs
Item tenn horses and tenn gueldings the depasturage of each weeklie worth one with another	iijs
Item tenn mares and of the said Mares tenn younge Coltes or foales each Coult or foale worth	xls
Item fortie waine or Cart loades of wood *scilicet* Willowes Ashes Popler Elmes Hawthornes and other firewood and underwood which was Lopped Stocked or Cutt downe and cut made up into faggotts billetts or kidds[20] each loade worth one with an other	xxs
Item fortie waine or Cartloades of firewood or underwood made and bounde up into faggotts or billetts each loade conteininge five score[21] kidds faggotts or billetts each score worth	iijs
Item fiftie burdens bundells or handfulls of hempe each burden bundell or handfull worth	xijd
Item fiftie burdens bundells or handfulls or flax each worth	xijd
Item fortie strikes or bushells of Apples each strike or bushell worth	vs
Item fortie strikes or bushells of Peares each strike or bushell worth	vs
Item fortie strikes or bushells of Plumbes each strike or bushell worth	iiijs
Item a hundred poundes of Cherries each pounde worth	viijd
Item two hundred pounds of Hopps each pound worth	xxd
Item thirtie hives or sholles of Bees and of them three hundred pyntes of honey each pynte worth	xxd
Item of the said Bees one hundred poundes of waxe each pound worth	xxd
Item one hundred peckes[22] gaunes[23] or keeves of Onions each pecke gaune or keve worth	xijd
Item one hundred peckes gaunes or bunches of Carrotts each peck gaune or bunch worth	xijd
Item one hundred peckes gaunes or bunches of Parsnipps each worth xijd	
Item one hundred peckes gaunes or bunches of Turnipps each pecke gaune or bunch worth	xijd
Item two hundred Cabbages each worth	viijd
Item all other garden herbes and seedes not menconed before the due value and worth thereof extendeth to the sume of	xxs

This list is still not comprehensive in that it does not include sheep and pigs, but it is interesting to note in all of the demands made for tithes that every possible cow and sheep is considered to produce young every year, and that every sheep will also produce a worthwhile fleece. As with other categories of business in these courts, the main legal pitfall for the unwary is that of over- or under-estimation of the quantity of material demanded and their values given; there was always a tendency to exaggerate in favour of one's cause. It is also important to try to place these causes in their local perspective. At the time of this particular dispute Leicester was suffering from religious and political turmoil which may have played its part in the generation of this cause.

Those who lived in urban areas were subject to demands for tithes on agricultural produce, however overstated. Many would have retained grazing rights if nothing else outside the town. There was only one major exception to the payment of tithes on agricultural produce and that was London. Here the extent of the built-up area, the complexity of the parishes, and the dominance of trade led to the provision of a rate tithe after the Reformation, levied first in 1545 at 1s. 4½d. for every ten shillings of rent; consequently no tithe suits for goods in kind would appear in the courts. The punishment for non-payment in London at this time was imprisonment, as opposed to the more lenient excommunication and the payment of costs elsewhere.[24]

Once the cause had been set out, the defendant could give his personal answers to each of the given articles of libel. It is at this point that a further disagreement often appears in the value of the items untithed; either estimate should be treated with caution. The items being tithed were probably those that were being grown in the parish at that particular time, but not necessarily in the quantities proposed by the plaintiff. The descriptions of the areas upon which the crops were grown can also give some idea of the state of enclosure of the parish, and whether this had been accomplished privately or by Act of Parliament.

Witnesses were very often called in tithe causes and, as this type of cause depended so much on the custom of the parish, the oldest members of the community often gave evidence, including their ages and occupations. Sometimes the questions posed in the interrogatories requested information relating to the personal wealth of the witness, which is rare information from any period, but was considered to reflect on their reliability.

The age of the witnesses in these causes can occasionally provide a great deal of information. Purvis has found in Yorkshire that some older witnesses had very long memories, recalling events prior to the Dissolution in some mid-16th-century causes.[25] Evidence given by Roger Crossley a Leicestershire parson[26] gives a surprising amount of detail about his migrations. He was:

> born in the parish of Grinden in Staffordshire was afterwards brought up at Leake and Horton until he was of the age of fourteen or fifteen years, from whence he went to a place called White houghe where he remained a year or thereabouts thence he went to Ilam and continued there about half a year, thence he came to Seale where he abode for ... about one year and three quarters of a year thence he went to Staunton near Ashby de la Zouch where he abode about a year thence he went to Ratby and was Curate about eleven weeks, thence he went to Foremark and stayed there about four years, thence he went to Crich and was there about fifteen weeks, thence he came to the vicarage of Thurnby where he has been vicar of Thurnby almost forty seven years.

One unusual individual, Maria Brookes, described her life on a farm in Leicestershire in 1636-7 in great detail.[27] Her husband, Clement, died during the progress of a tithe cause and she had to continue as head of the household, not only to run the farm but to carry on with the cause. She was but one example of a woman defendant in a tithe cause, which one might expect to be a male domain. Female plaintiffs are also recorded, widows of the clergy, or widows of the proprietors of tithes, who continued to instigate proceedings over a period of years. Women also appear as witnesses in some tithe causes.

Positions additional could be added to the process, requiring further personal answers and possibly more witnesses. As in all other causes, when matters had been exhausted, a sentence was read, usually in favour of the party maintaining the status quo. Following this, the usual monition would be issued for the payment of costs, for which bills would be prepared. However, as with other causes, matters could cease without any trace in the record, the only hint of a victory being the presence of tenders for payment lodged with the registry, or a stray bill of costs. Two tenders from Lichfield are shown in Fig. 5.3, neither giving information as to the parish involved, although this could be traced through the act books.

Prohibitions occur in tithe disputes more frequently than in other areas because business could easily be transferred to one of the higher temporal courts where double or triple value was sought. These documents were written on parchment and the text of the 18th-century example illustrated is as follows (Fig. 5.4):[28]

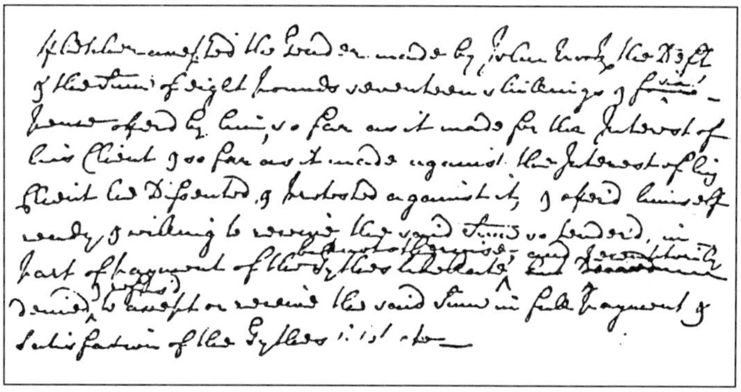

& Ablewhite accepted the tender made by John Ernly the Deft of the sum of eight pounds seventeen shillings & fourpence offered by him, so far as it made for the Interest of his Client & so far as it made against the Interest of his Client he Dissented & protested against it, & offered himself ready & willing to receive the said sum so tendered, in part of payment of the Tythes libelled but not otherwise and [illegible] denied & refused to accept or receive the said sum in full payment & satisfaction of the Tythes libell'd &c—

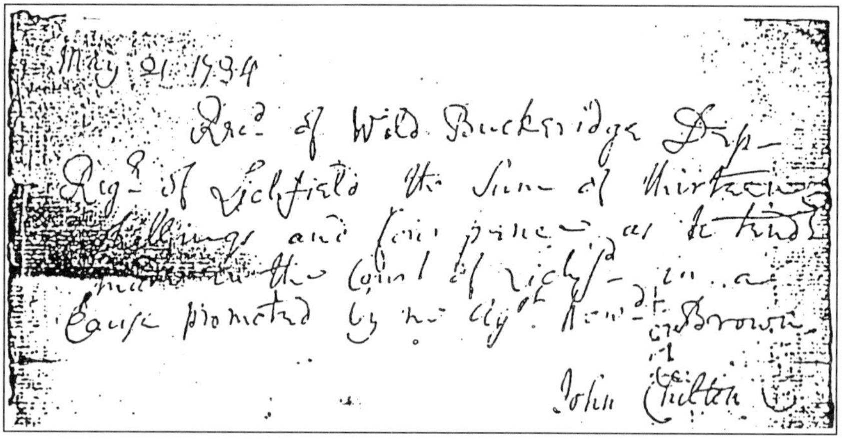

May 21 1734

Rec.d of Wild Buckeridge Dep.
Reg.r of Lichfield the Sum of Thirteen
shillings and four pence as tendred
into the Court of Lichf.d in a
Cause promoted by the Rev.d Mr. [illegible] Brown

John Chilton

Fig. 5.3 Two tenders for tithes from the Lichfield court, where the defendants had paid their money into the court.

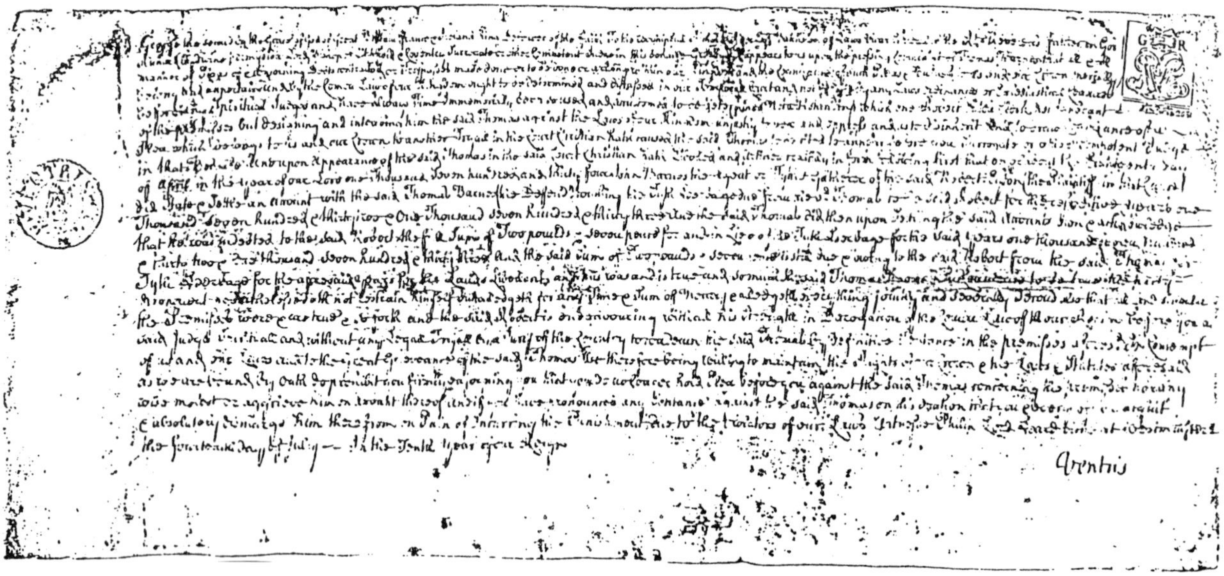

Fig. 5.4 Prohibition in tithe cause, transferring the legal action to a civil court.

George the second by the Grace of God of Great Brittain France & Ireland King Defender of the Faith To the Worshipfull Richard Rider Esquire Batchelor of Laws Vicar General of the Right Reverend Father in God Richard by divine permission Lord Bishop of Litchfield & Coventry Surrogate or other Competent Judge in this behalfe Greeting. It appears to us upon the pressing Complaint of Thomas Barnes that all & all manner of Pleas of & concerning Debts contracted or Trespasses made done or to be done or arising within our Kingdom and Cognizance of such Pleas & Business to us and our Crown specially belong and appertain and by the Comon Law of our Kingdom ought to be determined and discussed in our Temporal Court not [document damaged] by and Laws Ordinances or Ecclesiasticall Censure before any Spiritual Judges and have always Time Immemorially been so used and accustomed to be determined Notwithstanding which one Robert Eyton Clerk not Ignorant of the premisses but designing and intending him the said Thomas against the Laws of our Kingdom unjustly to vex and oppress and us to disinherit and to draw Cognizance of a Plea which belongs to us and our Crown to answer Tryall in the Court Christian hath caused the said Thomas to be cited to appear before you Surrogate or other Competent Judge in that Behalfe. And upon Appearance of the said Thomas in the said Court Christian hath Libelled and Articled craftilly in form following, first that on or about the Eighteenth day of April in the year of our Lord One Thousand seven hundred and thirty four John Barnes the Agent or Tythe Gatherer of the said Robert Eyton (the Plaintiff in that Cause) did State & Settle an account with the said Thomas Barnes (the Defendent) touching the Tyth Herbage due from the said Thomas to the said Robert for the respective years one Thousand seven hundred & thirty two & One Thousand seven hundred & thirty three. And the said Thomas did then upon Settling the said Accounts own & acknowledge that he was indebted to the said Robert the full Sum of Two pounds and seven pence for and in Liew of the Tyth Herbage for the said years one thousand seven hundred & thirty two & one thousand seven hundred & thirty three. And the said Sum of Two pounds & seven pence is still due & owing to the said Robert from the said Thomas for Tyth Herbage for the above said years for he Lands Libellents and this was and is true and so much the said Thomas knows in his conscience to be true the party Proponent neverthelesse doth not restrain himself but alledgeth for any Time & Sum of Money & alledgeth everything jointly and severally. Second also that all and singular the Premisses were & are true & so forth and the said Robert is endeavouring with all his Strength in Derogation of the Comon Law of our Realm before you as Said Judge Spirituall and without any Legall Tryall by a Jury of the Country to condemn the said Thomas by definitive Sentance in the premisses aforesaid. In Contempt of us and our Laws and to the Great Grievance of the said Thomas We therefore being Willing to maintain the Rights of our Crown & the Laws & Statutes aforesaid as we are bound by Oath do prohibit you firmly enjoyning you that you do no longer hold Plea before you against the said Thomas concerning the premisses nor any wise molest or aggrieve him on account thereof. And if you have pronounced any Sentance against the said Thomas on this Occasion that you & every of you acquit & absolutely discharge him therefrom of Pain of Incurring the Punishment due to the violators of our Laws, Witnesses Philip Lord Hardwicke at Westminster the fourteenth day of July In the Tenth Year of our Reign.

Ventris

Easter offerings

Easter offerings were not technically tithes, in that they were not related to the increase of the produce of the land. They were collected from each household simply to pay for the communion bread and wine. The usual sum at the Reformation, in rural areas, was a penny for each communicant in the household, which included children over the age of sixteen, and by the end of the 16th century this had risen to about 2d. for every adult over sixteen, including servants. Collections of bread, in relation to the size of land holding, are not unknown in rural areas an Easter offering in kind! Over time, small modus payments in lieu of tithes were included with payments for Easter offerings, which has led to some confusion between the two types of payment. As we have seen, these moduses might include a hearth penny instead of a tithe on firewood, a garden penny to cover tithes on vegetables and fruit as well as small sums in lieu of milk, barren cattle and foals. In some parishes they also contained a small sum for 'hands' or the remnants of a personal tithe modus on craftsmen, and in others a small charge was made for the 'house'. These were almost infinitely variable from parish to parish and, of course, over time. Again urban parishes presented their own problems in terms of population density, the number of people involved in trades, and the difficulties of knowing individual members of the community and their financial situation. There was also a much greater problem of non-attendance at church, which led to many individuals living within the parish being less well known to the clergy. This form of ecclesiastical taxation was the subject of much bitterness between Quakers and the established church and many who refused to pay Easter offerings were non-conformists.

These dues were often listed in the form of Easter books, or paschal rolls. These are rare survivals, but where they do exist, they can provide fairly complete lists of households in a parish, many of whose inmates do not appear in parish registers. They were the personal 'account books' of the incumbents and depended on clerical literacy for their production and the vagaries of fate for their survival. Existing cause papers show that they were used by the incumbent to record receipts of money in the presence of those paying, so that both parties could be sure that a record had been kept. In some rare causes, Easter offerings could be claimed by a layman but renting of Easter books was not common.

Occasionally, where a living was vacant, either through death of the incumbent, and lack of an immediate successor, sequestrators would be appointed to ensure that the revenues due to the church in the form of tithes and Easter offerings continued to be paid, so that the custom could not be seen to have been broken. Sequestrators' accounts often list the tithes collected in a parish together with the names of those who paid. Tithes could also be collected retrospectively after an incumbent had moved to another parish, and also after his death, and this latter type of cause could often be caught up in the testamentary business of the spiritual courts.

Chapter Six

Defamation

Under English law, every individual was entitled to a good name; to undermine this in public, or indeed in private, was an offence against both the secular law and that of the church, wherein the medieval concept of Christian charity demanded that individuals should not think ill of their fellow men. Litigation relating to damage to personal reputation began to increase from around 1500 alongside changes in the law whereby offence given by libel, or the written word was beginning to be separated from slander, the spoken word; a process that was developing no doubt in response to the spread of the printed word and the slow increase in literacy that resulted.

Defamation cases could be heard in the whole range of church and secular courts and proliferated during the 17th and 18th centuries. Legal redress was sought from the highest courts in the land at Westminster down to local manorial courts and justices of the peace where damages were claimed. The church courts, on the other hand, could only offer canonical correction in the form of public penance and some financial consolation in that the defamer had to pay the costs of the cause. The type of court used to hear a specific case was determined by the nature of the disputed words, and the legal niceties involved need further explanation. The dividing line seems to have been that any accusation of behaviour that would have resulted in a criminal indictment would be heard in the secular courts, and accusations of moral laxity would be taken to the church courts. In the heat of the moment or in wide-ranging gossip, accusations of all kinds of behaviour would fly, resulting in a mixture of defamatory words, which were generally heard before a secular judge, a typical example being 'thief and whore'. However, to suggest that someone was a whore or whoremaster, or guilty of adultery or fornication, would justify action in the church courts. In an attempt to reduce the number of litigants during the 17th century, the secular courts began to place the most charitable meaning on the words disputed, which tended to encourage the use of the church courts. A similar attitude was reflected in the church courts where 'words of passion' which had been spoken in the heat of the moment were not considered to be defamatory, the speaker being in a temporary state of madness.

A good reputation in society was, during the 17th and 18th centuries, dependent upon financial solvency and sexual conformity. The former was of some concern in the church courts where witnesses were questioned as to their financial status, and, of course, the latter was of vital importance. Phrases used to describe individuals of good reputation include, 'an honest man of good credit', 'discreet, honest and sober', and 'held in good esteem'. The use of the word 'honesty' in many of these causes is used in its sense of chastity rather than in its modern meaning. The attitude to personal reputation at this time is summarised in a letter where Thomas Barnett wrote in 1703 about his 'fear of losing my good name and credit which are dear to every one that hath the sense to know the value of them'.[1]

Three legal points had to be made in defamation cases. Firstly, the person defamed should have been of good character before the offensive words were spoken, and secondly that the words used had resulted in the loss of this reputation. The third point related to the circumstances under which the words were spoken; the more people who heard the accusation, the greater the damage that could have been done and thus emphasis was placed on the location of the offence. A malicious motive added weight to the prosecution; the words 'and I can prove it' being quoted in the initial libel also implied that the statement had not been merely made as 'hot words' in an argument.

The use of the church courts implied that damages were not sought by the plaintiff, merely the public humiliation of the defamer in the form of an official penance, or apology for the words spoken. Many of these causes arose from disputes between individuals from the same parish, and the use of these courts may have provided an informal system of social control on sexual behaviour and reputations in a gossip-laden society.

In the ecclesiastical courts defamation causes were heard both as office and instance causes. Those brought by the office related to words spoken against the clergy, primarily relating to the performing of their clerical duties, and these causes were variously categorised as 'Scandal to the Ministry and its Function' at Lichfield, or 'Opprobrious words against the Clergy' in Salisbury. These were treated as Office causes and are often filed as such in collections of court papers, and are described in Chapter Two.

Defamation causes were instance in form, where the injured party took the speaker of the words in question to court. Of the four permutations of plaintiff and defendant, male against male, female against female, male against female and female against male, the last two are commonest. In the few causes of defamation of one male against another, the words whoremonger and rascal or rogue[2] were generally the source of offence. These could be tried in secular and church courts, but were often heard in the more discreet surroundings of the church courts. Men could also be accused of fathering bastards which would not endear them to whose who paid their local poor rates. The number of these causes, however, was very small compared with the number of offended females who accused males of uttering potentially damaging words. Those involved in these causes in the church courts reflect a wide cross-section of the middling and lower levels of society, down to a few examples where individuals pleaded in '*forma pauperis*'.

By the 17th century, only words which implied sexual impropriety could give rise to instance causes in the church courts, and that alone, although a cause involving an implied theft was heard in the York courts in the late 17th century. One of the main allegations in this type of cause at Lichfield concerns accusations of one party being 'nought' [naughty] with another; in other words engaging in illicit sex in a society where marriage was the norm. In theory, such accusations could be seen as damaging to the marriage chances of single women and widows. However, the majority of the plaintiffs in the York courts[3] were married women, and it is interesting to speculate as to whether the woman was more anxious to clear her name, or her husband to avoid unspoken suspicions of cuckoldry! The implication of sexual disease would also be damaging to the marriage and to the potential marriage expectations in the case of death of either of the partners; such a slur on a personal reputation would be long-lasting in the countryside. Many causes were brought by spinsters and widows, obviously acting solely in their own interests although support would probably have been forthcoming from friends and family, but this is not apparent from the records. Obviously causes of this nature would have some effect on domestic relationships and Mary Rivington reported in 1704 that 'her husband is not soe kind to her as formerly' after Hannah Rhodes had defamed her reputation.[4] Several of the defamation cases at Lichfield also suggest that damage had been done to an individual's business by accusations of improper behaviour. Here of course certain categories of women were more vulnerable than others. Many widows became involved in business to support themselves and kept small shops or ale houses and their trade would be affected by a poor reputation.

Sharpe had shown that the majority of the causes at York involved the use of the word 'whore' against women and 'whoremaster' against men in samples from the 1590s and a century later.[5] The adjectives used in conjunction with the word 'whore' were many and various and include 'pox'd' and 'burnt'. These described the symptoms of syphilis or the French pox which became widespread in the 16th century. When used as an adjective it is merely a secondary allegation and would not require the case to be heard in a secular court, the main implication being that of sexual laxity. Another adjective used was 'carted'—a punishment whereby the lady in question had been paraded around the parish on the back of a cart, as a punishment for immorality.

Defamation causes where a woman was accused of being a named individual's whore, where there was the implication of a 'common fame' or local rumour, may well have led on to further investigation and a possible immorality cause for the Office to promote. The principal of 'smoke and fire' could be applied and many were afraid, not so much of the words that had been spoken, but of the suggestion that there may have been more to the accusation than met the eye. Statements like that made by Isabel wife of William James to the effect that Mary Tipler (wife of Samuel) 'had been taken in bed between two lawyers', could either reflect local gossip or lead to more of it, as well as investigation by the local churchwardens.[6] In fact, a small proportion of defamation cases did lead to accusations of immorality and to prosecutions in the courts.

It was also important in these causes that the words should have been spoken in a public place—the greater the number of people who heard the words spoken the greater the damage done to the individual concerned. It was a far more serious matter if they were spoken, or shouted, in a crowded market place than in a quiet street or over the garden fence between neighbours, although the punishment would have been the same. The work place was also seen as being important where fellow workers could hear the accusations, and words spoken in this type of setting are common from country parishes. Another location would be the roads to, and more importantly from, fairs where groups of people were travelling together, often in holiday mood, tired and full of alcohol on the homeward journey. Even those incidents which happened indoors could involve a number of people. William Bagnold, a weaver from Walsall recalled a:[7]

> great quarrel and noise in the house of John Massie in Walsall situate within about 8 yards of this deponents house this deponent being in his own house and hearing an outcry made in the said John's house went in great haste to the said John's house and found it locked and hearing a great bustle in the said house ran back to his house for an axe designing to force open the door but just as he this deponent came again to the door it was set open and this deponent went into the said Massey's house and there found the plaintiffs husband holding the said Massey fast by his cravatt or neckcloth and the articulate William Mousley the plaintiffs son beating the said Massey's wife and this deponent fell a chiding the said William and immediately Mr. Leigh the defendant came into the house being next neighbour to the said Massey and asked the said William if he designed to murder the woman in her own house and thereupon the said William gave the said Mr. Leigh many ill words and called him a Bandy legg'd rogue and a bandy legged dogg and the said Mr. Leigh called the said William a Clown and a Loggar head but never called him sonn of a whore or a bastard all the time of that quarrel for this deponent was with em both in the said house and at the said house door and on the Cill before the door all the time the said quarrel lasted and soe were his fellow witnesses namely the said John Massey and his wife, Elizabeth their daughter, and Elizabeth Hamersley by, also from the beginning to the end of the said quarrel.

Due to the variety of locations involved these causes tend to bring in the widest social range of witnesses.

A typical 'ale house' cause usually begins with the words being spoken 'in the back kitchen of the house of William Smith, known as the Black Horse, between the hours of nine and eleven in the evening'. This of course, readily translated into an 'alcohol-related' incident—a case of '*In cerevisia veritas*' in most cases. One delightful case reflecting the absurdities of life records Anne Steventon, wife of Thomas of Acton Reynolds in Shawbury parish in Staffordshire, taking Richard Gough to court for defamation. It would appear that he had called her a 'Jilt and a common Strumpet'.[8] The circumstances of the case were revealed by John Sherwood, Anne's brother-in-law, who explained that she had been helping in her husband's ale-house and that she had:

> draw'd a mug of Ale and set before the said Dependant [*Richard*]. He offer'd to pay her Two pence for the same upon which she said that the Twopence would pay for the Tobacco and she would take the Ale againe if He would not pay for it upon which she laid hold upon the mug and in the scuffle some ale being shed on the Table he [*Richard*] threw the remainder in her face and there upon she took his Peruke and rub'd the Table with it and struck him with it in the face.

This was probably a case of high spirits after the consumption of quantities of beer,[9] and, although insulting words had been spoken, there seems to have been no serious implication of sexual impropriety, merely injured dignity on Richard's part. For the local historian, the owners of small ale houses, and sometimes their frequenters, can be located, although not on any systematic basis.

An unusual 'public place' cause arose in Derby in 1735, where the deposition of William Horne of Derby, framework knitter aged about 30, reported (Fig. 6.1):[10]

To the first and second Articles of the said Libel the Deponent saith that about the latter end of January last past (the time more particularly the Deponent cannot now remember) he this Deponent and his fellow Witness Mr. John Heath[11] happening to be with the Defendant Mr. Richard Wright in his the said Defendants Chirurgery situate in Derby aforesaid heard the said Defendant say the said Plaintiff was a Whore; and that he could prove her one; who was just gone out of the said Chirurgery from the Deponent and his said Fellow Witness and the said Dependant. The Deponent saith farther that the said Plaintiff and Defendant had just before had some Words in a loud noisy manner, and the Deponent is certain that the said Defendant spoke of the said Plaintiff when he spoke the said defamatory Words and farther he cannot depose.

To the third article of the said Libel the Deponent saith that the said Elizabeth Lowe at the time the said defamatory Words were spoken was a person of good Character and much esteemed by her Neighbours as such and farther he cannot depose.

To the fourth article of the said Libel the Deponent saith that upon account of the said defamatory Words being spoken by the said Dependant, the good name credit and reputation of the said Plaintiff are much impaired and injured and farther he cannot depose.

To the fifth article of the said Libel the Deponent saith that the said Richard Wright at the time he spoke the said defamatory words was and now is a Parishioner of the parish of St. Michael in the Town of Derby in the County of Derby and Diocese of Lichfield and Coventry and farther or otherwise he cannot depose.

Repeated the Day and Year

aforesaid before me.

J. Stephenson Surrogate [*signed*] William Horne

From the interrogatories it would appear that the words had evidently arisen over a 'Mistake with twenty shillings'. The words would appear to have been spoken in front of two witnesses only and in a comparatively private place, although the door may have been open at the time. William also states that they were 'not then in the Church Yard' implying that the chirurgery was adjacent to it. This deposition also contains the phrase 'he could prove her one [a whore]', suggestive of an element of malice.

To summarise, there were four elements in these causes which were considered to be important:

a) The words spoken should have a moral implication whereby an individual was accused of some form of immoral behaviour which could have been followed up by the church courts.
b) The words should have been spoken in a public place.
c) The words should have been spoken in the hearing of a number of other people.
d) The words were to have been spoken to 'the diminution of the good name' of the party concerned.

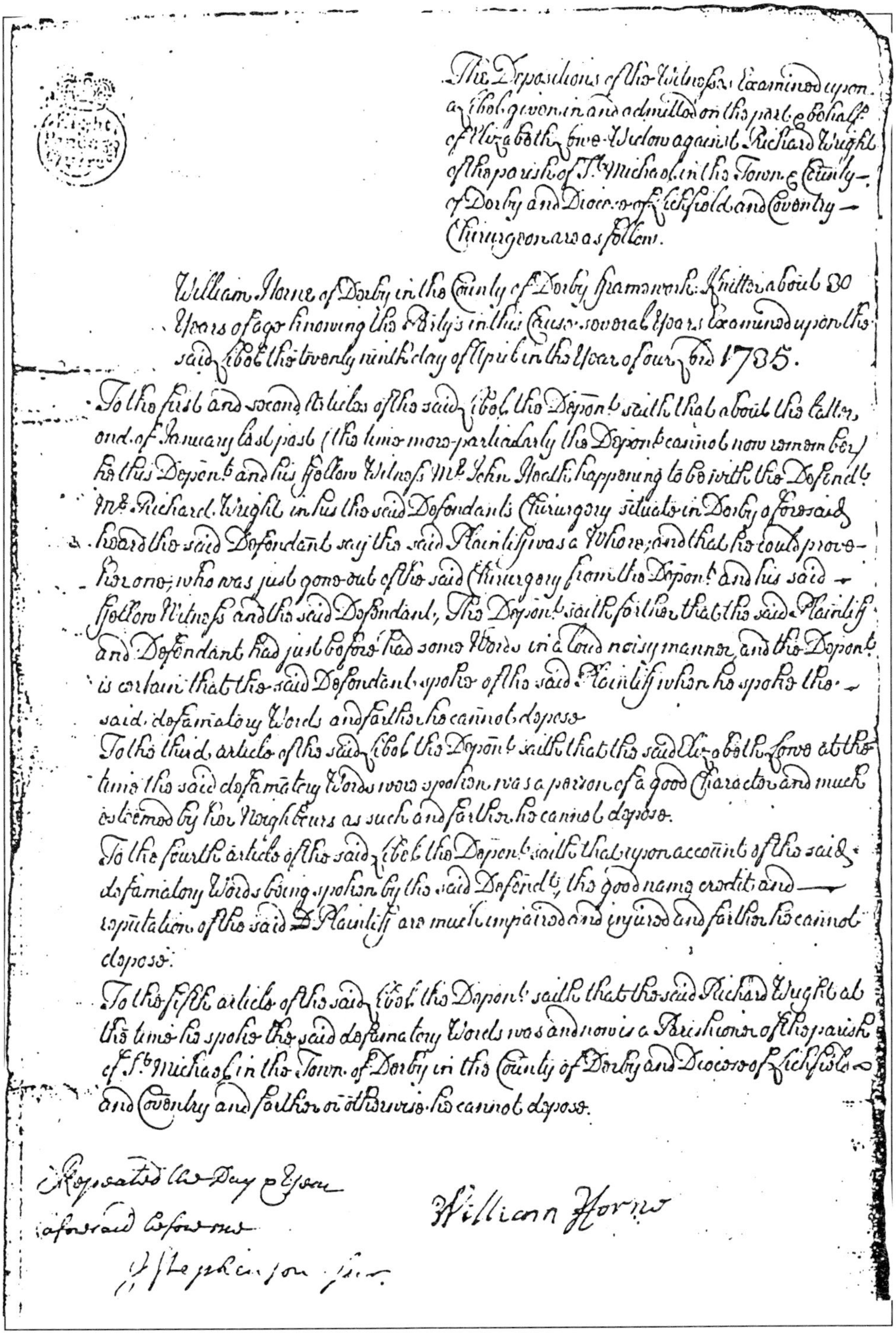

The Depositions of the Witnesses Examined upon a Libel given in and admitted on the part & behalf of Elizabeth Ewe Widow against Richard Wright of the parish of St Michael in the Town & County of Derby and Diocese of Lichfield and Coventry Chirurgeon are as follow.

William Horne of Derby in the County of Derby framework Knitter about 30 Years of age knowing the Partys in this Cause several Years Examined upon the said Libel the twenty ninth day of April in the Year of our Lord 1785.

To the first and second Articles of the said Libel the Depont saith that about the latter end of January last past (the time more particularly the Depont cannot now remember) he this Depont and his fellow Witness Mr John Heath happening to be with the Defendt Mr Richard Wright in his the said Defendant's Chirurgery situate in Derby aforesaid heard the said Defendant say the said Plaintiff was a Whore, and that he could prove her one; who was just gone out of the said Chirurgery from the Depont and his said fellow Witness and the said Defendant, The Depont saith farther that the said Plaintiff and Defendant had just before had some Words in a loud noisy manner and the Depont is certain that the said Defendant spoke of the said Plaintiff when he spoke the said defamatory Words and farther he cannot depose

To the third article of the said Libel the Depont saith that the said Elizabeth Ewe at the time the said defamatory Words were spoken was a person of a good Character and much esteemed by her Neighbours as such and farther he cannot depose.

To the fourth article of the said Libel the Depont saith that upon account of the said defamatory Words being spoken by the said Defendt, the good name credit and reputation of the said Plaintiff are much impaired and injured and farther he cannot depose.

To the fifth article of the said Libel the Depont saith that the said Richard Wright at the time he spoke the said defamatory Words was and now is a Parishioner of the parish of St Michael in the Town of Derby in the County of Derby and Diocese of Lichfield and Coventry and farther or otherwise he cannot depose.

Repeated the Day & Year aforesaid before me
J Stephenson Sur.

William Horne

Fig. 6.1 Deposition of William Horne of Derby.

This type of cause produced a great many citations at Lichfield, but comparatively few proceeded further. Private apologies would probably have been made to avoid further expense and the threat of public humiliation. The wording of the citations in the 17th and 18th centuries at Lichfield often gives the status of the plaintiff, in the case of women, as 'wife of', widow, or spinster. The defendant is named and often has an occupation given, together with the parish to which they belong. Even though these initial documents are the only surviving material in the majority of causes their information can be used to build up a picture of the social groups of the plaintiffs, as well as the towns or villages from which they were brought to court, together with the overall numbers of causes over time.

In those causes that did proceed further the next document, the articles of libel, would be give the general context of the cause, as well as the words that had been spoken. Where witnesses were called, the social context of the cause becomes very much clearer, often describing the location in terms of public house, workplace, the street or, on rare occasions, some festivities. The following transcript is included to give a broad understanding of the format of a libel and wording used in this type of cause. The first article justifies the cause in terms of Canon Law and the second article describes the words spoken and their context. This form of wording continued until the last cause of this type heard at Lichfield in 1852, with only minor alterations in the form of linguistic adornments. This initial article of libels comes from the Lichfield Courts and dates from 1736 (Fig. 6.2).[12]

In the Name of God Amen before you the Worshipfull Richard Rider Esquire Batchelor of Laws, Vicar General of the Right Reverend Father in God Richard by Divine permission Lord Bishop of Lichfield & Coventry and official Principal of the Episcopal Consistory Court of Lichfield aforesaid Your Surrogate or any other competent Judge in this behalf The Party of Mary Gewin the wife of William Gewin of the parish of Saint Chad in Shrewsbury in the County of Salop against Thomas Rogers of the parish of Stepleton in the said County of Salop & Diocess of Lichfield & Coventry & against all others intervening in Judgement before you by way of complaint, doth alledge and articulately propound in writing as follows, to wit,

1. First That all persons whatsoever that shall speak utter or declare any scandalous opprobrious or Defamatory words, tending to diminish injure or lessen the good name character or reputation of any other persons whatsoever against good manners, or have spoken or published any such words are to be admonished & compelled to retract the same opprobrious and Defamatory words, & to restore the good Nature fame & character of the Party injured, and to abstain from speaking or uttering any such words for the future and canonically punished and corrected, And this was & is true publick & notorious and the Party proponent alleges every thing Jointly & severally

2. Also that notwithstanding the Premisses in the foregoing Article mentioned the said Thomas Rogers in the Months of May, June, July, August, September, October & this instant Month of November in this present Year of our Lord 1736, in all some or one of the said Months, within the Parish of Saint Chad in Shrewsbury aforesaid or in some others parishes & publick places thereto adjacent, did publickly and Maliciously Defame the said Mary Gewin the Plaintiff in this Cause, then being and living in good fame, by uttering & publishing several scandalous and Defamatory words tending to diminish injure & lessen the good Name fame & reputation of the said Mary Gewin, and particularly the words following, or words to the like effect & purport, to wit, You thou or she (the said Thomas Rogers then speaking to, of, or concerning the said Mary Gewin the Party Agent in this Cause) are, art, or is a Whore, with several other words of Diffamation or Scandal, & with a Mind & intention to Defame her the said Mary Gewin before diverse credible Witnesses, And this was & is true Publick & notorious, And the Party proponent doth allege & Propound as above

continued ...

3. Also that the said Mary Gewin the Party Agent before the speaking uttering and declaring the Defamatory words in the foregoing Article mentioned, was a person of good credit, fame and reputation in her Neighbourhood, & for & as much commonly known reputed & esteemed and by reason of the speaking publishing and declaring the Defamatory & scandalous words in the said foregoing Article mentioned the good Name fame & reputation of the said Mary Gewin is very much impaired injured diminished & hurt amongst her Neighbours and other good & reputable people in the neighbourhood, and the party Proponent allegeth & propoundeth as before

4. Also That the said Thomas Rogers was & is of the parish of Stepleton in the County of Salop & Diocess of Lichfield and Coventry, and Subject to the Jurisdiction of this Court, and the party proponent doeth allege as above

5. Also That all & singular the Premisses aforesaid were & are true publick & notorious, and of the same there was & is a publick voice fame & report, Wherefore what is required in this behalf being done, the party proponent prays Right and Justice to be done and administered to him and his Client effectually, and the said Thomas Rogers to be Admonished and compelled to reclaim and retract the Defamatory and scandalous words in the foregoing Articles mentioned, and to restore the good name fame and reputation of the said Mary Gewin, and be likewise admonished from speaking uttering or declaring any such scandalous and Defamatory words for the future and thereto be compelled by Law, and the Party proponent likewise prays the said Thomas Rogers to be condemmed in all Costs of Suit already had or made or to be made in this Cause on the part & behalf of the said Mary Gewin, and being so condemmed to be compelled to pay the same to the said Mary Gewin or to her Proctor, by your Definitive Sentence or final Decree to be read or made in this Cause humbly imploring your office & so forth

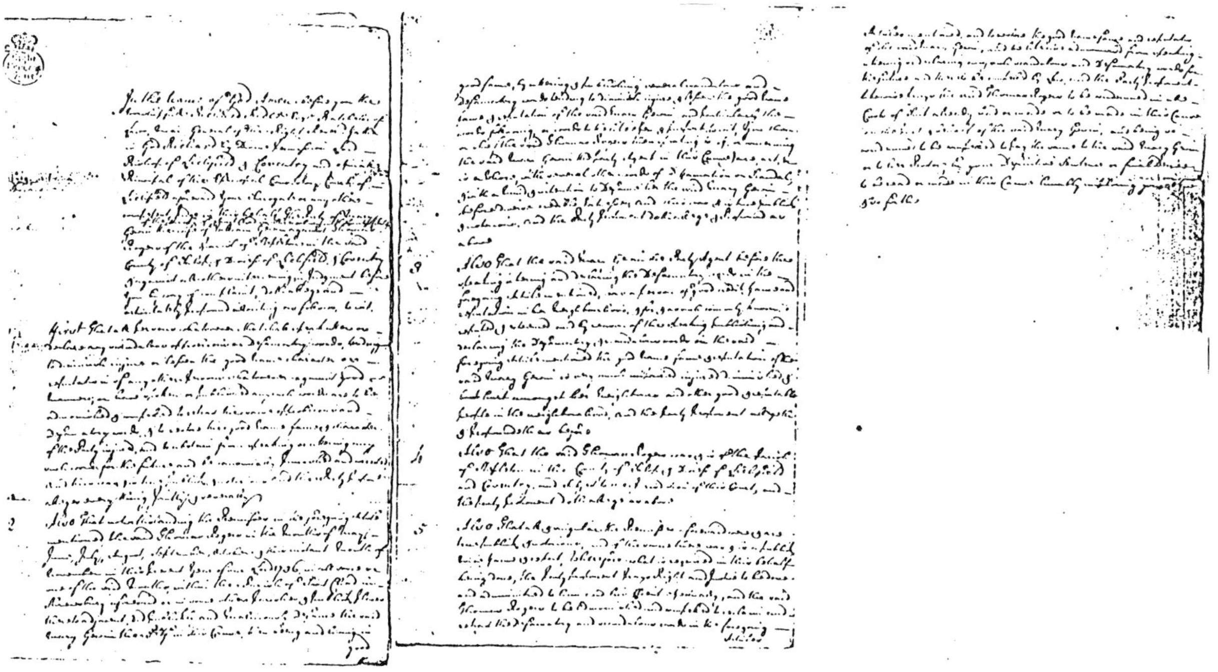

Fig. 6.2 Initial articles of libel in a defamation cause, Mary Gewin v Thomas Rogers of Shrewsbury, 1736.

When the initial articles of libel, the depositions of witnesses and the interrogatories all survive, the context of the cause becomes very much clearer (Fig. 6.3).[13]

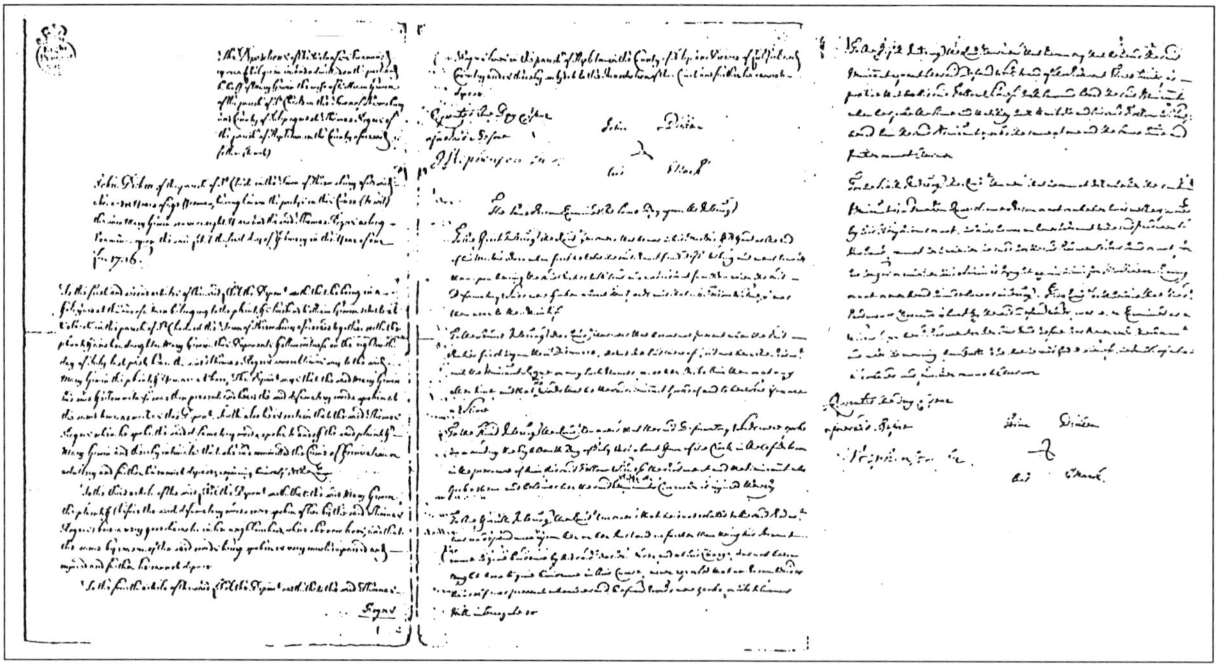

Fig. 6.3 Deposition of John Dicken and his replies to the interrogatories.

The Depositions of the Witnesses Examined upon a Libel given in and admitted on the part and behalf of Mary Gewin the wife of William Gewin of the parish of St. Chadd in the Towne of Shrewsbury and County of Salop against Thomas Rogers of the parish of Stepleton in the County aforesaid follow (to wit)

John Dicken of the parish of St. Chadd in the Town of Shrewsbury aforesaid above 28 Years of age, Yeoman, having known the partys in this Cause (to wit) the said Mary Gewin seven or eight Years and the said Thomas Rogers as long Examined upon the said Libel the first day of February in the Year of our Lord 1736

To the first and second articles of the said Libel the Deponent saith that he being in a Foldyard at the end of the barn belonging to the plaintiffs husband William Gewin situate at Welbech in the parish of St. Chadd in the Town of Shrewsbury aforesaid together with the plaintiff and her daughter Mary Gewin this Deponents fellow witness on the eighteenth day of July last past, heard the said Thomas Rogers several times say to the said Mary Gewin the plaintiff You are a Whore, The Deponents says that the said Mary Gewin his said fellow witness was then present and heard the said defamatory words spoken at the same time as well as this Deponent Saith also he is certain that the said Thomas Rogers when he spoke the said defamatory words, spoke to and of the said plaintiff Mary Gewin and thereby

continued ...

intimated that she had committed the Crime of Fornication or adultery and farther he cannot depose, referring himself to the Law

To the fourth article of the said Libel the Deponent saith that the said Thomas Rogers lives in the parish of Stepleton in the County of Salop and Diocese of Lichfield and Coventry and is thereby subject to the Jursidiction of this Court and farther he cannot depose.

Repeated the Day & Year aforesaid Before J Stephenson Surrogate — John Dicken his Mark

The Same Person Examined the Same Day upon the Interrogatories

To the First Interrogatory the Respondent Answers that he was in his Master's Fold Yard at the End of his Master's Barn when first he heard the said Plaintiff and Dependant talking and went towards them upon hearing the said Parties talk loud and was distant from them when the said Defamatory Words were spoken about Ten Yards and that his Fellow Witness was then near to the Plaintiff

To the Second Interrogatory The Respondent Answers that he was not present when the said Parties first began their Discourse, heard the End thereof, did not hear the Producent call the Ministrant Rogue or any Such Names, or see her Strike him then or at any other time and that the Words that he the said Ministrant spoke of and to her Were You are a Whore

To the Third Interrogatory the Respondant Answers that the said Defamatory Words were spoke on Sunday the Eighteenth Day of July last about Four of the Clock in the Afternoon in the presence of him, his said Fellow Witness the Producent and the Ministrant who spoke them and beleives her the said Producents character is injured thereby

To the Fourth Interrogatory the Respondent Answers that he is not related to the said Producent has no dependence upon her or her husband no farther than being his Servant came to give Evidence by his said Master's Order and at his Charge, has no been taught how to give Evidence in this Cause, never reported that no Person besides himself was present when the said Defamatory Words were spoke, or told Silvanus Hill interrogate so[14]

To the fifth Interrogatory the Respondent Answers that he can say that he heard the said Ministrant repeat the said Defamatory Words to and of the Producent Three times, is positive that his said Fellow Witness both saw and heard the said Ministrant when he spoke the Same and that they both to wit He and his said Fellow Witness heard him the said Ministrant speake the same at one and the same time and farther cannot Answer

To the Sixth Interrogatory the Respondent Answers that he cannot tell whether the said Ministrant is a Drunken Quarrelsome Person or not or whether his is well respected by his Neighbours or not, believes he was an honest Servant to the said producent's Husband, cannot tell whether he sued her the said Producents Husband or not for his Wages or whether this Action is brought against him for Mallice or Revenge or not or ever heard him declare as interrogate The Respondent doth beleive that the said Producents Character is hurt by the said Defamatory Words, was never Examined as a Witness for the said Producent her Husband before has never received the Sacrament and takes the meaning of an Oath to be that he calls God to Witness the truth of what is declared and farther cannot Answer

Repeated the Day & Year aforesaid Before J Stephenson Surrogate — John Dicken his mark

This witness is obviously speaking in support of Mary and there are suggestions of previous legal problems over unpaid wages.[15] It is also interesting to note that this witness describes himself as a yeoman; he was a servant to the Gewin family and he had never received the Sacrament. Was he therefore a nominal member of the Church of England or a dissenter?

The following are the interrogatories produced by Thomas Rogers to be put to the witnesses who appeared on Mary's behalf, to which the above answers were given (Fig. 6.4).[16]

Interrogatories to be administered on the Part and Behalf of Thomas Rogers, to all and Singular the Witnesses produced or to be examined on the Part and Behalfe of Mary Gewin, in a certain Cause of Defamation promoted by her against the said Thomas Rogers, and are as follows

First ask every Witness where and in what House or other Place was you when the Words libellate in this Cause were spoken? Was you, your Fellow Witness, the Producent and the Ministrant in the same Room or Place and where when the Defamatory Words libellate were spoke how far distant was you from the Producent, the Ministrant and your Fellow Witness respectively at the very Time the Words libellate were so spoken? did you see the Producent the Ministrant and your Fellow Witness att the same Time, or was you prevented from seeing them and which of them by Name, by any Wall Door or other Meanes whatsoever, at the Time it is pretended the Words libellate were spoke? and ask each Witness jointly and severally to each Particular Question

2. Also ask each Witness, was you by and present, when the Quarrell between the Producent and Ministrant began? did you hear the beginning and ending thereof and who began the same, did not the Producent call the Ministrant Rogue and other opprobious Words, did she not greatly provoke him, and strike him then or at any and what other Time? sett down the very Words that the Ministrant called the Producent as near as you can recollect or remember? declare the Truth by vertue of the Oath you have taken?

3. Also ask each Witness can you particularly remember the Day of the Month Week and Hour that the Words libellate were spoken, if yea, sett them down as near as you can remember, who was by and present when the said Words were also spoken, sett down their Names and Places of Abode? has the Producent received an Injury in her Character, Fortune or Reputation and how and which Way by the diffamatory Words being uttered as libellate, and ask each Witness as above

4. Also ask every Witness, are you any Way, and how, related or of Kin to the Producent and in what Degree have you any Dependence upon or Expectations from her or her Husband or any Way related to him and how? At whose Request Costs or Charges do you come to be a Witness in this Cause? Have you been taught or instructed how to depose or form your Deposition in this Cause, and by whom, and when? Have you not reported that no Person beside your selfe was by and present or within the hearing of the Ministrant when the Words libellate were spoke, and particularly have you not told one Silvanus Hill, or some other Person, and whom by Name, that you only or but one Person only was present and within the hearing of the Ministrant when the diffamatory Words were spoken and ask each Witness as above.

5. Also ask each Witness, were the Words libellate spoke once or twice or how often by the Ministrant, can you possitively swear that your Fellow Witness saw and heard the Ministrant at the very Time the Words were so spoken or did you hear them at one Time and he or she at another, Is not your said Fellow Witness A Domestick Servant to the Producent at this Time, and at the Time it is pretended the diffamatory Words were spoken, was he not thrashing for her or her Husband in a Barn at the very Time the Words libellate were spoken? what Wages are due to you from the Producent, and how old are you at this Time declare the Truth by vertue of your Oath and ask each Witness as above

Also ask every Witness do you not know and beleeve that the Ministrant is a peaceable sober Person and well respected by his Neighbours? Has he not been a faithfull and an honest Servant to

continued ...

the Producents Husband and hath he not as such been respected by them and their Neighbours untill he demanded and was oblidged to sue the Producent's Husband for his Wages due to him and do you not in your Conscience beleeve that the Producent prosecutes this Cause in this Court against the Ministrant out of Revenge to him and have you not heard her or her Husband declare the same or to that Effect? Is the Producent's Character Name or Reputation any Way impaired or lessened in her Neighbourhood by the diffamatory Words pretended to be spoken by the Ministrant? Was you ever examined as a Witness for her in any other Cause and what do you take to be the Meaning and Nature of an Oath and have you ever been a Partaker of the Sacrament of the Lord's Supper and how long since, and ask each Witness as above?

Also ask Mary Gewin only, is not your Fellow Witness a Poor Indigent Person? addicted to profane curseing and swearing? and of evill Life and Conversation and so commonly esteemed, and Known

And let each Witness sett forth the Reason of his or her Knowledge and sett forth the Truth to each Particular Question

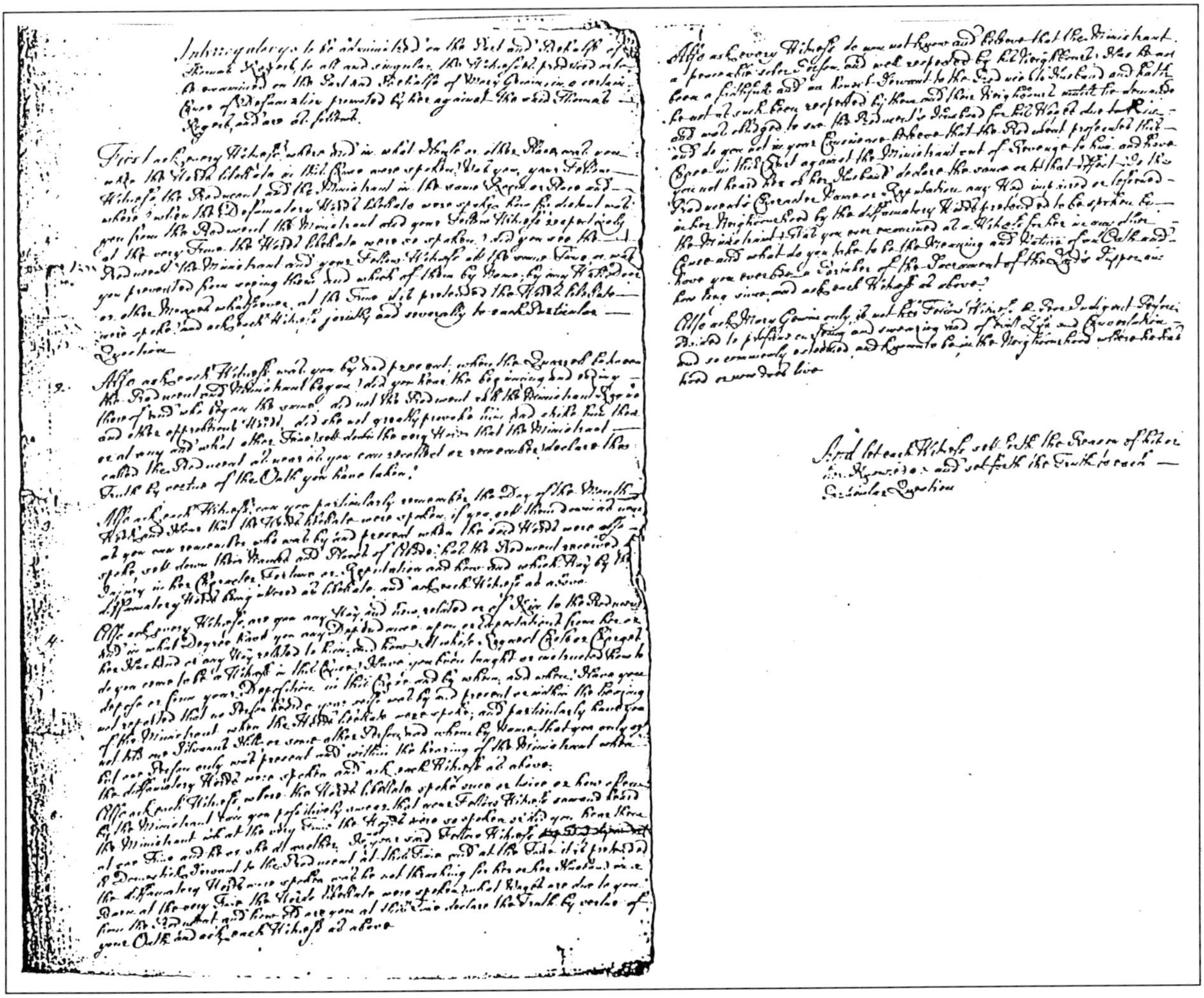

Fig. 6.4 Interrogatories on the part of Thomas Rogers.

The emphasis in these questions is usually placed on the number of people who could have heard the words that were said, where they were spoken, and the tone of voice used. However, in this cause, they reveal the underlying reason for the action taken in the church courts—another dispute in the secular courts. It is also interesting to note the slightly defamatory line in the questioning when it came to the character of the witnesses for the opposing party! The questions also demand a certain amount of personal information from the witness, and the relationships between the parties and their witnesses.

Very few individuals were accused more than once over a long period of time in the church courts, although they may well turn up in the secular courts; little work has yet been done in this field. There were cases of several individuals complaining of one person's behaviour on a particular occasion, usually members of the same family. Disputes within families in public places could also result in 'hot words' and thereby defamation suits, indicating tensions within households, often between unrelated members of the same generation, particularly brothers- and sisters-in-law.

After the initial citation, the other most common document is the schedule of penance, 'by which he [the guilty party] is obliged to give a public satisfaction to the church, for the scandal he hath given by his evil example'.[17] This was issued from the court and had to be signed in the church in which the penance was performed, by the minister, the churchwardens and in some cases the witnesses. It was then returned to the court for safe keeping in the Registry. The apology, in the case of defamation, was relatively simple. If the words had been spoken in a public place, then the penance, according to Burn,[18] was to take place in the local church during divine service; the guilty party was spared being clad in white sheets, but had to recant before the vicar and churchwardens, and the offended individual, if they chose to be present. The process was very similar to that enjoined in immorality causes, described in Chapter Two.

If the words had been spoken in a private place, then penance was performed in suitably private place, the house of the plaintiff, an 'honest neighbour' or the local clergyman. In some cases penance could be commuted to a financial donation to the benefit of the poor of the parish, but this did not seem to have been applied in the Lichfield diocese. The penance was certified and signed by the clergyman and churchwardens, and returned to the Registry of the Courts to confirm that justice had been done.

As we have seen, one final consideration to bear in mind is that the defamation in many of these causes may have been part of a larger quarrel. In some arguments, particularly those over church seats, words were often exchanged which the parties later regretted. It also worth checking records of the lower levels of the secular courts, some causes being recorded as having started in the house of the justice where another case was being heard, or on the way back from the assizes. In such circumstances people may well be predisposed to 'hot words'. In 1710 in the house of Justice Bracebridge at Atherstone, many such words passed between Bridget Bartlett and Hannah Rowley. The events did not take place in the hall of the house as one would expect, but in the kitchen where the cook was preparing the dinner. It would appear that George Bartlett, a carpenter, his wife Bridget and their daughter May were 'in low condition' because their 'goods had been seized'. They were obviously short of money and George had been accused of stealing an ash pole and an alder pole. All three of the Bartlett family were accused of being addicted to pilfering and Bridget had been charged by Hannah Rowley of 'cheating her of a gold ring'. These hot words then led to a cause in the church courts.[19] A similar situation ensued at Wirksworth in 1720 when Robert Symms and his wife Mary and Morris Higgett appeared before Justice Wilmot to settle a dispute about bread and afterwards they all retired to the alehouse of one Harrison, near Ashley Hay for a cup of ale, 'with a design to make friends between the parties'. Unfortunately, this turned into an alcohol-related cause when Morris unwisely suggested that William Candell, a married man, had been too familiar with Mary. Their next court appearance was at Lichfield.[20]

It is also interesting to note that the party uttering the words was told 'that for the future they refrain from uttering publishing asserting and reporting any such reproachful scandalous and defamatory words', in other words, 'to forever hold their peace'. Most would appear to have done so.

Notes

Introduction

1. Martin Ingram in his book on the church courts records the consistory courts of other dioceses only sitting during the Law Terms, but the evidence from the court books would suggest that the Lichfield courts were in fortnightly session through the year from September to July. Occasional documents from the Lichfield courts are dated by Law Term, a system that was in use in the courts of King's Bench, Common Pleas and the Exchequer.
   There were four terms in the year and their dates were:
   Hilary Term: 23rd January to 12th February
   Easter Term: Wednesday fortnight after Easter Day to the Monday following Ascension Day
   Trinity Term: Friday after Trinity Sunday to the Wednesday fortnight after
   Michaelmas Term: 6th November (if a weekday) to 28th November.
2. Royal Commission on Historical Manuscripts, *Record Repositories in Great Britain: a geographical directory*, 9th Edn., 1991.
3. Richard Burn, *Ecclesiastical Law*, 6th Edn., 1797.
4. C.T. Martin, *The Record Interpreter*, 2nd Edn., 1949.
5. Dorothy Owen, *The records of the established church in England*, British Records Association, 1970.
6. J. S. Purvis, 'Select Sixteenth Century Causes in Tithe from York Diocesan Registry', *Yorkshire Archaeological Society*, Vol. 114, 1949.
7. R.M. Helmholz, ed., 'Select causes in defamation to 1600', Seldon Society, Vol. CI, 1985.
8. Hilda Grieve, *Examples of English Handwriting*, 1150-1750, Essex Record Office, 1974.
9. The courts of York followed their 'custom of York', described by Carson Ritchie and the Courts of London also observed slightly different procedures.

Chapter One

1. Elton, R.G., *The Sources of History: Studies in the Use of Historical Evidence in England 1200-1640*, 1969, 40.
2. Burn, Richard, *Ecclesiastical Law*, 6th Edn, 1797, Vol II.
3. Conset, H., *The Practice of the Spiritual or Ecclesiastical Courts*, 3rd Edn, 1708.
4. Grey records that the vicar general was responsible for the 'Correction of Manners and punishment of Vice and all other Parts of Episcopal Jurisdiction, except that of Hearing Causes'.
5. LJRO/B/C/5/1784 Misc (admission of Thomas Buckeridge)
6. Addy, John, ed., *The Diary of Henry Prescott, Ll.B, Deputy Registrar of Chester Diocese*, Vol. I Record Society of Lancashire and Cheshire, Vol. CXXVII, 1987, p.xv. This book gives a unique insight into the life and work of a court official at this period.
7. LJRO B/C/2/98 Court Book.
8. It was declared illegal to use any language other than English for legal documents by the acts of 4 Geo. 2, c.26 and 6 Geo.2, cc.6, 14.
9. A contumacious person was one who demonstrated contempt for the courts by simply not appearing when cited to do so.
10. LJRO Court Book B/C/2/98 f290.
11. From 1639 at Lichfield, the fiat was either written onto the original will or a small slip of paper and filed in the Registry, together with the inventory.
12. Through this book the modern term, 'v', has been used between the parties in the causes, although 'cna' appears on documents generated before 1733.
13. LJRO B/C/5/1734/Office: Tatenhill, OD v Lucas.
14. LJRO B/C/5/1784/6/Office: Coventry, Hand v Bartlam.
15. LJRO B/C/5/1734/Testamentary: Sarah Ryley dec of Shenstone: Letters of request.
16. In summary pleading there does not appear to have been any necessity to produce a libel. In criminal

proceedings pleaded in plenary form the libel is described as 'the articles' and in testamentary causes this first plea is described as the allegation.

17. NUMD LB 237/3/1/1, Tithes: Casson v Howard, 1733.
18. Ibid.
19. LJRO B/C/5/1852/Defamation: England v Sampson: Compulsory.
20. LJRO B/C/5/1737/Tickets for witnesses.
21. Examples of the information that can be obtained from depositions can be found in 'Oxford Church Courts, Depositions 1542-1550' by Jack Drake.
22. NUMD/LB 237/3/19/1, Matrimonial: Beeston, Allegation apud Acta: Robinson v Robinson.
23. This is a typical example of the more complex legal contractions sometimes used in the earlier document. It is technically nonsense in that the words are in a contracted form and need to be expanded, but there is insufficient information to do so.
24. LJRO B/C/5/1707/Chesterfield: OD v Burbeck, positions additional.
25. Burn Vol. III, p.338.
26. LJRO B/C/5/1734/Wem: Defamation: Wicksteed v Thomas: Sentence.
27. LJRO B/C/5/1734/Wem: Defamation: Wicksteed v Thomas: Bill of costs.
28. LJRO B/C/5/1734/Shrewsbury, St Chad: Clandestine Marriage: OD v Joseph Edwards: Excommunication.
29. LJRO B/C/5/1736/Tixal: OD v Beardmore: Absolution.
30. The significavit was so called from the use of the verb 'to signify' used in this request.
31. LJRO B/C/5/1764/115/Tithes: Manlove v Moor: Significavit.
32. A mainprize was a surety for the appearance of a prisoner

Chapter Two

1. Grey, Richard, *A System of English Ecclesiastical Law*, 1730.
2. An inhibition was described by Burn as being a writ, 'in nature of a prohibition'. This could be issued by a higher spiritual authority to a lower one. A true prohibition would only be issued by a temporal court, and was quite common in tithe disputes, where financial gain was claimed.
3. Jones, M.D.W., 'The ecclesiastical courts before and after the civil war: the office jurisdiction in the dioceses of Oxford and Peterborough'. B. Litt thesis, Oxford 1977. Hereafter Jones, M.D.W., Thesis.
4. The 'cure of souls' refers to the spiritual responsibility of the parson towards his parishioners.
5. LJRO B/C/5/1707/Ellesmere: Clergy discipline: OD promoted by Dicken v Ottiwel.
6. Li stands for librum, a pound, hence 5li means £5.
7. LJRO B/C/5/1707/Ellesmere: OD promoted by Dicken v Ottiwel: Testimonial.
8. Jones, M.D.W., Thesis.
9. Recusant includes all non-conformist groups, as well as Roman Catholics.
10. LJRO B/C/5/1686/Visitation citation.
11. LJRO B/C/5/1734/Brawling, OD promoted by Gell v Ward: Allegation.
12. The ordinary was another name for the bishop.
13. This was written in larger lettering than the rest of the text of the document, enhancing the seriousness of the words.
14. LCRO 1/D/41/4/54 King v Errington. This cause was taken on appeal to the Court of Star Chamber.
15. LJRO B/C/5/1734/Chesterfield: Wheatley v Minister and Churchwardens: Church seat, allegation.
16. Marcombe, D., *English Small Town Life: Retford 1520-1642* (1994).
17. LJRO B/C/5/1708 Owen v Critchlow.
18. LJRO B/C/5/1734 OD v Sherratt, Penance.
19. NUMD, Penance, PN366, 1729-40.
20. Burn, Vol 2, pp 513-5.
21. LJRO B/C/5/1764/132a,b.
22. The origin of this office lay in the medieval period when clerics were given assistance with the 'celebration of Divine Office', and one of the duties of the parish clerk or aquaebajalus was that of carrying the holy water (Burn Vol. III, p.66). According to Gray, the parish clerk had to be least 20 years of age and known to be of 'honest conversation'. He also had to be literate and, in some parishes, have a 'competent skill in singing'. He was appointed by the incumbent, unless customarily elected by the vestry. Non-payment of his salary was an offence that could be taken to the church courts, but those who had failed to pay could only be admonished to do so—in other words, given a mild reproof.
23. Every parish elected two churchwardens who served for one year, and they were chosen in Easter week. The custom of the parish was again important; often one churchwarden would be selected by the parish, the other by the incumbent, or both by joint decision. Their accounts had to be presented

within one month of leaving office. This was an ancient office whose main function was to maintain the church, its fitments and environs. They were also given the dubious task of reporting on the faults and misdemeanours of their fellow parishioners.

24. LJRO B/C/5/1735/Faculty, Leigh.
25. LJRO B/C/5/1737/Faculty, Norton in the Moors.
26. LJRO B/C/5/1760/Faculty, Ashbourne.
27. LJRO B/C/5/1699/OD v Thomas Holland.
28. LJRO B/C/5/1722/Breaking of tomb, Holke v King.
29. Morris, Richard, *Churches in the Landscape* (1989).
30. LJRO B/C/5/1792/Church levies, Hayfield.
31. LJRO B/C/5/1844/Faculty, Derby St Alkmund: bill of costs.
32. LJRO B/C/5/1735/Fees, stipend and salary, citation *quorum nomina*.

Chapter Three

1. Burn quotes the preamble to an Act of Edward III in 1344-5 wherein it was stated that 'causes testamentary notoriously pertain to the cognizance of holy church', Vol 4, p.230.
2. Probate normally had to be sought from the archdeaconry court in which the testator lived, unless they held property in two archdeaconries within the same diocese; in which case probate had to be sought from the bishop's court. Those with property in two dioceses had to seek probate from the Archbishop's court either the Prerogative Court of Canterbury, known as the PCC, or the Prerogative Court of York, known as the PCY. The former court claimed probate in those cases where individuals held property in both provinces.
3. The oath was taken by the executor to swear that the will was that of the testator. In the province of York, the oaths of both the executor and one of the witnesses to the will were required (Burn III, pp.250-1).
4. The original wills were filed in the Lichfield diocese and presumably copies were given to the executors or administrators.
5. Technically this was known as 'proving the will in common form'.
6. The archaic form 'legatory' is often used in these causes.
7. A credible witness was one neither 'infamous nor interested' and whose principal function was to attest the will and the sanity of the testator.
8. LJRO B/C/5/1707/24a/Testamentary: Tutbury, Castle Hays: Coooper, Robert: Nuncupative will.
9. Excessive consumption of alcohol was considered to engender a form of madness and render the drinker incapable of making a will.
10. LJRO B/C/5/1707/63/Testamentary: Gilbert, Rebecca widow dec: Interrogatories.
11. LJRO B/C/5/1736/6/Testamentary: Bland, Hannah: Personal answers of John Bland.
12. Literally, seat filled. This refers to the fact that the Bishop was officially in office but not in this case allowed to exercise his jurisdiction, having been suspended by the Archbishop of Canterbury.
13. LJRO B/C/5/1735/Testamentary: Tamworth: Repington, Edward: renunciation.
14. LJRO B/C/5/1753/113/ Testamentary: Leek: Fogg, Henry: inventory.
15. LJRO B/C/5/1737/27/Testamentary: Shiffnall: Horner, Richard: renunciation.
16. LJRO B/C/5/1736/60/Testamentary: Thompson, Mary: personal answers of John Parker.
17. LJRO B/C/5/1735/96/Testamentary: Wem: Sadler, Joseph: deposition George Bromhall.
18. LJRO B/C/5/1707/166/Testamentary: Wright, Jane: deposition of Mary Judd.
19. LJRO B/C/5/1737/30/Testamentary: King, John: declaration instead of an inventory.
20. LJRO B/C/5/1735/33/Testamentary: Shrewsbury: Hancock, Thomas: probate account.
21. The charge on an account is sometimes given as the 'Onus'.
22. LJRO B/C/5/1735/45/Testamentary: Madeley: Wagstaff, Alice Catherine: citation with intimation.
23. LJRO B/C/5/1735/1/ Testamentary: Alstonfield: Applebey, Mary: guardianship of minor.
24. LJRO B/C/5/1737/23/Testamentary: Garret, Joseph: election of guardian.
25. LJRO B/C/5/1736/46/Testamentary: Shottle: Medley, Joseph: Caveat.

See p.131 for a table of consanguinity and affinity which gives an accurate translation of the Latin names of many of the relationships given in the preamble of the allegation in the earlier cause papers.

Chapter Four

1. Ingram, M., in Outhwaite, R.B., Ed. *Marriage and Society: Studies in the Social History of Marriage* (1987).
2. Pers comm Narita Pike.
3. From the Latin verb *spondere*, to promise.

4. Burn, Richard, *Ecclesiastical Law*, 1797.
5. Swinburne, Henry, *A treatise of Spousals, or Matrimonial Contracts*, 1686.
6. LJRO B/C/5/1598/Matrimonial: Bancrofte v Waterhous.
7. Emmison, F.G., *Elizabethan Life: Morals and the Church Courts*, 1973.
8. Pers comm John Addy.
9. Grey, Richard, *A System of Ecclesiastical Law*, 1730, p 145.
10. LJRO B/C/5/1735/Office: Citation, *quorum nomina.*
11. LJRO C/5/1624: Boyer v Blunston: libel.
12. The feast of St Michael tharkangell (St Michael the Archangel) was held on 29 September. This was also a quarter day when rents were due and financial matters settled.
13. The word 'mencorat' does not appear to exist and some form of the verb 'maritat', to marry, would be more appropriate.
14. 'Sponsalitica' was the Latin for spousal, from the verb sponso, to marry.
15. Rogers, Francis Newman, *Ecclesiastical Law*, 1842, p.343.
16. Ibid.
17. LJRO B/C/5/1707/Matrimonial: Dunton v Dunton: deposition.
18. 'Seled' in the text should probably read 'selecta', Cordelia having to answer the second article at the request one of the parties in the dispute.
19. LJRO B/C/5/1744/56/Matrimonial: Eaves v Eaves: bond.
20. LJRO B/C/5/1753/13-30/Matrimonial: Sley v Sley.
21. A corn meeter was one who officially measured corn in the market.
22. LJRO B/C/5/1756/15-27/Matrimonial: Haynes v Haynes.
23. Burn, Richard, *Ecclesiastical Law*, 1797.
24. LJRO B/C/5/1742/10-18/Matrimonial: OD v Rolley.
25. LJRO B/C/5/1754/14-42/Matrimonial: Wolseley v Wolseley.
26. Doctors Commons was another name for the College of Advocates in London, where judges of the higher church courts lived in a collegiate manner.
27. LJRO B/C/5/1737/Matrimonial: Taylor v Taylor: personal answers.
28. LJRO B/C/5/1743/1-7/Matrimonial: Morley v Morley.

Chapter Five

LCRO Leicestershire County Record Office

1. Burn, R., *Ecclesiastical Law*, 6th edn 1797 (hereafter referred to as Burn).
2. Murrain was a cattle plague.
3. LCRO 1D41/4/279: Payne v Salisbury, Claybrooke.
4. LCRO 1D41/4/243: Messenger v Wright, Stoney Stanton.
5. LCRO 1D41/4/XII, 12-23: Watson v Forrian, Congerstone.
6. LCRO 1D41/4/VII, 107: Johnson v Mould, Seale.
7. 7 & 8 Wm.III c.6, 1836.
8. Aftermath was the grass that grew following the hay harvest.
9. LCRO 1D41/4/XIV, 6: Blunt v Coates, Leicester St Margaret.
10. Derives from *jacere*, to lie.
11. LCRO 1D41/4/XV, 124-7: Staveley v Marshall, Cossington.
12. LCRO 1D41/4/XX, 31-40: Hunt and Smart v Dorman, Fleckney (Wistow).
13. There are two definitions of the word chrisome. The first suggests that it was a white robe in which a child was baptised, signifying innocence which, if the child died within a month of baptism, was either used as a shroud, or the garment or its value was given to the church. Another explanation was that it was in fact a headcloth to cover the chrism on the head of the newly baptised, which again would be given to the church if the child died.
14. Lammas, 1st August.
15. Martlemas, 11th November.
16. *An Exact Abridgement of all the Statutes*, 1689, p. 593.
17. LJRO B/C/5/1735/Tithes: Chesterfield: citation, *quorum nomina.*
18. LCRO 1D41/4/XIV, 6-18: Blunt v Coates, Leicester St Margaret.
19. *Scilicet*—namely, that is to say.
20. A kidd was a unit of measurement of firewood, the size of a bundle.
21. There were 20 items in a score.
22. A peck, as a unit of measurement of dry goods, contained two gallons or a quarter of a bushel.

23. A gaun was a tub, with a capacity of about a gallon.
24. Burn Vol IV, p.533.
25. Purvis, J.S., 'Select XVI Century Causes in Tithe, from the York Diocesan Registry', *Yorkshire Archaeological Society*, Records Series, Vol. CXIV (1949).
26. LCRO 1D41/4/VII, 107: Johnson v Mould, Seale.
27. LCRO 1D41/4/XX, 126-32: Rogers v Brookes, Blaby (Countesthorpe)
28. LJRO B/C/5/1737: Tithes, Eyton v Barnes, Prohibition.

Chapter Six

1. LJRO B/C/5/1703, Defamation: Tamworth, letter. Thomas had been accused of jilting Anne Leigh and was trying to clear his own name.
2. The words rascal and rogue did not imply a defined crime, by the word whoremonger was of real concern to the church courts.
3. Sharpe, J.A., 'Defamation and Sexual Slander in early Modern England: The Church Courts at York', *Borthwick Papers No. 58* (1980)(Hereafter Sharpe).
4. LJCO B/C/5/1704, Defamation: Pentrich, Rivington v Rhodes.
5. Sharpe.
6. LJRO B/C/5/1700, Defamation: Ladbroke, Tipler v James.
7. LJRO B/C/5/1705, Defamation: Walsall: Mousley v Leigh: deposition of William Bagnold.
8. LJRO B/C/5/1745/178, Defamation: Shawbury: Steventon v Gough.
9. Many of these causes related to beer rather than wine or 'strong liquors' reflecting the social status of the parties involved.
10. LJRO B/C/5/1735, Defamation: Derby: Lowe v Wright.
11. John Heath described himself in his deposition as a chapman.
12. LJRO B/C/5/1736, Defamation: Shrewsbury St Chad: Gewin v Rogers, libel.
13. LJRO B/C/5/1736, Defamation: Shrewsbury St Chad: Gewin v Rogers, deposition.
14. Silvanus Hill was another individual involved in the cause.
15. This may have been taken to the local Justice of the Peace or Quarter Sessions, or simply to a local mediator, but demonstrates the fact that many of these causes arose as part of a larger quarrel.
16. LJRO B/C/5/1736, Defamation: Shrewsbury St Chad: Gewin v Rogers, interrogatories.
17. Burn, R., *Ecclesiastical Law*, 6th edn. 1797, Vol. III, p.77.
18. Burn Vol. II, p.138.
19. LJRO B/C/5/1710, Defamation: Atherstone, Rowley v Bartlett.
20. LJRO B/C/5/1720, Defamation: Wirksworth, Symms v Higgett.

Table of Affinity

This is taken from Gray's System of Ecclesiastical Law, 1730, and is included for reference in testamentary business so that the less obvious relationships can be identified from the Latin versions used in early cause papers. Relationships in bold type are those of consanguinity (blood relations), and those in italic, affinity (relations by marriage).

A Man may not marry his:		A Woman may not marry her:	
Avia	Grandmother	***Avus***	Grandfather
Avia relicta	Grandfather's Wife	*Aviae relictus*	Grandmother's Husband
Prosocrus, vel socrus magna	Wife's Grandmother	*Prosocer, vel socer magnus*	Husband's Grandfather
Amita	**Father's Sister**	***Patruus***	**Father's Brother**
Matertera	**Mother's Sister**	***Avunculus***	**Mother's Brother**
Patrui relicta	Father's Brother's Wife	*Amitae relictus*	Father's Sister's Husband
Avunculi relicta	Mother's Brother's Wife	*Materterae relictus*	Mother's Sister's Husband
Amita uxoris	Wife's Father's Sister	*Patruus mariti*	Husband's Father's Brother
Matertera uxoris	Wife's Mother's Sister	*Avunculus mariti*	Husband's Mother's Brother
Mater	**Mother**	***Pater***	**Father**
Noverca	Stepmother	*Vitricus*	Stepfather
Socrus	Wife's Mother	*Socer*	Husband's Father
Filia	**Daughter**	***Filius***	**Son**
Privigna	Wife's Daughter	*Privignus*	Husband's Son
Nurus	Son's Wife	*Gener*	Daughter's Husband
Soror	**Sister**	***Frater***	**Brother**
Soror uxoris	Wife's Sister	*Levir*	Husband's Brother
Fratris relicta	Brother's Wife	*Sororis relictus*	Sister's Husband
Neptis ex filio	**Son's Daughter**	***Nepos ex filio***	**Son's Son**
Neptis ex filia	**Daughter's Daughter**	***Nepos ex filia***	**Daughter's Son**
Pronurus *i.e. relicta nepotis ex filio*	Son's Son's wife	*Progener* *i.e. relictus neptis, ex filio*	Son's Daughter's Husband
Pronurus *i.e. relicta nepotis, ex filia*	Daughter's Son's Wife	*Progener* *i.e. relictus neptis, ex filia*	Daughter's Daughter's Husband
Privigni filia	Wife's Son's Daughter	*Privigni filius*	Husband's Son's Son
Privignae filia	Wife's Daughter's Daughter	*Privignae filius*	Husband's Daughter's Son
Neptis ex fratre	**Brother's Daughter**	***Nepos ex fratre***	**Brother's Son**
Neptis ex sorore	**Sister's Daughter**	***Nepos ex sorore***	**Sister's Son**
Nepotis ex fratre relicta	Brother's Son's Wife	*Neptis ex fratre relictus*	Brother's Daughter's Husband
Nepotis ex sorore relicta	Sister's Son's Wife	*Neptis ex sorore relictus*	Sister's Daughter's Husband
Neptis uxoris ex fratre	Wife's Brother's Daughter	*Leviri filius* *i.e. nepos mariti ex fratre*	Husband's Brother's Son
Neptis uxoris ex sorore	Wife's Sister's Daughter	*Gloris filius* *i.e. nepos mariti ex sorore*	Husband's Sister's Son

Set forth by the most Reverend Father in God, Matthew Parker, Archbishop of Canterbury, Primate of all England and Metropolitan, 1563.

Further Reading

Ecclesiastical Law

Not all of the earlier law books on this list will be available from record office or public library shelves; they may have to be sought out in university libraries, but they do represent the books available to the lawyers of the 18th century. Books on the other subjects should be reasonably easy to obtain.

Richard Burn, *Ecclesiastical Law*, 4 Volumes (1797)
S. Degg, *The Parson's Councillor and Law of Tithes* (1676)
Richard Grey, *A System of English Ecclesiastical Law* (1730)
Carson Ritchie, *The Ecclesiastical Courts of York* (1953)
F. N. Rogers, *A Practical Arrangement of Ecclesiastical Law* (1840)

The church courts

John Addy, 'The Diary of Henry Prescott, LlB, Deputy Registrar of Chester Diocese', Vol. I, *Record Society of Lancashire and Cheshire*, Vol. CXXVII, 1987.
Colin R. Chapman, *Ecclesiastical Courts, their officials and their records* (1992)
Jane Cox, *Hatred Pursued Beyond the Grave* (1993)
F.G. Emmison, *Elizabethan life, morals and the Church courts* (1973)
R. Houlbrooke, *Church courts and people during the English Reformation, 1520-70* (1979)
Jack Howard-Drake, *Oxford Church Courts: depositions 1542-1550* (1991)
Ronald Marchant, *The Church under the law: justice, administration and discipline in the diocese of York, 1560-1640* (1969)
Brian Woodcock, *Medieval ecclesiastical courts in the diocese of Canterbury* (1952)
R.M. Wunderli, *London church courts and society on the eve of the Reformation* (1981)

Immorality

John Addy, *Sin and society in the seventeenth century* (1989)
G.R. Quaife, *Wanton wenches and wayward wives* (1979)

Testamentary matters

John Addy, *Death, money and the vultures: inheritance and avarice, 1660-1750* (1992)
A. J. Camp, *Wills and their whereabouts* (1974)
Henry Swinburne, *A briefe treatise of testaments and last wills* (1590)

Tithes

E.J. Evans, *The contentious tithe* (1976)
J.S. Purvis, 'Select XVI Century Causes in Tithe, from the York Diocesan Registry', *Yorkshire Archaeological Society*, Records Series, Vol. CXIV, 1949
S. Toller, *A treatise on the law of tithes*, 3rd Edn. (1822)

Marriage

Martin Ingram, *Church Courts, Sex and Marriage in England, 1540-1640* (1987)
Henry Swinburne, *A treatise of spousals or matrimonial contracts* (1686)
Lawrence Stone, *The Road to Divorce* (1990)
Lawrence Stone, *The Family, Sex and Marriage in England, 1500-1800* (1979)

Defamation

R. Helmholz, 'Select Causes on Defamation to 1600', *Selden Society* Vol. CI (1985)

J.A. Sharpe, 'Defamation and slander in early modern England, the church courts of York', *Borthwick Papers No. 58* (1981)

Latin

Eileen Gooder, *Latin for Local History*, 2nd edn. (1986)

Charles Trice Martin, *The Record Interpreter*, 2nd edn. (1949)

Thomas Morell, *An abridgment of Ainsworth's Dictionary, English and Latin* (1857)

Janet Morris, *A Latin glossary for family and local historians* (1989)

Dorothy Owen, *The records of the established Church in England*, British Records Association (1971)

Handwriting

H.E. Grieve, *Examples of English Handwriting, 1150-1750* (1954 and subsequent editions)

Record Offices

J. Foster and J. Sheppard, *British Archives* (1982 and subsequent editions)

Royal Commission on Historical Manuscripts, *Record Office Repositories in Great Britain* (1991)

Glossary of Latin Words and Phrases

Aec	etcetera
Æditauus	parish clerk
Aedes	lawyers chambers
Agnus	lamb
Allegatio	allegation
Apud	by, at or near
Assignatio Cururatio Gratis [Ass Cur]	Assigned curator gratis (free of charge)
Avena	oats
Bovis	bull, ox
Causa decima [causa xma]	causa decima or tithe cause, the 'x' being an abbreviation for the number ten
Causa diffinis	defamation cause
Causa sponsalitica	cause relating to marriage contract
Caveat	a warning, entered into the court records
Celebs	bachelor
Cerevisia	beer, ale
Chirurgus	chirurgeon or surgeon
Compertum	fact, or detection, found at visitation
Compotus	account
Concordus est	act book entry to the effect that an agreement has been reached
Contra et adversus [Cna]	against
Coram vobis	before, in the presence of
Crimina delicta vitae	criminal life
Decima	tithe, tenth
Decimae garbarum	bound tithes, i.e., those of grain crops
Deponere	to depose
Et ponit ut supra	and propound or depose as above
Ex officio mero	mere office of the judge
Ex parte [ex pte]	on the part of
Exposit ultra vires inventarii, sumam	expended above inventory by the sum of
Fenum	hay
Fiat	written authority
Gallina	hen
Hordeum	barley
Hujusmodi [hmoi]	of this sort, this
Humulus	hops
Hypodidascalus	under master in school
In dei nomine	in the name of God
In forma pauperis	a form of pleading wherein the plaintiff claims to be worth less than £5, or a pauper
Lana	wool

Lesionis fidei	breach of faith
Litis contestis	contestation of cause
Ludimagister	schoolmaster
Molindum aquaticum	watermill
Molindum ventricum	windmill
Natus	born
Nosco	know
Obstetrix	midwife
Œconomus	churchwarden
Officialis foraneus	commissary
Officium dominum [O.D.]	office of the judge
Omnia bene	all is well
Ovis	sheep, goats
Pars actrix	plaintiff
Pars rea	defendant
Partis [ptes]	party in a cause, counsel
Perjorium	perjury
Ponere	produce in court
Pratum	meadow
Processus	legal proceedings in a cause
Propter laevitiam	on account of cruelty
Pro salute anima	for the health of the soul
Quorum nomina	form of citation, naming several defendants
Restat in manibus	literally, resting in hand. Sum remaining in credit in a probate account, after debts had been deducted
Rimor	to search, to examine documents
Scabellum	stool or a bench, church seat
Sede plena	bishop enthroned and in charge of his Diocese
Sede vacante	vacant see
Separationis a thoro mensa	separation from bed and board the nearest available option to divorce in the modern sense of the word, although the parties were forbidden from remarriage
Separationis a vinculo	separation from the bond of marriage, by virtue of nullity
Sequuntur	as follows
Significavit	a writ to civil authorities requesting the detention of an individual who had remained exommunicate for more than forty days
Silva cedua	coppice wood
Sponso	to marry
Subtractionis feodo [subnis feodo]	subtraction of fee
Subtractionis legatio [subnis leg]	subtraction of legacy
Temere	rashly, unadvisedly (relates to administration of estates)
Triticum	wheat
Uxor	wife
Vehicula	cart or waggon
Vidua	widow
Viis et modis	by ways and means
Vinculum	bond

English Legal and Technical Terms

Absolution	acceptance of an individual back to the church after excommunication
Act book	book containing records of legal business carried out by courts at each session
Affidavit	sworn statement
Allegation [Alln]	an unproved assertion
Allegation apud acta	allegation with an act of court
Apparitor	court official whose duties included the delivery of citations to defendants
Archdeacon	church official, with administrative authority over a unit of a diocese
Archdeacon's official	judge in the archdeaconry court, chosen by the archdeacon
Articles [Arles]	articles, usually of a libel, but can relate to interrogatories
Articles of exception	those items in the articles to which a response has been made
Assize court	civil court, which sat in county towns one a year to try serious crimes, including theft, murder and rape
Bishop	also known as the ordinary, who was in charge of the diocese
Canon	a rule of the church, binding upon the clergy
Chancellor	the most senior member of the court, nominated by the bishop to act as his surrogate and whose office combined the roles of vicar general and official principal
Church levies	also known as leawans or church rates, monies collected for the repair of parish church, at a rate set by the church wardens or the vestry
Citation [Cio]	citation, or initial document or summons in a cause
Citation, viis et modis	a citation by ways and means which would be attached to the defendant's door and then to the door of the local church
Citation with intimation	citation with additional notice of action to be taken should there be no objection
Commissary	a deputy assigned by the bishop to take statements
Compurgation	clearing of the defendant's name by witnesses
Compulsory	document demanding the presence of witnesses
Condign	suitable
Contumacy	contempt of court, shown by failure to appear when requested by citation—the individual would be declared contumacious
Correction business	causes generated by the office of the judge for offences against the church and its ministers
Custom	regular usage of certain practices but not legally binding
Declaration instead of inventory	statement by an administrator or executor explaining why it had not been possible to produce an inventory of the estate
Decree	a judicial decision or command
Defamation	or diffimation, verbal abuse now described as slander
Defendant	one against whom an accusation had been made
Definitive sentence	sentence given at the end of a cause

Deponent	one who deposes, that is to say, a witness
Deposition	statement by a witness
Easter offerings	small sums of money paid, sometimes in four instalments during the year, towards the cost of communion bread and wine. This often included small tithe modus payments by the end of the 16th century.
Ex-communication, greater	the exclusion of an individual from all christian company
Ex-communication, lesser	forbidding of an individual to take part in divine service or to partake of communion
Instance business	causes between parties, usually for defamation, marriage or tithes
Interrogatories	series of questions to be put to witnesses by one or other of the parties involved in a cause
Inhibition	document to inhibit, or restrain, the activities of a court, usually issued by a higher ecclesiastical authority to a lower one
Interlocutory sentence	sentence given on a particular legal point during the cause
Justice of the Peace	or J.P., individual before whom small disputes could be brought
Letters of request	or letters requisitional. Letter sent to the bishop of another diocese, requesting him to cite an individual sought in a law suit
Libel	a set of articles issued at the beginning of a cause
Mainprize	a surety for the appearance of a prisoner
Monition	mild reproof
Notary public	one who writes down the acts of court
Note English	a note in English which accompanied the citation, prior to 1733
Official principal	the court official responsible for hearing causes between parties
Peculiar	an area outside the jurisdiction of the bishop
Penance	a public apology for a moral crime, particularly defamation and immorality
Personal answers	the responses of one individual to the allegation or articles of libel, or to a decree
Plaintiff	the individual who brought the cause to court
Plenary pleading	a full form of pleading in instance business, which generated a wide range of documents
Prebendary	an official of a cathedral, who was paid for his services
Probate	granting official permission for one or more individuals to interfere in the estate left by a named individual, either as executors or administrators
Probate courts	courts which dealt exclusively with the proving of wills
Proctor	a lawyer in the church courts, usually a notary public
Prohibition	a paper preventing further action in the church courts, and transferring the business to a civil court. This was used in tithe disputes where more money was claimed.
Propound all acts	to gather facts together at the end of a cause
Quarter Sessions	civil courts which sat four times a year to hear criminal cases
Registry	office of the registrar and place of storage of documents
Respondent	one who answers, or the defendant
Sententia	final judgment at the end of a cause
Significavit	writ directed to the civil authorities to detain an individual in prison, who had remained excommunicate for a period exceeding forty days
Summary pleading	a simple form of pleading used in office business, which generated few documents
Surrogate	one who stands in for another
Term probatory	period of time for the assembling of evidence and production of witnesses

Term to conclude	period of time after all the evidence had been gathered together during which the final sentence in a cause would be decided
Tithes	the tenth part of agricultural production, to be paid to the church
Transmission of documents	the process by which documents were copied by the clerks of one court and sent to those of another
Vicar general	the bishop's official who heard causes relating to moral matters

Index of People and Places

This list includes only plaintiffs and defendants in causes and those witnesses who gave evidence. There are many other names given in the cause papers cited, churchwardens, clergy, court officials, too numerous to index.

Subject Index

Numbers in **bold** type indicate the page numbers on which the document illustrations appear.